SO YOU WANT TO WORK IN THE FASHION BUSINESS?

SO YOU WANT TO WORK IN THE FASHION BUSINESS?

A Practical Look at Apparel Product Development and Global Manufacturing

MAURICE J. JOHNSON
EVELYN C. MOORE

Prentice Hall
Upper Saddle River, New Jersey 07458

Library of Congress Cataloging-in-Publication Data

Johnson, Maurice J., 1949–
So you want to work in the fashion business? : a practical look at apparel product development and global manufacturing / Maurice J. Johnson, Eveyln C. Moore.
p. cm.
Includes index.
ISBN 0-13-857889-3 (paperback)
1. Clothing trade—Vocational guidance. I. Moore, Evelyn C., 1951– . II. Title.
TT497.J64 1998
746.9'2'023—dc21 97-34259
CIP

Production Editor: ***Adele M. Kupchik***
Managing Editor: ***Mary Carnis***
Acquisitions Editor: ***Elizabeth Sugg***
Director of Manufacturing and Production: ***Bruce Johnson***
Manufacturing Buyer: ***Ed O'Dougherty***
Marketing Manager: ***Danny Hoyt***
Editorial Assistant: ***Emily Jones***
Formatting/page make-up: ***Stephen Hartner***
Printer/Binder: ***Banta, Harrisonburg, VA***
Cover Design: ***Robert Barker***
Photos that do not display credit lines are the work of co-author Maurice Johnson

Printed in the United States of America
10 9 8 7 6 5 4 3 2 1

ISBN 0-13-857889-3

Prentice-Hall International (UK) Limited, *London*
Prentice-Hall of Australia Pty. Limited, *Sydney*
Prentice-Hall Canada Inc., *Toronto*
Prentice-Hall Hispanoamericana, S.A., *Mexico*
Prentice-Hall of India Private Limited, *New Delhi*
Prentice-Hall of Japan, Inc., *Tokyo*
Simon & Schuster Asia Pte. Ltd., *Singapore*
Editora Prentice-Hall do Brasil, Ltda., *Rio de Janeiro*

To Jesse, Peter, Zach, and Philip,

Who had to live through this project
Minute by minute,
hour by hour, day by day,
month by month.

CONTENTS

PREFACE

For Students and Others Interested in Fashion

by Maurice J. Johnson

HERE'S WHAT THIS BOOK IS NOT

- It is *not* a fashion history book, from Louis XIV to Madonna.
- It is *not* "How to Design a Pleated and Matched Plaid Skirt."
- It is *not* an examination of the rise and fall of the American department store.
- Nor is it a technician's guide to patternmaking, grading, and cutting.

There are several really excellent textbooks that cover the above in great detail. We will give you just enough information on these subjects to interest you, not confuse you.

HERE'S WHAT THIS BOOK IS

- This book is an attempt to give you the *real* flavor of the garment-making industry.
- It will hopefully be a "reality check." What a job *feels* like, especially in wholesale, manufacturing, designing, and private-label product development. More and more jobs of the future, including buying, will require a working knowledge of the technicalities of apparel product development.
- This book should give you a general but practical "how to" when it comes to designing and producing a line of clothing.

Unit 1 focuses on the fashion industry today. Potential job seekers need to have creativity and talent, but they must also be able to recognize and respond to the wants and needs of customers. How does the industry identify and address different customers? What segments of the fashion business world are growing? Which are going away?

Unit 2 provides a close look at the development of garments by following the process of wholesale and private-label product development, step by step. Our attempt is not just to show you what the steps are but to show you how to do these steps, from the first concept right through to the retail marketplace. We also let you in on a few of the dark little secrets that exist in the wholesale–retail relationship.

Unit 3 is about the scale and future of manufacturing. It's one thing to make one blouse for one season. It's another to do it on the mass scale that is required today. Incredible new developments in computerized designing, patternmaking, and production have already changed the industry radically. What's coming next? What's all this talk about offshore sourcing, and where will manufacturing be done in the twenty-first century? Will there still be an industry in the United States?

Unit 4 includes some inside tips for your future career. From decades of experience in the industry, we're going to predict where some brand-new opportunities might lie—for your new career, or maybe even for your own new business. So that you will also sound like a pro, we have given you a brief glossary of terms which you're going to want to hold on to. Fashion jobs don't come with interpreters. Finally, we asked some of the veterans to share their sage advice with you.

This book will give you the *big picture*, but with sufficient detail to be able to:

- Decide if this field is right for *you*.
- Put subsequent specialized fashion and garment construction courses into perspective.
- Serve as a *common sense* (rather than glamorized) foundation for a fashion career.
- Help students with the transition from the (known) world of school to the (unknown) world of business. (That's why this book has two authors: Evelyn, as a teacher, knows where you're coming from; Maury, as an industry veteran, knows what you are walking into.)
- But best of all, this book has not been written by just two people. You'll be hearing *many* different voices. We have been honored by support and input from all corners of the fashion industry. Each chapter includes messages from members of the countries' largest stores, leading manufacturers, and design teams. These are firms you'll recognize, such as Liz Claiborne, Donna Karan, Tommy Hilfiger, Polo, Pamela Dennis, Saks, and Marshall Field's.
- Above all, this book should help all readers (students, industry members, and those simply curious) to get a sense of where the (intense, creative, and often funny) garment business is going in the 21st Century, rather than where it has been.

So, read on, and have some fun as you do! After all, as they say in "the business," we are talking about clothes, not brain surgery!

PREFACE

For Instructors
by Evelyn C. Moore

Fashion surrounds us and is a part of our lives; in what we wear, in our home, work or school environments, where we shop, and even in the entertainment world: music, TV, and the big screen. Therefore, it is no surprise that each year more and more students enroll in fashion programs. Some programs start as early as high school now and serve as a foundation for students to enroll in college programs offering both associate and bachelor degrees. It would seem, then, that the transition to the working world should be logical and easy. We are all surrounded by fashion, we all wear clothing, everyone needs clothing. It has to be an easy business to move into—but it is not!

Students quickly discover that the fashion industry is a business, and they must wear many hats to be successful. Not only must they be visionary enough to project fashion trends and styles for consumers up to two years in advance, they must also be able to work effectively in the business world: negotiating prices, construction costs, and deliveries. In addition, they must understand the economic and political world, to decide how and where products should be manufactured. Fashion designers of the 1990s must design and construct textiles and garments using state-of-the-art computer technology. In the past few years, the fashion world's approach to sales has pushed fashion advertising into an entirely new realm.

As I watch my colleagues teaching garment construction classes, I can easily see why students clearly understand what they have to do to find success in that particular field. First, my colleagues identify the goal and the students have a chance to discuss what a garment or product needs to be successful from the design and construction end. At that point there is an explanation of "why" and then a natural movement to a demonstration on "how to." Then students have the opportunity to learn themselves by working on their own project. Why should the approach towards learning about the business component of fashion be any different?

As I taught a course on the business of manufacturing, I found myself seeking the advice of people in the industry. I had exhausted all the textbooks. They were all about what was; or they were pages and pages talking at the students about what they should know; not one book really explained how. Industry leaders kept telling me that I had the responsibility to teach students how to learn the forecasting twists, technological turns, consumer needs, and manufacturing demands of the fashion business world! The industry echoed a common woe—fashion graduates are often artistically talented, but:

- They do not have the foundation to analyze and interpret the trends in order to make forecasting projections and to market products successfully.
- They do not understand the steps to make work boards, cost sheets, or spec sheets.
- They often lack an awareness of the world, of cultures, customs, and even politics, to help them understand why and where products are being produced.

Never did I imagine undertaking this overwhelming responsibility alone. Yet I knew that I had an obligation to help my students make the journey successfully from the classroom to the fashion industry. The journey had to be steady, with stopping points, allowing them to gather their skills and abilities and make the transition to the fashion world with a solid business foundation, one built with *explanation!* Over the years I relied heavily on the industry for help, and I developed many wonderful relationships. One constant and supportive ally has been Maury Johnson, vice president and general merchandise manager at Associated Merchandising Corporation in New York City. Maury undertook the responsibility of wearing a second hat and of helping many of us in colleges throughout the United States. We would ask Maury to conduct industry field trips and explain to our students the steps in developing products. We would ask him to speak when he was in our town, and we sought his advice on what knowledge the industry felt was important for our college graduates to know before entering the job market. After awhile, as we compared notes, sought the advice of other industry leaders, and listened very carefully to the fears our students expressed, we knew that it was time to write a "how to" book on the business of product development and manufacturing.

We knew the explanation had to be multifaceted, so that students could find their own niche. So together Maury Johnson and I have developed a textbook that shows students what is really going on in the fashion business, in addition to some fundamental skills that will be needed for students to know how to succeed in the fashion industry. We encourage you to use this book as a *workbook*.

The book is divided into four major areas:

- Where the industry and consumers are going.
- The step-by-step process of developing and producing garments.
- An introduction to the technology of products, involving both the tools and the "where."
- A look at the future as seen by the successful leaders of today.

As your students move through the book, take time to discuss the points carefully, and make time each week to have students learn "how to," just as they do in their design and construction courses. If you remember, I wrote that my design colleagues identify the goal, discuss why, then move to a demonstration on "how to," followed by the students doing their own work. We have provided you with techniques to be utilized in teaching the "how to" in each chapter. We do not consider these activities a chapter afterthought, but rather, an integral part of the journey from the classroom to the design room. The activities have made a big difference with my students. By guiding students through step by step, they have the opportunity to use trade publications, absorb industry lingo, and develop a solid understanding of what it will take for their designs to end up on the selling floor. There is no reason that a class discussing business has to be all lecture. Hands-on has always been the first step to on-the-job training and what better place to start than in the classroom. No matter what job path they follow in the industry, the process will demonstrate for each student that fashion designers, merchants, sourcers, and product developers (whether or not their name is on the label) are, indeed, visionary business people: forecasting the trends, producing the products, giving beauty to our world, and ending up with financial success. We hope both you and your students enjoy the journey!

ACKNOWLEDGMENTS

First and foremost, thanks to all 40 "Inside Scoop" industry people who *really thought about* what they wanted to tell future fashion business-people.

Thanks for help in content: Maurice Zucker, Geri Sussman, Judy Smith, Barbara Dugan, Dianne Ige, John Fleming (Dayton/Hudson/Marshall Field), Kim Roy (Liz Claiborne).

For reviewing sections for industry accuracy: Julia Hughes, Howard Cohen (Host Apparel), Lezlie Johnny (Alan Stuart), Paul Rosengard (Randa Neckwear).

For sharing time, insights, and factory tours: Alan Glist, Lawrence and Alan Behar, Wendell Watkins.

For graciously providing visuals: Del Rose (Gerber Garment Technology), Rick Ludolph (Lectra Systemes), Marie-Pierre Stark-Flora (Promostyl), Carrie Kim and Cara Metz (Unite), Jennifer Sommers (Malden Mills), Vanessa Lau (East Sun Button).

For really wonderful and important guidance and advice: Diann Valentini and Barbara Wycoff of the Fashion Institute of Technology, New York City.

For their kind understanding and profound generosity: Zach Solomon and Bill Baer.

For explaining the differences between the fashion world and the publishing world: Judith Rothman.

For flying cross-country to type, proof, encourage, and console—and for passing along her writer's gene: Marian Johnson.

For those who contributed their professional talents to the production of this book: Stephen Hartner, Elizabeth Sugg, Emily Jones, Mary Carnis, Miguel Ortiz, Mark Cohen—all of Prentice Hall. We owe special gratitude to Prentice Hall's Adele Kupchik, Senior Production Editor, for her patience, responsiveness, and warmth. Thanks to our gifted artists, designers, illustrators, and photographers: Mary Lisa Caramico, Michael Carnegie, Trudi Trudeau-Lopez, David Coulter, Sergio Sani, Bob Barker; and to Barbara Zeiders, copy editor, for giving the text such sensitive and meticulous treatment.

A very special thanks to the reviewer who not only "got" what we were trying to do but also made a helpful and important contribution on almost every page of the book: Lynda Gamans Poloian, New Hampshire College. Heaps of gratitude to the experts who shared their expertise in training: Bernice Murray, Vercelli Corporate Images, Inc.; Guy Adamo, Berkeley College; Pam Kuchenmeister, Meridian Educational Corporation; Grace I Kunz, Iowa State University; June Fischer, Art Institute of Atlanta; Nancy L. Cassill, University of North Carolina, Greensboro.

Thanks to the Art Institute of Fort Lauderdale for providing full access to students, classrooms, and instructors. But most of all, thanks to those students! This project has always been about them: their insistence on information that *means something* to them and their high expectations of the job market. It was their constantly repeated questions of "But how do *I* do this?" and "Where do *I* start?" that gave us the framework for the entire book.

Students pictured in the book represent some of the future of the fashion world and it was great fun to give them the chance to make their first contribution to the industry: student photographers J. Colin Dunn, Cathy Holt, and Jason VanBlaricum, and student designer Izabela Guta. Thanks for showing us your talents before the industry has had a chance to meet you!

Maurice J. Johnson

Evelyn C. Moore

ABOUT THE AUTHOR

Maurice J. Johnson

A native of Appleton, Wisconsin, Maurice (Maury) Johnson received his B.A. degree in German language and literature from the University of Wisconsin–Madison, including one year's study at the University of Freiburg, Germany. After receiving an M.A. degree from Cornell University in comparative/German literature and deciding to take a break in his studies, he consulted Cornell's Career Center for short-term work options. The Center suggested entry-level training positions in banking, insurance, or retailing. Since retailing sounded "more interesting" than the other two, he interviewed with major New York department stores plus one New York–based international buying office, the Associated Merchandising Corporation. AMC's international connections sold him! Twenty-three years later, Maury was a corporate officer of AMC, as vice president and general merchandise manager. His responsibilities included product development, global sourcing, and marketing for department and specialty store clients in the categories of men's, children's, and women's private-label apparel.

In previous positions at AMC, he was also involved in wholesale fashion and market coverage and reporting, research of consumer and market trends, and in-store consulting. Store clients included Dayton's, Marshall Field's, Bloomingdale's, Foley's, Filene's, Strawbridge and Clothier, Carson Pirie Scott, Parisian, Eaton's (Canada), Harrod's (London), De Bijenkorf (Netherlands), and Matsuzakaya (Japan), among others. In recent years, however, AMC narrowed its services primarily to product development and sourcing. Maury's staff, ranging from 15 to 45 people, included many young people who had some department store background but no product development experience. It was his job to teach them this skill and to ensure their success. It was also his challenge to integrate these young people with the industry veterans, designers, and divisional managers already on staff.

Together, this group helped design, source, and market private-label apparel for member stores. It also organized exciting "buy meetings" with samples collected each season from their world travels. These meetings, attended by American department store buyers, were held in New York, Los Angeles, Paris (France), Florence (Italy), and Hong Kong.

Maury has made over 60 overseas trips, mainly to the Far East, Southeast Asia, Europe, Turkey, and Israel. He was included in one of the earliest groups of Americans to attend the Canton Fair, when China began to allow foreigners to visit. Special research trips were also made to locate new apparel makers in Portugal, Egypt, Uruguay, Argentina, Brazil, Malaysia, and the United Arab Emirates. The volume of shipments from overseas markets under his jurisdiction ranged from (a retail dollar equivalent of) $200 to $400 million per year.

ABOUT THE AUTHOR

Evelyn C. Moore

A graduate of Youngstown State University with a degree in business administration, Evelyn Moore worked her way through the ranks at Ohio's Strouss Department Store, a division of the May Company. Her departments included children's, pre-teens, and intimate apparel. In that experience, she found the opportunity to participate in the May Company executive training program classes exciting and rewarding. The classes, designed and presented by seasoned store leaders, were jammed with practical firsthand knowledge. After gaining experience as a sales associate, clerical, assistant buyer, and buyer with Strouss, she realized that her first love was training and development. Learning directly from the pros made her realize there is a wide gap between college courses based on definitions and theory—versus the needed on-the-job skills.

As a result, she went back to school for certification in grades K–12, secondary, and adult education programs. Then, upon entering the teaching arena, she found there were many other students like her, asking "OK, what do I do first?" "How do I start?" "What advice do you have?" But now they were asking her! Evelyn decided to look for a *practical, step-by-step approach.* On the job, she had found successful merchandisers, designers, and other business people who took the time to share this very specific advice. She also treasured their encouragement: their words "Just try," "Don't worry about failure," "What do you have to lose?", "It will be a good experience," and "Just do the best you can!"

All of this led Evelyn to find ways to make learning easier—to show students "how to." She has let her students "take over" the role of learning by giving them *tools* that are practical and relevant. In her first book, *Math for Merchandising, A Step-by-Step Approach,* she starts at the very beginning: how to use a calculator. In *So You Want to Work in the Fashion Business?*, a wider-ranging book, she hopes students will find many helpful tools that will apply directly to their first jobs in the fashion industry.

Evelyn has been an adjunct instructor at the Art Institute of Fort Lauderdale and a member of the Broward County Schools Marketing and Diversified Advisory Board. The latter is a group of community business and college leaders throughout Broward County seeking to address the curriculum needs of high school students who are planning to enter the business market upon graduation or who might consider postsecondary training and education. Evelyn was also a 1996 honoree in *Who's Who in America's Teachers*. She resides in Fort Lauderdale, Florida, with husband, Jesse, and sons, Peter and Zachary.

ILLUSTRATIONS, ART WORK, AND PHOTOGRAPHY

Illustrations and Art Work

Caramico, Mary Lisa, 59, 60, 113, 114, 115, 116, 117, 158, 160, 167, 168
Carnegie, Michael, 9, 11, 44, 83, 106, 152, 153, 154, 155, 211, 233, 237
Trudeau-Lopez, Trudi, 132, 140, 143, 145

Photos of store logos

Antique Boutique, 70
Banana Republic, 43
Barney's New York, 73
Bergdorf Goodman, 65
Bloomingdale's, 87
1411 Broadway, 194
1407 Broadway, 194
Brooks Brothers, 67
Burdine's, 69
Contempo Casuals, 70
Dillard's, 16
Disney, 46
Express, 16
(The) Fashion Center Information Kiosk, 194
Fashion Tower, 3
Fendi, 65
Gap, 16
Giorgio Armani, 79
Gucci, 64
J.C. Penney, 38
K-Mart, 37, 71
Liz Claiborne, 46
Lord & Taylor, 15
Macy's, 16
Marshall's, 71
Maus and Hoffman, 85
Miami International Merchandise Mart, 196
Neiman-Marcus, 72, 76
Old Navy Clothing Co., 80
Polo Ralph Lauren Factory Store, 71
Prada, 6
Saks & Company, 16
Sears, 69
St. John, 72
Target, 37
Versace, 65
Walmart, 37

Photography Credits

Cover by Coulter, David
Color Inserts 1-4 by Coulter, David
Field Gear Catalog, courtesy of Dayton's, Hudson's, Marshall Field
Photos courtesy of Alan Stuart, 23, 162, 163, 173, 174, 175, 176, 177, 180, 181, 185, 186
Photos courtesy of the Art Institute of Fort Lauderdale, 4, 19, 21, 23, 60, 95, 213,
Photo, Davis, Vicky, courtesy of Davis, Vicki, 263
Photo, Dennis, Pamela, courtesy of Dennis, Pamela, 105, 262
Photo, Dittrich, Al and family, courtesy of Dittrich, Al, 267
Photos courtesy of Gerber Garment Technology, 215, 216, 217, 219, 221, 222, 223

Photo, Glist, Alan courtesy of Glist, Alan, 251
Photos courtesy of Harwood Companies, 159, 165, 179, 181, 187
Photo, Hilfiger, Tommy by Scavullo, Franceso, courtesy of Tommy Hilfiger, 4, 262
Photos courtesy of Ike Behar, 171, 177, 179, 180, 182, 183, 184,185
Photo, Johnson, Maurice J., by Carabetta, Philip 270
Photos by Johnson, Maurice J., 4, 5, 6, 7(1-2), 8, 10, 17, 19, 20, 21, 22, 23, 24, 25, 28, 29, 32, 50, 53, 54, 60, 61, 62, 64, 66, 73, 74, 81, 84, 86, 87, 88, 93, 94, 95, 105, 109, 119, 148, 149, 157, 159, 165, 171, 172, 173, 174, 175, 176, 177, 178, 179, 180, 181, 182, 183, 184, 185, 186, 187, 196 (Solomon), 199, 213, 214, 226, 234, 236, 240, 245, 254, 261, 262, 263, 264, 265, 266 and store logos
Photos courtesy of Lectra Systemes, 217, 218, 220
Photo, Moore, Evelyn C., by Moore, Zachary T., 270
Photos, Malden Mills, by Vogt, Ethan, 246; Liss, Steve, 246
Promostyl's "Women's Fashion Planner," courtesy of Promostyl, 90-91
Photos by Sani, Sergio, 92
Photo of UNITE, by Metz, Cara, 243

Student Photographers

Photo by Dunn, J.Colin, 31
Photo by Holt, Kathy, 7
Photos by VanBlaricum, Jason, 31, 85

Student Designers

Fabric rendering art work by Guta, Isabela, 24

UNIT 1

The Fashion World versus The Real World

CHAPTER 1

So You Want To Work In The Fashion Business?

The two most important words on the cover of this book are *work* and *business*. Often, people are drawn to this field because they expect it to be exciting and glamorous. It often is, but it is still a business! The fashion industry is not a hobby, it is not an ongoing conversation about what people like to wear, and it is not an endless fashion show. What is it? It's a high-energy fast-paced business that controls billions of dollars of consumer spending around the world. Everyone wears clothing. It's just that simple (and big).

Fashion Tower Building, New York City

The best news from this simple fact is that clothes are here to stay. In music, the World War II generation listened to music on large, fast-turning records called "78s." The generation growing up in the 1950s had smaller single records called "45s." The baby boomers had long-playing albums, "33s." Each of these was quickly replaced by the next generation of even-newer technology: cassette tapes; Beta, then VHS; CDs; videodisks. These will also soon be replaced. But with all this going on, everyone was and

THE INSIDE SCOOP

Tommy Hilfiger

Tommy Hilfiger needs no introduction. His company is probably the single biggest fashion success story of the 1990s. Here's what Tommy himself has to say about the fashion business:

> I know a lot of people see the fashion business as a "glamour" industry but it is, first and foremost, a business. In addition to the designer, it takes a team of people to turn a vision on a sketchboard into a successful product. And, once you have that product it takes another team of people to market and sell your overall vision to the buying public. When I started out in this business over 25 years ago all I had was my name and a dream of one day being a successful designer. Thanks to the talent of my creative staff and the business acumen of my marketing and sales teams, Tommy Hilfiger has become a brand name that is recognizable all over the world.

Photo by Francesco Scavullo, courtesy of Tommy Hilfiger.

still will be wearing clothes. It's a fundamental human need. These clothes may be made via newer technology and in a different corner of the world, but thankfully, there will always be a garment business.

Wendell Watkins, vice president of manufacturing for the Harwood Companies, Inc., says: "Clothing is second only to food as a basic human need. There will always be an apparel industry; which means there will always be opportunities." Students like you, with a keen eye for color and a love of fashion, are looking for opportunities to work in this industry. A fashion student quickly learns that the best designers are also the most visionary business people, able to analyze and interpret business, economic, and consumer trends. They must know how to design, construct, and market fashion products successfully. Just designing is not enough.

It is also important for newcomers to realize that fashion is mostly work, just like any other job. Hope Cohen, vice president of domestic licensing for Polo Ralph Lauren, put it perfectly: "If it wasn't work, they'd call it something else!" So what you will discover is that discipline and dedication pay off in fashion as much as they do in any other field.

YOU'RE PROBABLY THE EXCEPTION!

How do you know if you're the right fit for the fashion industry?

- You like clothes, don't you?
- You follow fashion reports in magazines and on TV?
- People have always told you that you were a great dresser?
- You were the only one in fifth grade to wear black head to toe?

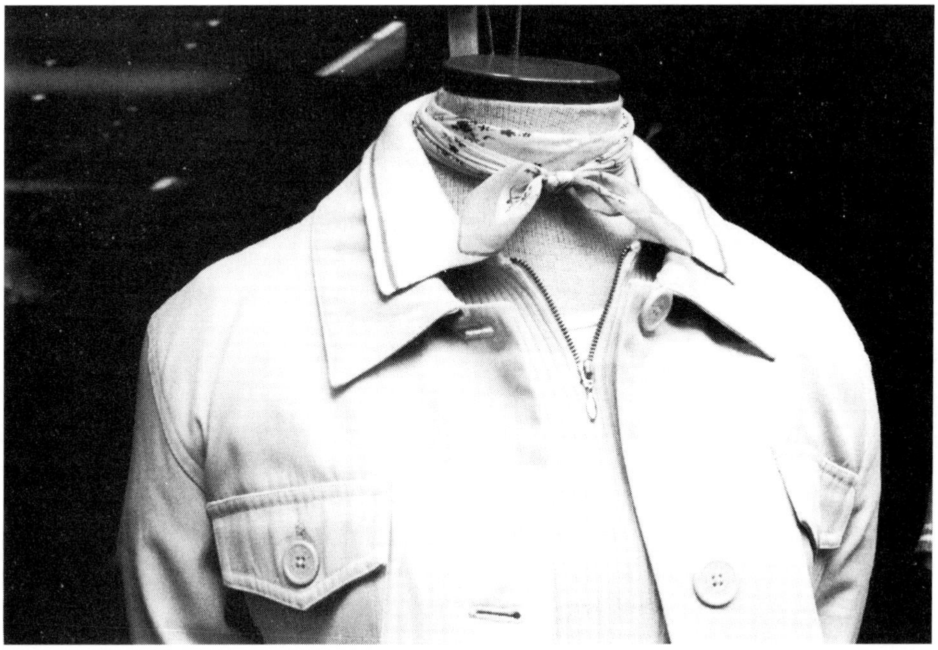

"Prada" Store Window

These all sound like the perfect qualifiers to pursue a career in fashion. They are, in fact, reasons often given by people working in the industry. Well, here's the first shock:

- You may be a great dresser, but most people are not—and
- They're the ones who are buying the clothes!
- The majority of American customers unfortunately have a minority of taste and style (see Figures 1-1 and 1-2).

The irony of this situation is that anyone who is actually interested in fashion is not a typical customer. As a result, these people tend to be bad "fashion barometers." What they find interesting or new in fashion might well be just too interesting or too new for most people.

Most customers don't want to look so fashionable that they stand out from the crowd. OK , a tiny few do, but this represents a very small number of customers. In fashion theory, these people are often called *innovators*. Those that quickly catch on to what these innovators are wearing are called *early adopters*. Those that pick up a fashion trend just as it is peaking or declining are called *laggards*.

But remember: This is a fashion business. To have enough business, you have to have a lot of customers. Your chances of landing a job that caters only to the **fashion-forward** innovators are very small indeed. Before you panic and say, "But I don't want to design boring clothes!", let's make one point clear: Even though this is work, it is work in which you can and need to use your special taste, creativity, and interests.

Fashion-forward
A more fashionable person than most.

Figure 1–1

You thought your customer would look like this. . . Photo by student Cathy Holt.

Figure 1–2

But, chances are, she'll look like this...

IS THERE A PLACE FOR YOU? CAN YOU FIND CREATIVITY WITHIN LIMITATIONS?

Here's a test to see how you might do in the garment business: What was your reaction in grade school when the teacher gave you two pieces of construction paper, four popsicle sticks, a ruler, and two rubber bands (Figure 1-3) and said: "Make an airplane out of this"? If you tingled with excitement at

THE INSIDE SCOOP

May Cygan

May studied fashion merchandising at Ursuline College, in Pepper Pike, Ohio. Included in the curriculum was a junior year at the Fashion Institute of Technology (FIT) in New York. She graduated with a B.A. from Ursuline plus an FIT associate degree.

It was the year at FIT that opened my eyes. I was exposed to all parts of the industry (**production**, **buying**, fashion design). Two days a week I interned at Joseph and Feiss, a men's clothing maker. (This wouldn't have happened in Cleveland!)

The city intrigued me, but I had to return to Ohio to finish. My first job was for Lerner Stores in East Cleveland, preparing branches for visits by the buyers. When I met the New York buyers, I knew I had to get back to New York. So, I packed one bag and moved in with friends in the city. FIT's placement office helped me land a job at Positive Attitude Dresses, as assistant to the **merchandiser** and designer. It was a great first job—I did **presentation boards** for salespeople, **swatched spec sheets** for the **patternmakers**, and was even allowed to order all the buttons and trim.

But I wanted more focus to my career, so I went on an interview for **technical designer** at the Associated Merchandising Corporation, even though I was not really interested in that particular job. But through that interview, I met several people at AMC, and one thing led to another, and I landed a merchandising job in **Infants** and Toddlers.

When I started my fashion study, I had tunnel vision like everyone else. I was sure I only wanted to work in **Juniors** on **7th Avenue**. Well, here I am in Infants and Toddlers, and I *love* it! My advice? Just try something; it might be great!"

Production
The process of making a garment.

Buying
Retail stores "buy" merchandise from wholesalers to "sell" to consumers.

Merchandiser
The person who takes the garment designs and executes them in real fabrics, trims, and constructions.

the challenge, you're probably going to do well in the fashion industry. Creativity in the "real world" is as often a matter of finding creative solutions to practical challenges as much as it is a matter of "expressing oneself." The reality of what you can and can't work with should not be viewed as a restriction, but as a "dare." You need to view "the possible" rather than "the impossible." The most brilliant achievements are often a matter of making a lot out of very little.

In garments there are lots of technical limitations—in fabric, in sewing. There are sociological limitations, too—in what "average" people will wear. These limitations become the "rules of the game" for a designer. Almost always, cost is a major *limiter*. It is easy to make a glamorous gown out of luxurious material that costs $30 per yard, but it takes a lot more skill and ingenuity to make something glamorous out of material that costs $2.50 per yard. But it can be done! The market for $1000 dresses is a lot smaller than the market for $59.99 dresses! So, chances are, in your job in the fashion industry, you're going to need this skill and ingenuity.

In menswear, one of the major limiters is what a "guy" will wear. American males tend to be skittish about clothes. They really don't want to stand out

Figure 1-3

Artwork by Michael Carnegie.

from a crowd. Menswear designers and merchants tend to sweat over the smallest details to achieve a balance between "new" and "too new." They have to find the one-millionth new version of a **paisley** pattern, or that just-right color. Designers have found that men can accept one new idea in a garment (maybe color, maybe fabric, maybe a slight **silhouette** change) but not more than one.

In kidswear, the major limiter is usually price. Parents will spend only so much on a garment that will be quickly outgrown. The trick is to find a way to apply the most novelty or "cuteness" for the least amount of labor and materials.

A designer or design team faces similar tasks and challenges season after season. Those with longevity are able to come up with fresh, original, but still practical solutions year after year. Repeating exactly the same solution season after season is as dangerous as being too original season after season. Going back to our "airplane" example: It is a fine line, but if you can make not just one, but two or three different airplanes out of your construction paper and popsicle sticks, you are really on your way (Figure 1-4).

> ***Presentation Boards***
> Visual aids such as pictures, drawings, and swatches mounted on foam-core boards, to help illustrate a concept or a line.

> ***Swatched***
> A swatch is a small piece of fabric that is representative of the actual type and quality of a larger lot of fabric.

> ***Spec Sheets***
> Garment measurements are listed in a standardized fashion, allowing for accurate and consistent measurements. (*Spec* is short for *specification*.)

> ***Patternmakers***
> People who can take a designer's sketch of a garment and translate this into specific pattern pieces.

> ***Technical Designer***
> A technician who knows how to adjust garments to achieve proper fit and to compensate for variables such as shrinkage.

> ***Infants***
> Children's clothing from newborn to size 24 months.

> ***Juniors***
> The fast, young, teenage female customer segment. Sizes generally run from 3 to 13.

THE INSIDE SCOOP

SIMON GRAJ

Simon founded Graj+Gustavsen in 1990 after years in wholesale and retail. The company develops concepts, **brands**, **packaging**, **store design**, and **licensing** ideas for client wholesalers and retailers such as Nordstrom, Edison Brothers, the Discovery Channel, Hickey Freeman, and Gap. In 1997, he teamed up with Spike Lee to form Spike Lee Productions, a new clothing company. We consider him among the most original thinkers in the industry.

On creativity and originality:

You have to have the courage to go through the void of "not knowing"—and trust that you *will* know at some point. Don't jump to quick conclusions. If you wait, you will be inspired.

In the flow, accidents occur. And these are the best things! In fact, you go through this whole exercise so you can allow accidents to happen. You can be more original and creative if you are not looking to reinforce what you already know or what someone else already knows. If you are aimed at only the things you already know, you won't allow these accidents to happen.

In the process of observing, you can learn anything you need to know. Designers are reporters. If you lose this fact, you will fail. You'll be locked into too few ideas. You have to see the flux, the panorama. You've got to keep having fresh experiences.

Everyone has a capacity for genius. You just need to give up the things that keep you from experiencing it!

7th Avenue
The main avenue in New York City along which garment manufacturers' showrooms are located. Used to denote the entire ready-to-wear industry. Signs along 7th Avenue now also say "Fashion Avenue."

Paisley
A classic rounded, swirling, and highly detailed pattern.

So let's take a look together. From our classroom experience we know that the first thing you'll want to hear about is the job market. In Chapter 2 we outline lots of jobs and wonderful opportunities. Then you'll find out where these jobs are going and what you need to learn to get them and then how to find *your* place in the fashion world.

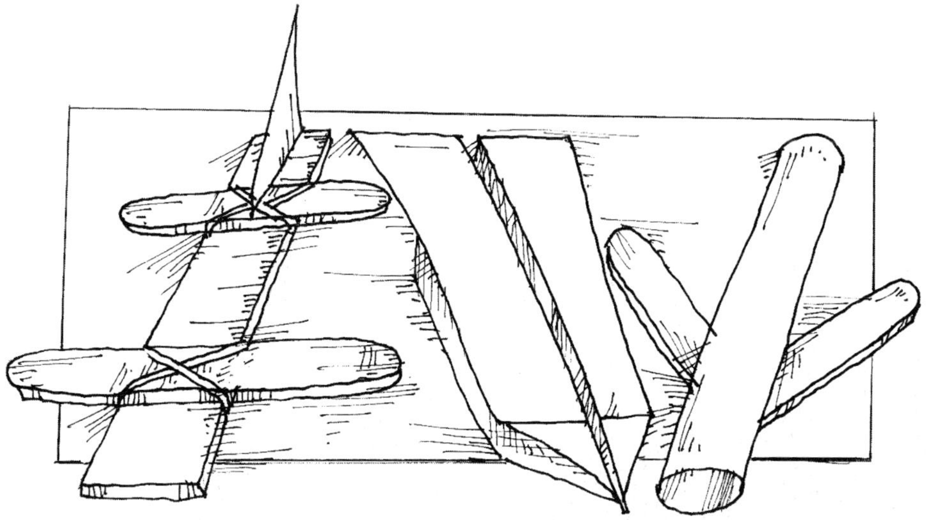

Figure 1–4

Artwork by Michael Carnegie.

Silhouette
Used to mean the model or style of a garment.

Brands
Usually refers to wholesalers' labels that are advertised and widely recognized by consumers.

Packaging
Anything that accompanies a garment when it is presented to the customer: a box, a protective bag, a paper hang-tag, or other device.

Store Design
The way a store is planned, laid out, and set up.

Licensing
The practice of buying or selling a brand or name from one company to another.

SO YOU WANT TO WORK IN THE FASHION BUSINESS?

Here's How to Begin. . . Chapter 1

It is always a lot of fun at the beginning of a course to find out about the person sitting next to you and learn why he or she wants to be in this wonderful, fast-paced, ever-changing industry. Take a moment and get to know the future fashion pros. Together, learn about their fashion philosophies, visions, and have some fun at the same time!

The Fashion Quiz

Thinking about your life in general, list three things that you love to do (dancing?, organizing?, sleeping in?) Then, list three things that you hate to do (washing dishes?, cleaning your room?, math homework?). We've had fun doing this in class and then suggesting what job in the fashion industry might be a good fit based on these likes and dislikes. (For example, if you really hate math, being a buyer is not a good choice.)

But it's also important to keep your list and come back to it at the end of the book. See if you can pick out where you'd fit into the industry. Or perhaps some of your likes and dislikes will have changed as new opportunities are explained.

Fashion Failures

Most fashion magazines do an annual feature on the "best and worst" of fashion, but obviously that's only once a year. Everyone should bring into class any current magazine and try to find the fashion failures in the issue. What is important is to identify the "mistakes," but make sure that you share your reasoning.

Fashion Faux Pas

Oops—we all wear the wrong outfit at the wrong time at least once in our lives. Think over the last few weeks and what you have seen on TV: It could be a news or entertainment piece that really screamed: Oops!

Fashion Fixes

Each of you has said sometime, to someone, "If only that person would dress differently!" Pick a leading national figure, male or female (could be a political figure, an actor, actress, sports hero, any well-known public figure), and write one paragraph on why you don't think the person's look suits his or her image, and then write one paragraph on what you would suggest.

Fashion Firsts

Although you can have a lot of fun laughing at crazy costumes and finding fashion mistakes, take a moment and identify a fashion leader. Again, choose a leading national figure and write one paragraph on why this person makes a strong statement as to who he or she is and stands for in appearance. Then identify a fashion leader in your own peer group.

SO YOU WANT TO WORK IN THE FASHION BUSINESS?
Here's How to Begin. . . COURSE-LENGTH PROJECT: A Fashion Business Journal

Probably one of the most important keys to success is knowing what is happening in an industry. The fashion industry is all about change—you can get out-of-date in a flash. Before reading further, it is important to gather your working tools and supplies. Your first and most important tool will be a fashion business journal. A journal gathers ideas and opinions. It is important to note that a journal is strictly personal: There is no "right" opinion nor is there a "wrong" opinion. What this journal will do for you is to keep you well versed on the current events of the industry. You will be using this journal throughout the course to help you develop your own insight and to analyze and interpret the trends of today and tomorrow.

FASHION BUSINESS JOURNAL

Maintain a notebook, divided into three parts.

Part One: "The News": Watching the Trends, Learning the "Lingo," and Identifying Who Is "Growing" and Who Is "Going"

Each week you are to clip out:

a. One article from the business section of the local newspaper relating to fashion or retailing
b. One article from *Women's Wear Daily* or *Daily News Record* reflecting an industry activity
c. One article from a business publication such as *Newsweek* or *Time*

Write two or three sentences about the content of the article and two or three sentences on how this might affect the fashion industry.

Part Two: "People Watching": Focusing on How People Are Responding to Fashion Trends

Every three weeks you are to people-watch.

a. Visit a local mall or shopping area. As you observe the shoppers, make notes about what people are wearing. Compare and contrast, in writing, the leading fashion trends being promoted versus what is actually being worn.
b. At the end of the course, write a synopsis discussing areas that manufacturers could target for growth and how you would address current fashion trends if you were on the job.

Part Three: "Fashion Influences": A Little of This and a Little of That!

a. Every day you see, hear, or read something that reflects a fashion trend—it could be something you see in a movie, on a TV show, at a sporting event, or even something being targeted on the news. Maintain a miscellaneous section in your journal and jot down something each week that relates to the fashion industry: It could be a reflection from the past, something current, or a feature that you feel will have an impact on fashion's future. For example: Have you seen a fashion trend emerge that is a direct result of a movie that was just released?

b. Sometimes, even "unrelated" pictures, ideas, or thoughts influence design. You might be struck by:

Paint samples
Photos of places or things
Headlines
Typeface styles
Placemats, napkins, flower petals—who knows?

Good designers are constantly on the lookout like this. You'll be amazed how collecting these ideas when you see them will help you remember good design ideas when you need them.

CHAPTER 2

Segments of the Garment Industry: Where the Jobs Are

WHERE TO START? RETAIL NEVER FAILS!

If you're not lucky enough to have "connections" to land a job in the fashion industry, the single best way to break in is by getting a sales job in a retail apparel or department store. If you can do this in tandem with study at a fashion institute or technically focused college majoring in design, retailing, or business, you will be well on your way. Barbara Dugan, divisional vice president of personnel of the Associated Merchandising Corporation, puts it this way: "Focus your energies on related work. Even summer work shows an interviewer that you've thought about the path you'd like to take."

Retailing, by definition, is the sale of goods and services, and even though you may not want to work on the selling floor forever (and your dreams are to be in a designer's studio), it is the best place to start. On the front lines you will encounter many different customer groups and levels of buying power. It's a chance to learn about customers firsthand: their wants, needs, habits, and attitudes. The broad variety of retail is also a wonderful advantage for you when you need to decide which part of the industry is for you: women's, men's, children's, accessories/shoes, home furnishings.

Having working experience with an important retail company on your résumé is always going to serve you well. No matter what end of the industry you specialize in, having front-line retail experience will always be viewed as an important plus! The sector of the industry with by far the greatest number of jobs is retail. In fact, this is one of the largest job markets in the country. For apparel, jobs are available at a wide variety of retail stores, which you will find outlined in Chapter 5. So, if you start out as a sales associate, even seasonally or part-time, at a renowned chain such as Federated, May Company, Dillard's, Nordstrom, Dayton-Hudson or Saks Fifth Avenue, you'll have a good learning experience.

If department stores aren't for you, national specialty chains such as Limited and Gap would also be great on your résumé, even if their product lines are a bit more narrow in scope. Either avenue is fine, because both the leading department stores and the national specialty stores believe that good training is essential to success. It's training that you need right now.

Let's take a look at three different career paths that you can focus on within retail: sales, store operations, and merchandising (or buying).

Sales

After front-line retail sales experience, many companies will encourage leading retail sales associates to concentrate on a specific category or classification of merchandise or even a single designer line. These positions are called *selling specialists.* In this position you become a liaison for the store, the buying office, and the manufacturer. You are responsible for optimizing sales through presentation, promotion, and good customer service. This job involves a keen eye for color and presentation, strong communication skills, and some good merchandising math skills to complete departmental paperwork. Being a selling specialist is a wonderful career opportunity because it opens avenues to both merchandising and design, since you might work directly with the leading designers and manufacturers.

DMM
Divisional merchandise manager; supervises several buyers in a related area, such as all children's wear buyers.

Store Operations

Some sales employees advance to department manager or group manager. These supervisory jobs are centered around training, educating, and scheduling sales and stock people. Keeping track of inventories, setting the floor, and anything else that makes the branch store run are included in the manager's responsibilities. Store managers are also concerned with personnel, building maintenance, and security. Given the fact that there are now fewer chains of stores but each with more branches, it stands to reason that there are more

GMM
General merchandise manager; DMMs report to this senior manager, who is responsible for an entire merchandising division of the store, such as all ready-to-wear or all men's and kids.

THE INSIDE SCOOP

DENNIS ABRAMCZYK

Dennis is the executive vice president and chief operating officer of Ralph Marlin Neckwear. Prior to working in wholesale, he spent 25 years advancing through the ranks of Federated Department Stores (Boston Store) and Carson Pirie Scott. He started right from college on the executive training squad in Milwaukee.

> I really believe in a career path that gives you both stores and buying office {merchandising} experience. My path was trainee, assistant buyer, branch area manager, buyer, assistant store manager, **DMM**, **GMM**, director of stores, GMM. You are much more well rounded after that. You can appreciate what the other half goes through!

store operations jobs than ever before. Conversely, however, this means that merchandising jobs are becoming fewer.

Merchandising

> **Buyer**
> Retail store employee responsible for purchasing the right merchandise for the store's customers; usually, buys for only one or two departments.

Merchandising is involved in the selecting, buying, and distribution of assortments of items to various branch stores, and the coordination and planning of sales and promotions. The career path is generally from assistant **buyer** to associate buyer to buyer. Often, stores will move you back and forth between the merchandising line and the stores line.

As you can see from Dennis's career path, you could end up as a manager of a number of buyers as a divisional merchandise manager, or move all the way into senior management as a general merchandise manager.

Very important skills for merchandising are analytical and mathematical skills (generally the use of Lotus and/or Excel) and aggressive negotiating abilities. You can't be shy when you are demanding that a vendor give you markdown money. (*Markdown money* is money given by the wholesaler to a buyer when that wholesaler's merchandise has not sold as well as expected. The buyer adds this to his or her profit statement to improve it.)

Being a buyer is a tough, demanding job. Hours tend to be very long, and the workload is considerable. Buyers are typically responsible for lots of things over which they have only limited control. There is a high turnover in buyers because either they get promoted, or they move into another field, one with a little less hectic pace.

But what if you find out while selling that you do not want the dollar responsibilities that management requires—it just isn't you? Yet fashion is in your blood and you have the pulse of knowing the "right" colors, trends, and fashions. You are creative but don't see yourself as a clothing designer? Don't worry, there are still some other wonderful opportunities for you. Success can also be found in the visual and promotion areas.

Visual Display and Promotion

First, take a look at the job of visual display. Figure 2-1 shows students learning display skills in class. But trust us, this is not just changing mannequins. That is only one of many job responsibilities. Visual display coordinators are responsible for setting the entire image of the store: presenting a good floor set, creating exciting visual displays to educate customers, and presenting merchandise physically in ways that will maximize sales. What is a *floor set*? It starts with a floor plan, identifying where racks and merchandise should be placed to create a strong flow of traffic through the store and to present the merchandise most effectively. Often, you will hear this called a *plan-o-gram* or *prototype* (Figure 2-2). In fact, because store image and presentation is one of the few areas where stores can distinguish themselves from the competition, this area is growing. The leading companies—Federated, Limited, Gap, and Target—all have corporate planning offices that prepare plan-o-grams that are implemented nationwide to maintain continuity in presentation.

Visual display and presentation can be a steppingstone for other creative opportunities. With continued success and experience, you might find yourself

Figure 2–1

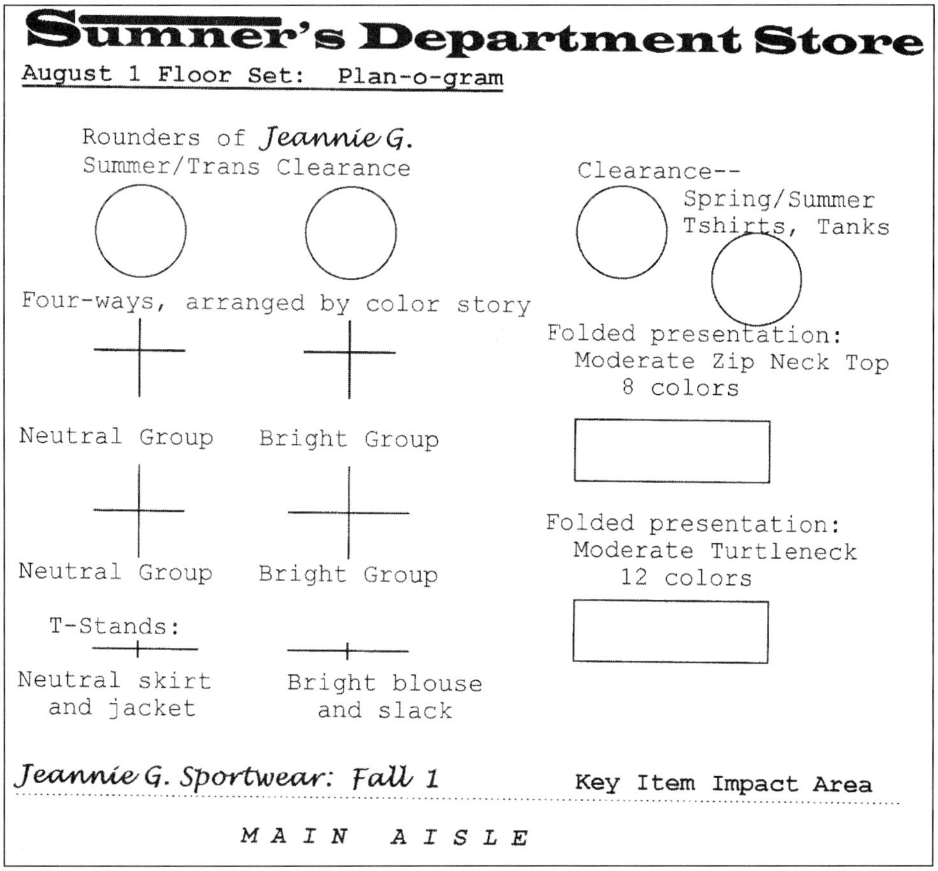

Figure 2–2

Fashion Office
Store's fashion director and staff.

Trunk Shows
Store events in which a designer or wholesaler will bring an entire collection to show to preferred customers.

Designer Firm
A wholesaler at the top end of the price scale; the brand is usually the designer's own name.

moving to the store **fashion office** as a fashion coordinator, or to the marketing and public relations offices. Here creativity branches out to fashion shows, **trunk shows**, and public relations activities involving the local community.

Stay in Retail or Maybe Try Wholesale?

Some of you will find that staying in the retail segment of the fashion industry suits you just fine. But others might still be anxious to find a place in the design and merchandising world of fashion. If so, start pointing yourself toward that segment of the industry. But even after your (very helpful) experience in retail sales, don't expect to land a job as head designer for Prada—you've still got lots to learn. Nevertheless, that retail background is going to pay off right away. It will help you land a position on the wholesale side. Here's Zach Solomon, who has been the president of both Perry Ellis and Ellen Tracy: "Many wholesalers look to hire people with retail experience for several reasons:

- For their understanding of the buyers that they are dealing with.
- For their retailer's mentality and math skills.
- For the department store training, which teaches planning and discipline.
- For the ability to visualize stock assortments by store (How is the tops-to-bottoms ratio? Skirts to slacks? etc.)"

THE INSIDE SCOOP

KEN MASTER

Ken is the director of manufacturing for DKNY Men's.

On persistence and resourcefulness:

After getting my B.A. in economics, I became a project manager for a mechanical construction company for five years in Philadelphia. But then I decided to change career paths and explore the fashion industry. So I got a job at The Cupcake Café at the corner of 39th and 9th on the edge of the garment district in New York City. Every time I gave someone change, I said, "Your change is $12.50, and do you have a position open at your garment business?' Sure enough, someone asked me to come in for an interview!

I ended up at a small **designer firm**, Patricia Clyne, as **assistant production manager**. They were wonderful to me! Being such a small **design house**, I became involved in many jobs, ranging from **cutting**, **sewing**, patternmaking, to **shipping**. There were only six of us, so we had to get involved in everything.

From there I went to Bugle Boy (at this interview I stressed that I had a full year and a half of experience). As assistant merchandiser, I learned the import end of manufacturing (10 trips a year to Hong Kong, each trip three to four weeks long)!

After another job in between and yet more experience, I began to network and was hired as corporate production manager at Donna Karan Co. Since then, I was promoted to director of manufacturing of DKNY Men's, and I've been here ever since.

On your first full-time industry job, even with your retail experience, remember that you probably have less to offer your employer than your employer has to offer you. Stay humble but enthusiastic, positive, and eager. The more a boss sees that an employee is eager and willing, the more that boss will teach and entrust responsibility to that employee.

Remember that you are on your new job to learn, not to run the joint. If the job is difficult but you are learning a lot, do your best to tough it out as long as you can. (Being able to handle a difficult situation or a demanding boss is a very valuable skill—you're going to need it again, we promise you.)

Michael McKeithen, **CAD** designer, puts it this way: "Go for the go-fer jobs. That's where you will get your initial exposure to the fashion industry. The smaller the company, the better. If you can hang out in one of these jobs,

Student Brent Vandling preparing fabric for draping.

Assistant Production Manager
Helps the production manager who is the wholesale firm's employee responsible for having all garments made and shipped.

Design House
Same as *designer firm*.

Cutting
The part of the production process in which the individual pattern pieces are cut out of bolts of fabric.

Sewing
The assembly or sewing together of the various garment components.

Shipping
Boxing and transporting the finished products to stores.

CAD
Computer-aided design. The process of designing garments, prints, and patterns on a computer screen.

the experience you get will be worth it!" But if the situation is really bad or if you stop learning because all you're doing is straightening shelves, move on. Do not allow someone to demean you. If it's not right, it's perfectly OK to move on.

You need a training situation in the wholesale and manufacturing sector that is positive enough so that you can stay long enough to learn and start establishing a résumé with a good amount of time at each employer. May Cygan illustrates the winning attitude: "In this business, you've got to be willing to schlep! I had three other roommates at FIT who thought I was nuts to work two days a week without pay. During market weeks, I even came in on Saturdays. But during this internship, I was exposed to product development and showroom sales. As a result of this experience, I was able to 'ace' my product development exam, without studying—while my roommates struggled." By the way, May went on to a highly successful product development career at the Associated Merchandising Corporation in New York. Her continued demonstration of willingness paid off.

Wholesale
The level of company in the supply chain that produces or contracts merchandise, which it then sells to retail stores.

Wholesale and Manufacturing

There are a number of different kinds of jobs in **wholesale** and **manufacturing**, but they are more geographically localized than retail. For wholesale, most are in New York or Los Angeles. Actual manufacturers that are located in the United States tend to be concentrated in the southeast and in Pennsylvania, Texas, and California.

Manufacturing
The actual production of garments.

Next we look in very general terms at the types of jobs that exist in wholesale.

Design

Flat Patternmaking
Drawing out the pattern pieces on a flat table.

Computer Patternmaking
Drawing out the pattern pieces on a computer screen.

Most people have heard of garment design. It requires specialized technical and art training, with skills in both **flat** and **computer patternmaking**. There is a lot of competition for these plum jobs. Be willing to start with anything remotely related and work up to a design position. Strong draping skills, with a keen eye for color and texture, are essential. The more technical skills you can acquire (**garment construction**, **fabric construction**), the more successful you will be when you design. Designers must have first-rate skills to create, produce, and promote their products (Figure 2-3). They must always be looking for ways to be leaders.

Garment Construction
The assembly of a garment; also, the level of quality detail that is included in a garment.

Textile Design

Fabric Construction
The technicalities of thread, yarn size and machinery used to produce a specific fabric.

Textile design is a combination job between pure art (pattern, print design) and technical concerns (printing techniques, weaving techniques). Many companies use freelance help to provide fabric design, particularly prints. There are large print services that show and sell thousands of print designs to mills, wholesalers, product developers, and retailers. The future for originality hinges on exciting fabrications. Many leading designers—Donna Karan, Jhane Barnes, and Pamela Dennis, to name just a few—are concentrating their efforts in textile design to create these new and interesting fabrics.

Figure 2–3

Designer Valerie Gary of Alan Stuart Menswear. (And yes, this is what a real designer's office looks like...) Courtesy of Alan Stuart.

There are many other technical jobs in the fiber and fabric markets. Usually, this type of technical career starts in a technical or engineering school.

Merchandising

A merchandiser expedites the process of putting together the wholesale or private-label line. Responsibilities include planning styles and inventory quantities, delivery by delivery. Also critical is keeping track of the status of the line

Student Izabela Guta rendering a fabric print.

Original fabric and matching rendering. Courtesy of Izabela Guta.

from concept to delivery. The merchandiser works closely with the designer to put the line together and with the production department to get the line made up. This is a real troubleshooting job.

Whatever goes wrong becomes the merchandiser's responsibility to fix. You need to be able to work with a wide variety of people and to coax and cajole to get things done. This job is very interesting because it gets involved in all aspects of garment design and production. It also carries tremendous responsibility and can be nerve-wracking at times. For a merchandiser's job, time spent as a retail buyer is an advantage, as these jobs are somewhat related. Both require strong knowledge of assortment planning and merchandising math.

THE INSIDE SCOOP

Dianne Ige

Dianne has been a buyer for the Boston Store, Milwaukee; a merchandise consultant and product developer for AMC; head of sales and marketing for Natori; in wholesale merchandising and sourcing for Polo Ralph Lauren and Gant; and then once again in retailing with Bluefish.

> The number one quality you will need for success in wholesale is *flexibility*. You also have to be able to see far enough down the road to anticipate changes and potential problems—and then bob and weave to keep things on track. You've got to be *proactive* rather than reactive. A wholesale merchandising job is very demanding. Don't think people will thank you for keeping up with it through long hours and tremendous effort. That is simply what you are expected to do.
>
> There are many things that come along that you can't control. You should try not to waste negative energy on these situations. Learn from experience, yes—but then let it go. If you can keep a sense of humor about these daily 'disasters,' it will be easier for everyone.

Production

Production work is mostly technical, with some candidates actually coming up from front-line or supervisory factory jobs. There are also administrative jobs that have to do with scheduling and tracking. In the production department, people often wear many hats. Being responsible for coordinating fabric delivery to factories, scheduling raw materials for construction, and shipping finished orders to stores takes a great deal of coordination and customer service ability. A strong knowledge of sewing and other individual production operations pays off here. In addition, this job has to deal with the complexities of import paperwork and U.S. Customs. The production department controls the flow of the product, making sure that there is always enough work (not too much, not too little) and that everyone has the right skills, training, and machinery to construct a garment properly.

Sourcing

If a wholesaler imports a line, the process is slightly different. Overseas contractors need to be located (*sourced*) and then controls put in place to make sure that production is executed correctly at a very long distance. This job requires frequent overseas travel and a sensitivity to cultural differences. Wholesale merchandising is the most direct background for this, in addition to considerable technical knowledge of both garment and fabric construction. Many newcomers are excited about this opportunity to travel, but remember, you go when and where the job requires, not necessarily when and where you want to go. Some positions require that you be away from home as much as six months a year (although three is more likely). This takes a toll, so you need to assess realistically if your personal obligations will allow this type of commitment.

This is not a job for beginners. Probably two to three years as a retail buyer and five to eight years as a wholesale merchandiser would provide a suitable background.

Sales and Marketing

For this job you've got to have the right personality! There are lots of really strong salespeople in the wholesale markets, and they have spoiled the retail buyers to the point where you're probably going to have to put up with quite a lot from the buyers, your customers. Buyers are trained to push hard for anything they can get, reasonable or not. You will be on the other side of that table. You've got to walk away with some of your profitability left and with that buyer still a customer. That's not always easy.

A sales professional must be "up" every day. You must be pleasant to even the most unpleasant buyer. Salespeople test themselves every day. Unlike many other jobs in fashion, a salesperson does have instant gratification—when an order is placed (or instant rejection when it is not!).

Sales in the wholesale market

Showroom Sales
A wholesale sales position based in a showroom (usually New York), to show the line to retailers who visit.

There are two principal roles for salespeople. You could be on the staff of a leading designer or manufacturer as a **showroom sales** *representative.* This means that you would be responsible for showing and selling the line in the showroom, usually in New York. You'd work closely with the buying offices, visiting buyers, press, and advertisers. You might also help coordinate fashion events during key market weeks. These reps often also participate in regional or national trade fairs.

Another job in sales is that of an *on-the-road representative.* Independent sales reps often work with two or three manufacturers. A rep will cover a geographic territory and show the lines to stores in that territory. Reps make sure that merchandise is delivered and presented well, and serve as a liaison between designers and stores. The job of a sales rep is very demanding and somewhat unstructured. Reps set their own appointments and keep their own schedules, yet they are responsible to maintain a certain volume level of sales. Each manufacturer or designer pays a commission to the sales reps for their sales, but the reps often must pay their own business expenses and personal tax liabilities.

What sets a really good salesperson apart is product knowledge. Having been involved in design and/or merchandising is an advantage. Also helpful, again, is that retail experience! Retail buyers (your customers) will feel that you understand them and speak their language if you have been a buyer previously. A salesperson also needs a clear understanding of the retail marketplace. For example, if you sell your line to a mass merchant, is this going to make it impossible to sell to department stores? Each order that is written often has some sort of repercussion, good or bad.

Finally, let's talk about a new kind of job that has grown tremendously in the past decade.

Vendor Sales Specialists or Merchandise Coordinators

Vendor sales specialist or merchandise coordinator almost sounds like the selling specialist job we talked about in the retailing section. You're right. Many people who really want to move into the design field find themselves taking a retail sales path and ending up as a merchandise coordinator for a manufacturer or designer. What's the difference?

Leading firms including Claiborne, Polo, Ellen Tracy, Anne Klein II, Ungaro, Donna Karan, and Nike, employ specialists who are responsible for a specific geographic territory. Instead of being employees of one store, these specialists work with all the stores in a region to train the sales associates about upcoming deliveries and events. Product knowledge seminars are presented at the onset of the season so that the salespeople will understand the particular vendor's look and quality. Customer loyalty is built through trunk shows and merchandise seminars held for retail consumers.

The latest refinement is the emergence of an independent organization to provide this service to a number of manufacturers. Merchandising Concepts Group in Philadelphia has been operating since 1995. Nick Eggleston, a principal of the firm, describes the service as "bridging the merchandising service gap between wholesale and retail." This company contracts with several manufacturers. The staff will go into each branch of chains that carry these lines on a prescribed schedule, to perform tasks such as straightening that manufacturer's fixtures, putting stock on the floor, doing special inventories, or providing extra sales help for special promotions. These jobs provide a very good introduction to the industry and they are needed in almost every city in the country.

Finally, though it may be difficult to believe, the two fields of fashion (retail and wholesale) do meet to form a hybrid kind of job, described next.

BUYING OFFICES AND RETAIL PRIVATE-LABEL PRODUCT DEVELOPERS

A **buying office** is usually a group of retailers working together under one corporate organization. For example, Burdines, Rich's, Macy's, and Bloomingdales are all part of the Federated corporate buying organization. There are also offices such as Atkins (Bon Ton, Stone and Thomas, Elder Beerman) or Doneger (hundreds of accounts), which have member stores but do not own them. Just as there are fewer department store chains, there are now fewer buying offices. We discuss next the two main services provided by buying offices.

> **Buying Office**
> An association of retail stores; used to share and provide several different services to the member stores.

Retail Consulting and Direction

The main responsibility of someone in retail consulting and direction is forecasting consumer, fashion, lifestyle, and buying trends. This research enables store buyers to select products that are right for their target market in styling, price, fabrication, and color. The resident buying staff is also responsible for locating new and exciting vendors by constant "shopping" of the wholesale showrooms. They often visit their member stores to be sure they have a clear perception of the stores' profiles and customers. At times they will write "test" orders for stores on new lines, follow up on buyers' orders, communicate between vendors and stores, and prepare for market weeks. (Examples are Atkins and Doneger.)

Some store groups have taken this one step further, with centralized buying. The corporate (or resident) buyer has the authority to place some (or all) of the orders for the member stores. Strongly centralized organizations, striving for maximum clout and uniformity, use this technique. (Examples are the May Company and Federated.)

Group Product Development

> ***Product Development***
> Creating a garment from start to finish. Done by wholesalers and private-label staff.

Group **product development** personnel are responsible for finding, designing, and developing product lines that are in synch with each member store's target market (Figure 2-4). Then they go out worldwide to find manufacturers to produce these products at competitive prices. Needless to say, this is a growing and demanding field. To some extent, stores are becoming their own designers, thus requiring employees who understand retail, design, *and* sourcing. (Examples are Associated Merchandising Corporation and Mast Industries.)

For group private-label product development, prior experience is usually also retail buying, but in some cases it can be wholesale merchandising and designing as well. Ironically, with more of the large chains pulling product development back under their corporate wing, there has been a huge shift, with many of these jobs moving out of New York. Currently, some of the largest centers include:

Figure 2-4

Tonya Bott and Geri Sussman of the Associated Merchandising Corporation discuss a proposed Children's style.

St. Louis, Missouri	May Company
Columbus, Ohio	The Limited
Andover, Massachusetts	Mast Industries (The Limited)
Little Rock, Arkansas	Dillard's
Minneapolis, Minnesota	Dayton-Hudson Corp.
Dallas, Texas	J.C. Penney
Troy, Michigan	K-mart
Chicago, Illinois	Sears
San Francisco, California	Gap

There are some other, more specialized job opportunities as well which we describe next.

FASHION AND COLOR SERVICES

Fashion and color services tend to be individuals or small companies that sell predictive fashion and/or color information to various companies at all levels of the industry. These jobs are real "purist" jobs, and there are few to go

Sketching
Drawing fashion figures or doing technical drawings of garments.

MAC Illustrator
Artist who works on Apple MAC equipment, preparing graphics or illustrations.

Hangtags
The small paper tags that are attached to garments to communicate information to consumers.

THE INSIDE SCOOP

TONYA BOTT

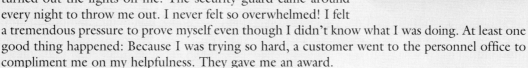

Tonya picked the University of Cincinnati to get her B.A. in fashion design for one major reason: They insisted on a series of co-op job experiences as part of the course of study. She had six different co-ops: Lord & Taylor and Neiman Marcus on the retail selling floor, at AMC, at Sarne Handbags doing merchandise **sketching** and presentation boards, at Edison Brothers as a **MAC illustrator** for labels and **hangtags**, and at Mast Industries making size specs. She is now the women's knitwear designer for Gillman Knitwear.

On the importance of getting out in the world:

Lord & Taylor was my first coop job. But I didn't know how to handle the workload. I worked so late every night that they turned out the lights on me. The security guard came around every night to throw me out. I never felt so overwhelmed! I felt a tremendous pressure to prove myself even though I didn't know what I was doing. At least one good thing happened: Because I was trying so hard, a customer went to the personnel office to compliment me on my helpfulness. They gave me an award.

Anyway, from this experience I knew that I didn't want to work in the retail end of the business. But I didn't know what I wanted. When I came to AMC [Associated Merchandising Corp.], I knew right away that this was it: product development.

The co-op program was a tremendous learning process. I found out what I did and did not want to do. Then, in trying to land a permanent job, I got no response from résumés and cover letters. But I did call people I had met on co-op, and that's how I got my first job—at AMC!

around. Current providers include the people who have established themselves through decades of accomplishment as on-target color and trend forecasters. Their credibility is based on their past record of accuracy. This could be an eventual career goal after some years at both retail and wholesale. You need an incredibly good fashion eye and lots of energy to keep selling yourself over and over.

In Chapter 6 we outline some of the companies providing this service.

FASHION PROMOTION AND AD AGENCIES

Jobs in fashion promotion and ad agencies are primarily journalism jobs (copy writing) or art jobs (illustration). Keep in mind that the majority of artwork is now produced on computers. The most common operating programs are Adobe Illustrator and Adobe Photoshop. You must have computer skills—there is no getting around it.

Another very stimulating field is fashion photography (Figure 2-5). You must be a photographer first and foremost—fashion becomes a specialization within that (Figure 2-6). But it must be one of the most exciting specializations!

If you have background or training in graphic design, writing, or marketing but want to work in fashion—large retailers and wholesalers tend to have some on-staff positions. Most others in the industry will go to freelancers or ad agencies to get this kind of help. But then there is that one, wonderful job that you never dreamed could be real. (See Inside Scoop, Dina Colombo.)

Figure 2-5

This fashion photo captures both the age and attitude of the customer. In addition, it shows the baggy jean more effectively than a posed shot would. Photo by student J. Colin Dunn.

Figure 2–6
Fashion photography class. Photo by student Jason VanBlaricum.

There is one other specialized area within marketing, show promotion.

Fashion Show Promotion

There are a handful of agencies in New York and Los Angeles that specialize in organizing, publicizing, and mounting fashion shows. The leading firm in New York currently is KCD. When Marc Jacobs received an influx of operating capital to design the first Louis Vuitton ready-to-wear line, "he said that the extra money was used to hire the efficient powerhouse of production and public relations, KCD, and that for the first time, he wasn't spending hours worrying about staging, models, seating, and lighting" [*New York Times*, April 9, 1997, "Two Take the Money and Produce," Amy M. Spindler]. To

THE INSIDE SCOOP

Dina Colombo

Dina is one of Evelyn's former students at the Art Institute of Ft. Lauderdale. She is now the director of publicity for DKNY Men's, Kids', Jeans, and Activewear.

On hitting the glamor jackpot:

I returned to New York after graduating. In my exit interview at the Art Institute, I was told that Donna Karan International occasionally calls for **interns**. After a week home, I called the Donna Karan public relations office and volunteered to intern for them. They needed help because the collection show was just a week away. I really wanted to work in sales, but this opportunity was in publicity. (I got a chance to try sales later and hated it!) Now, I wouldn't leave PR for anything!

In public relations, I work a lot with fashion magazines—advising on samples, working on stories. Fashion editors call and we decide together what is best for their shoot. DKNY is also very involved in the music industry. Occasionally, we lend clothes to big-name singers. I review head shots and listen to their music to make sure that everything fits the image of DKNY. I'm also involved in dressing celebrities for the Grammys, Tonys, Emmys, and Oscars. At times I've had to fly out to California to meet them. Recently, I was invited to the Oscars and went to all the parties afterward!

Internship
Also called *cooperative education.* To work for a company in the field, at a small salary or perhaps no salary. The point is to gain firsthand experience.

work in this field, you must be creative, original, flexible, and calm. Being fashionable in appearance also doesn't hurt.

Now that you've had a look at what opportunities exist for you, let's move on to Chapter 3 and learn what direction the industry is taking. You need to know what's going up and who's coming down. You don't want to pursue a fashion job for a whale-bone corset supplier!

SO YOU WANT TO WORK IN THE FASHION BUSINESS?
Here's How to Begin. . . Chapter 2

Often you will hear people say, "It's not what you know but whom you know," that will get you a job. This statement does have strong merit—and here's an idea of how you can start meeting the right people and not only learn about the industry but also start to meet the people who are making it happen. Industry leaders call this *networking*, and without a doubt it is the best way to secure a position in any industry. Develop strong networking skills as you seek out part-time jobs or internships, and as you grow in your professional career. Networking will help guide you to the field that will complement your strengths. It is so disappointing to work at a job that doesn't allow you to grow creatively and professionally. Networking is a great way to find out what you like and don't like.

Informational Interviews: This Is Your First Step

How to conduct an informational interview:

a. Ask your instructors, guest speakers, or even people you meet at your current job to suggest someone they might know in a field that interests you or in a field you are learning about.

b. Phone the contact person and ask for a brief meeting to learn about the industry. You are not asking for a job, so these are easy phone calls to make. Identify who you are, who referred you to the person, and tell him or her that you are simply looking for some advice about the industry.

c. Schedule a brief appointment. Remember that this person is taking time from his or her job responsibilities, so make sure that you are prepared.

d. Arrive on time, appropriately dressed. Make sure that you again emphasize that you are looking for advice, and ask if you can take notes. Here are some suggested questions to ask:

1. What are your job responsibilities?
2. With whom do you work or to whom do you report?
3. What are your greatest challenges?
4. How did you start out in this field?
5. What suggestions do you have for a newcomer to the industry?
6. Can you recommend any other people with whom I should speak?

e. Keep the meeting brief even if you would love to stay longer. Tell the interviewee how much you respect his or her time and ask if you might return sometime.

f. Follow up with a thank-you note. Make sure you tell the person how much you learned and that you hope to meet again. You never know—that person might be your next boss!

Try to meet at least one new person every quarter. By the time you graduate you will have many new contacts in your field, and with your education you will then be able to say that your first job came from what you know and from whom you've met.

As you move through this course, we want you to continue informational interviewing, but we also want to encourage you to get as involved as possible. Take a look at some advice for the near future.

Industry Shadowing: Now It's Time to Learn Some More Details

You're probably wondering what this means. We can assure you it doesn't mean sneaking around—it means having a chance to see the "action." Here are some suggestions on how to arrange a day in the industry.

After you have conducted a couple of informational interviews, you might find yourself wanting to learn more but not quite ready to tie yourself down to an internship or part-time job. One of the greatest opportunities is to shadow someone in the industry for a day. Using the same approach as you did with the informational interviews, call someone whom you have interviewed and ask if you can spend a day observing what goes on in the person's office or factory. Many college campuses have faculty employment advisors who can also assist you with an appropriate contact. Again remember to arrive on time, and to be dressed appropriately. Make sure that you again emphasize that you are simply there to observe and learn, and ask if you can take notes.

Here's some advice: Stay in the background observing the people and the activity. This is a perfect entry for your fashion journal. Write down your thoughts and feelings about the people, the types of jobs, and the atmosphere. What did you like? Even more important, what didn't you like? When your day is over, follow up with a thank-you note and point out something specific that you learned. You never know whom that person might be talking to in the industry.

OK, how's this for lucky? The Fresh Air Fund in New York provided a day of garment industry shadowing for their young people—with Tommy Hilfiger, himself! They "learned about fabrics, dyes, product quality, and all the different jobs in the fashion industry, like working in retail or accounting, or organizing shows." [*New York Times*, May 25, 1997, "Job 'Shadowing' Helps Children Discover Different Paths to Success," Stacey Hirsch].

Internships: This Is Your Chance to Find Your Niche Before You Look for a Job

Sometimes you will hear people call this *on-the-job training*, and sometimes, an *apprenticeship*. No matter what it is called, it can be your key to a future job opportunity. If nothing else, participating in a voluntary internship allows you the opportunity to work in several areas while you discover your niche.

Here are some suggestions on how to arrange an internship: Using your industry contacts, your school placement services, or even through a course requirement, everyone should dedicate a specific period of time to learning on the job, most often without compensation. Working hand in hand with industry pros, watching the business operations, giving a hand when needed, will allow you to find the tempo and creativity that suits you. Volunteer eight hours a week in the industry for about 12 weeks at a time. During that time you will really "see" firsthand what a job or company is like.

Here's some advice: Try to involve yourself in at least three internships during your formal educational training. This will give you an opportunity to explore a few different fields and evaluate which avenue—design, construction/production, or marketing/sales—suits you best. In the end you are far better prepared to interview; you not only know what the industry is looking for but your résumé will reflect your intensity and dedication to learning about the fashion industry.

CHAPTER 3

Changes in Today's Fashion Industry

You have just learned about the current job situation and where most jobs are. But there are big changes brewing in the industry that will produce more of some jobs, fewer of others. For example, if you are interested in designing clothes, there will be jobs but maybe not exactly where you had pictured them. To understand this, let's clarify four different types of designing jobs:

1. A designer brand with the designer's own name on the label (Tommy Hilfiger, Ralph Lauren, Betsey Johnson, Calvin Klein).
2. A design team with someone else's name or brand on the label (Levi's, ABS, Christian Dior). Name designers who fall into this category often also *license* other companies to design and produce products under their designer names. Calvin Klein underwear, for example, is made by Warnaco. You could be a designer for Warnaco, designing Calvin Klein underwear (with his direction, of course). Your name only goes on the paycheck, but consider that status enough.
3. Product development for department stores or mass merchants. These people design for the store's own private brands (Penney's Arizona, Macy's Club Room).
4. A buyer for totally private-label stores. The label on the clothes matches the name on the door (Gap, Limited, Abercrombie and Fitch, Talbot's). These buyers are expected to design *and* buy.

The first two types used to be the only design jobs. They're probably what you thought you'd be doing. In the past decade, however, jobs in product development and private-label design are becoming increasingly commonplace, even though they are not "pure" design jobs. They usually also encompass buying, merchandising, and/or sourcing as well. This reinforces why it is important to get as much broad experience as possible. Don't over-specialize too soon. Right now there is a relatively small pool of people who are fully trained to do this hybrid job. It is likely that you may handle one of these jobs in your career.

The next two segments of the book will give you some background on two other significant industry changes:

- There is a trend to have bigger companies control more of the functions that separate companies used to do, including design.
- There is a worldwide demand for lower prices, which means that a designer has to make more and more out of less and less.

Both these changes will affect where fashion jobs will (and won't) be in the future.

THE BIG GET BIGGER: AND IT STARTS WITH THE NATIONALIZATION OF RETAIL

Not too many years ago, every community had its own local department store plus an array of **"Mom and Pop" specialty stores**. Sure there were also the mass merchants such as Sears, Penney's, and Montgomery Ward, but even they carried special things for the local audience. Well, the 1990s are changing

> ***"Mom and Pop" Specialty Stores***
> Small, single-unit retail stores, often family run.

all this. The smaller operators are mostly dropping out, thanks to mergers and acquisitions. leaving only the strongest national retailers. Long-distance control has become possible via computers and electronic data transmission. "The top five department store chains are all national operators and control 73% of industry sales. The Big Three discount players—Wal-Mart, K-mart, and Target—control 80% of the discount sales [*Daily News Record*, Sept 2, 1996, "Managing the Productivity Loop Paradox"]. [Note: The *Daily News Record* (May 23, 1997) lists the top five department store chains as J.C. Penney ($24 billion), Federated ($15 billion), May Co. ($11.6 billion), Dayton/Hudson/Marshall Fields and Mervyns ($7.5 billion), and Dillards ($6.2 billion).

Specialty Store Chains
Large retail chains that do most of their business in shopping malls (for example, The Limited, Gap)

Most industry observers feel that there is still more consolidation ahead of us. Many believe that in the near future we will have four or five department store chains, two or three mass merchants, and a handful of **specialty store chains**. These retailers will span the entire country. Even 10 years ago, no one would have dreamed that the individually powerful department store chains of Federated (Bloomingdale's, Lazarus, Rich's), Allied (Sterns, Bon Marche), and Macy's would all be merged into one nationwide megacompany! Even country boundaries no longer contain retailers. The Swedish furniture chain IKEA has stores in virtually every part of the globe. The biggest retailers have the most buying and advertising power, making it almost impossible for smaller stores to compete.

$200 Million Retail Volume
The total gross sales volume (in retail dollars) that a store achieves in one year.

In the 1970s, a department store chain of **$200 million retail volume** was a force to be reckoned with. By the mid-1990s, a chain operation generating $2 billion was more like it. More buying and selling power is now being concentrated in far fewer hands. "Since 1990, over 100,000 retail firms have filed for bankruptcy protection, a 60% increase over the 1984 to 1989 period" [*Daily News Record*, May 23, 1997]. As a result, all the secondary players along the supply chain, including wholesalers, manufacturers, and material suppliers, are getting squeezed out of business.

What in the World Is This Leading To?

Niche
Small spot or place; used commonly to mean specialization in a distinct target market.

Before you panic, let's quickly point out that everything in life is cyclical. It's our feeling that as soon as the retail market is dominated almost totally by a handful of huge stores, the time will be exactly right for small companies to pop up with an original concept, or with an offering that is needed in just a small local area, or who find some other **niche**. There will always be room for a fresh retail concept. For example, giant J.C. Penney is testing the idea of targeting

the content of selected stores to African-American customers [*Women's Wear Daily*, July 18, 1996]. The Gap has renewed itself by reinventing Banana Republic, and tested several lower-priced concepts before hitting it right with Old Navy.

Dale Nitschke, senior vice president of Daytons/Hudsons/Marshall Field, put it this way: "On a grand scale, it's true that the big will get bigger. Stockholders will continue to want a return on their investment. And technology is becoming so important—and expensive—that only the big guys will be able to afford it. Still, there is room for smaller players to survive and succeed. Guests [customers] are always looking for unique fashion, and a personal touch. The 'Big Guys' struggle to deliver that."

Even if these very clever supercompanies know how to hit a huge chunk of the U.S. populace, there will always be some customers whom they can't address. That's where the new, small entrepreneur comes in, as Dale says. But with the huge nationalization of retail, focusing on fewer and fewer chains, the competition is aggressive among the designers and stores to develop collections that represent top-notch style and quality, with competitive pricing. So the pressure is on *everyone*, big and small alike!

THE VALUE SQUEEZE: EVERYONE'S GOT TO GET SMARTER!

What does the garment business boil down to? A customer sees a garment, likes it, decides if it is a good value, and buys it. That's it! As simple as this sounds, it is also simple (though a bit scary) to realize that this customer has hundreds of different places to buy the same garments. A garment retailer is in competition with every other **outlet** offering garments. Customers are no longer "loyal" to one store or another—they will generally shop anywhere that gives them what they want at the price they want to pay.

> ***Outlet***
> In a general sense, an outlet is any retail store, but *factory outlet* has become the dominant use of this word—so there is often some confusion.

Before the nationalization of retail, customers had vastly fewer choices. Retailers could get away with offering less value because there was less competition. There was room for everyone to make a nice living. Well, no more! Today's customer is extremely savvy about what does and does not constitute a good value. Even at the lower end of the scale, a retailer such as Wal-Mart offers quality that is really very good, certainly good enough for millions of U.S. customers. With their buying power, they can sell at a very sharp price, which means great value for the customer.

The same process is happening all the way up the price ladder. Even designers have realized that they can't get away with an outrageous price just because of their fashion image. When a leading manufacturer or designer produces product, the flow of activities usually follows this path:

designer → fabrics → manufacturer → marketing →
→ sales → advertising → customer service → store

Everyone in that flow has to get paid. For everyone to get paid, the product has to be exciting, dynamic, and worth enough to cover all these expenses.

However, customers (rebounding from job losses, downsizing, and cutbacks) have started focusing more on prices. The national retailers had to find a way to get the same exciting garments but at lower prices than previously. The answer became simple, but painful. Eliminate some of those people, such as the marketing, advertising, and sales departments, and the same product could get made, but sold at a lower price. Then the flow of activities above might be changed to this:

designer → fabrics → manufacturer → store

> ***Estimated Gross Margin***
> Gross Margin is the measure of profitability used in the retail industry, generally expressed as a percentage of total department or division sales, so it becomes the portion of the total retail dollar volume that can be considered as profit (before expenses).

Not only are the middlemen getting eliminated, the entire supply chain is getting squeezed—hard.

Gross margin is a measure of profitability in retail stores. It is expressed as a percentage of total dollar sales before deducting for general expenses. The National General Merchandise Group of Stores saw its **estimated gross margin** drop from 34.0% in 1986 to 29.6% in 1994 [Combined Annual Retail Trade, April 1996, U.S. Bureau of Census, current series, Business Reports series BR/95-9V].

Each step in the process, from acquiring fabric through construction and distribution, is being examined for cost savings. Through trial and error, the industry is learning what can be cut and what can't be cut, while keeping the customer happy with the end product. Here's Dale Nitschke again: "It's the supply chain side that will be key to success in the next 20 years. You can still squeeze efficiencies out of it. The person who can deliver the fastest and best will be the winner."

Manufacturers are always looking for ways to lower costs, because the lower the costs, the lower the selling price to the consumer. Finding lower labor costs has been the major solution for most manufacturers. Chic jeans opened its first plant outside the United States in Mexico in 1996. "As of January 1, [1997], wholesale prices for Chic's average stonewashed jeans were reduced to $11.75 a pair from the 1996 back-to-school price of $13.44, according to Robert F. Luehrs, president" [*Daily News Record*, January 3, 1997, "Chic's New Mexican Plant Will Let Firm Cut Prices"].

Price matters a lot to the consumer. This is really tricky territory. It's very easy to cheapen a product just enough so that the customer gets turned off by that garment. This usually happens after multiple wearings and washings. (You've probably got something in your closet that after several runs through the washing machine, you no longer wear. Perhaps it shrank too much, or faded, or lost its shape.) This is a big turn-off, and both brands and stores that have sold inferior merchandise have been put out of business. This means that if a manufacturer has to find a way to keep the price of a product down, there is no margin for error. Cost cutting has to be found in areas that don't affect quality. Everyone in the process needs to work smarter. For example, if you can find a way to manufacture a blouse for 25 cents less (which doesn't sound like a lot), that could mean that the blouse could be sold for $1.00 less at retail. A dollar less starts making a real difference. The trick is to save that 25 cents without letting it show in the final product.

Because the public is so much more knowledgeable about good value and good performance, increased knowledge is now necessary in every job in the garment industry. Retail buyers need to know much more about the manufacturing process than they did in the past, so they can recognize the best values and the technicalities of garment performance. With all of this, many retail buyers have become involved in product development. This means that they act as their own wholesalers. The buyers themselves determine their customers' preferences in coloring, sizing, and styling. They work directly with manufacturers (often the same manufacturers that produce goods for top-name designers) to develop products that might have the same fabric and cut as designer brands but with prices typically 20 to 50% less than those of designer name brands. The reason that prices can be 20 to 50% lower is not because there is necessarily any difference in product quality, but because some of the middlemen have been eliminated.

House Brands, Private Brands
Store-owned labels that are developed by and for that store alone.

Let's take a look at some examples of familiar brands in stores that are popular quality products, well priced and yet are **house brands** or **private brands**. This means that the buyer was instrumental in the design of the product. It also means that if the customer wants that brand, the only store they can find it in is the one that developed the product. So now, when we said earlier to you that when a customer sees a garment, likes it, decides if it's a good value, and buys it, you can add another feature for private-label items—the customer can buy it only in that store, because they can't find it anywhere else (Figure 3-1).

Here are some familiar private brands:

J.C. Penney	Arizona Jeans Worthington Hunt Club

(*Note:* "About 50% of Penney's apparel sales come from house brands" [*Investor's Business Daily*, April 4, 1997])

Saks Fifth Avenue	Real Clothes The Works
Federated	INC Alfani

("In 1997, private label and private branded goods are expected to represent well over $2 billion at retail" [*Daily News Record*, April 23, 1997, "Federated Brands Now 14% of Mix"]

Daytons/Hudsons/Marshall Field	Field Gear
Target	Merona Gilligan and O'Malley
Sears	Canyon River Blues
K-mart	Jacqueline Smith
Wal-Mart	Kathy Lee

(*Note:* Kathy Lee 1996 retail volume: $500 million. [*Women's Wear Daily*, May 7. 1997])

Figure 3-1

Men's department store private brand: Field Gear. Courtesy of Dayton's, Hudson's, Marshall Field.

Private-Label Product Development

In the past five to 10 years, many stores have plunged into private-label product development seeing all the advantages but not understanding the drawbacks. It is really hard to create truly professional-looking garments, and soon you will know many of the reasons why. There have been successes, especially in those companies that are 100% private label—Banana Republic, Disney, Warner Brothers. Department stores with a very clear brand vision have also been successful, such as Dayton/Hudson/Marshall Field with "Field Gear."

Pros

- *Exclusivity.* This is now probably the leading reason given for private label. If no one else is carrying these items or these (private) brands, you don't have to put yours on sale the minute your competitor does.
- *Control.* A good brand name has consistent fit and a consistent level of quality so that consumers can count on it season after season. If a store wants to develop a private brand with the same consistency, the best way to do it is the same way a wholesaler does—full product development from beginning to end, as we show in Unit II. The retailer will also be able to control the flow of inventory coming in each month under this brand.
- *More profitable.* Profitability goes hand-in-hand with exclusivity. If no one else has this item under this brand, the store can get whatever price the market will bear. Also, with the middlemen eliminated, the store can take more of the markup for itself. First quarter 1997 earnings at Federated "were bolstered by increased sales of private label clothes, which carry higher profits" [*New York Times,* May 15, 1997, "Federated Has Profit on Store-Brand Sales"].

Cons

- *You're all alone.* Oh, the mistakes we've seen buyers make. Until now, buyers were never expected to be product developers. They were to sit in a showroom and pick out their favorites from a line that had been put together by the professionals on the wholesale team. Since there is no wholesaler in private label, if the buyer makes a mistake, there is no cushion, no partner; no markdown money from the wholesaler, no returns, no coop advertising dollars. For example, Saks' sales fell short of expectations in the first quarter of 1997 "because the company's store brand clothes were too trendy for customers" [*New York Times,* May 16, 1997, "K-mart Posts Profit, and Earnings Gain at Saks and Gap"]. Remember—the buyer is buying a specification product from a contractor or manufacturer. That means

> ***Letter of Credit***
> A legal and binding agreement between (in our case) an importer, that importer's bank, and the local contractor. It gives contractors full assurance that they will be paid by the bank when they meet the obligation and deliver.

that if the garments come out as specified but look really ugly, that's the buyer's fault (and markdown), not the contractor's. And we've seen ugly!

- *Ties up funds.* Most financial arrangements with contractors require that some funding or financial guarantee (often a **letter of credit**) be posted by the store at the start of the process. This process could take nine months or more! This ties up the store's money, which means these funds can't be used for anything else during that (long) period. When buying from a wholesaler, stores have gotten in the habit of paying for the merchandise well after they've already started selling it. That's a big difference. Yet another risk in buying as much as nine months in advance is that fashion garments have a relatively short selling life. You might buy short skirts when they are hot, only to have them "drop dead" before you can deliver yours!
- *This is no place for amateurs.* As you will see in Unit II, buyers doing private-label product development have to go through the same elaborate, involved, and above all time-consuming product development process as a wholesaler would. And this they do on top of their normal duties (Figure 3-2). It is very hard to do both jobs well, especially since customers have learned to reject private brands that don't look every bit as good as national brands.

There are certainly advantages to private-label product development, but the disadvantages are separating the successful from the unsuccessful. Either stores make major commitments to staff and infrastructure (Federated, May

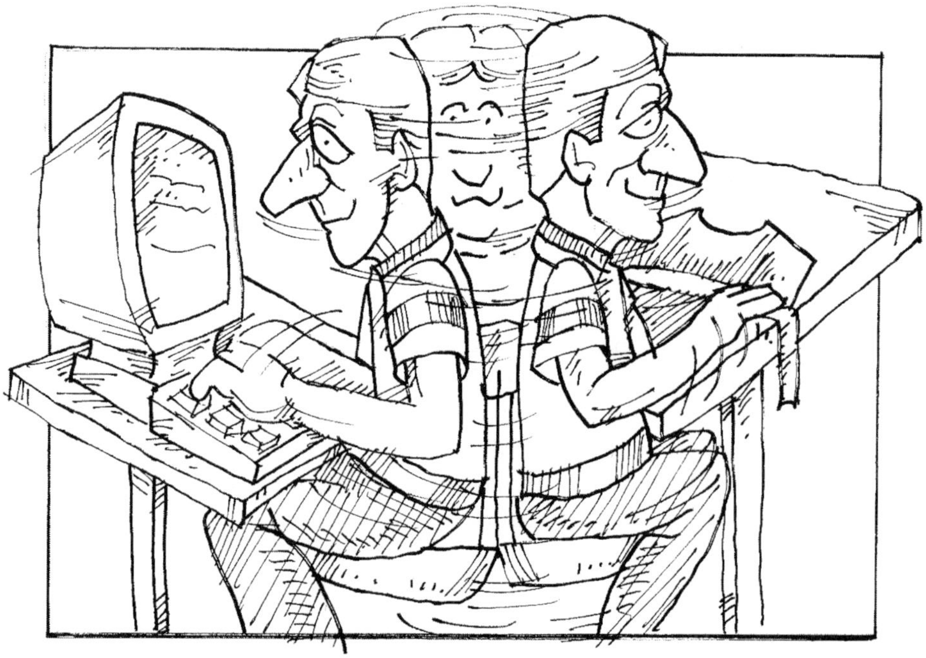

Figure 3-2

Artwork by Michael Carnegie.

Co., and Gap all certainly have), or else they will probably continue to struggle making private label profitable. As a side benefit, buyers involved with product development often say that this experience has also made them much better **line buyers**. This means that when they work with **sales reps** showing designer labels or branded lines, they know when a salesperson is "stretching the truth" or when a garment is over- or underpriced.

A product development buyer, through firsthand experience, is often able to determine how their private-label garment stacks up with industry quality standards. That information can then be passed on to salespeople on the floor, marketing people, and advertising agency staff, the folks who literally talk to customers. Being able to explain the washing and wearing **performance** of a garment in addition to the finishing details, styling, and color can make the difference between a good sales pitch and a great one. Since there are hundreds of places for a customer to buy, you've got to be able not only to offer the customer a better value—but also to explain to this customer why yours is a better value.

What this also means for you is that the shift toward more product development in the fashion industry opens more job opportunities. "Penney's is looking to build its home grown brands, including Arizona, estimated at about $1 billion in sales" [*Women's Wear Daily*, January 10, 1997, "Penney's Creates Unit to Develop Its Brands"]. Dillard's "is seeking to boost private label from just under 10% of assortments to around 15% in two years. About 15% of Federated Department store's assortment is private label, and Federated hopes to increase that to 20%." [*Women's Wear Daily*, January 21, 1997, "Mervyn's Exiting South; Dillard's to Buy 10 Units"].

In the past, buyers typically came from the fashion marketing, merchandising, or business wing of education. But with the growth of product development in the large national chains, buyers are being pulled from the design world as well because of their patternmaking, textile, and construction skills.

> ***Line Buyers***
> Retail store buyers who shop and buy preset manufacturers' lines (as opposed to buyers who do product development).

> ***Sales Reps***
> Wholesale salespeople, often independent and on commission. Rep is short for representative.

> ***Performance***
> How a garment holds up under washing and wearing conditions.

CUTTING OUT THE MIDDLEMEN: THE VERTICALIZATION OF FASHION

Yes, fashion is caught in a price squeeze: Labor and material costs are going up, but customers refuse to pay more. All participants in the garment supply chain are looking for ways to cut costs. One of the more recent developments involves an electronic connection between these participants. **Electronic data interchange**, known commonly as EDI, has connected wholesalers with retailers and fabric suppliers with wholesalers. Quite simply, this system allows the partners in garment making and selling to get more complete and timely information from each other. For example, wholesalers can get a steady stream of selling information from retailers. With this information, they can quickly make up the needed replacement goods—for what is actually selling versus what is not selling. Orders can also be transmitted back and forth electronically, in some cases automatically, without having to wait for an overbusy buyer. This entire setup has been dubbed **Quick Response** or QR. As all the players get bigger, this technology becomes critical to make sure that the supply lines keep the appropriate merchandise flowing into stores.

> ***Electronic Data Interchange (EDI)***
> Automatic exchange of information between companies, made possible by direct computer-to-computer linkage.

> ***Quick Response (QR)***
> Refers to the process of being able to produce and/or replenish merchandise in a compressed time frame.

Another aspect of more directly connecting the partners is an ongoing trend to have the primary partners speak directly with each other:

Fiber/fabric/trim producers
work directly with
Garment makers
who work directly with
Retail sellers.

It is the middlemen who used to facilitate this process who are getting squeezed out of business:

- *Fabric converters*, who would source fabrics for garment making.
- *Buying offices*, which would scout the wholesale market and put together "group purchases" between stores.
- *Wholesale road salespeople*, who would work with small accounts across the country.

More and more of these functions are being subsumed by one of the three principal partners. To go one step further, the industry is starting to see a partnership or even an ownership between the levels. Wholesalers such as Guess, Claiborne, Polo, and many others have opened their own retail stores. As noted earlier, retailers such as Limited, GAP, Disney, Talbot's, and Ann Taylor do their own design and product development and contract directly with factories. This means that these private label retailers act entirely as their own wholesalers. Fabric mills are adding sewing production, so they are fully vertical. *Vertical* means that a company does two or three of the steps in the production/selling process that would normally have been done by two or three separate companies selling to each other.

Dyer
Companies that dye fabric.

Finisher
Companies that specialize in providing the additional treatments needed by most fabrics before they can be used (for example, brushing, coating).

We've seen factories in places like Turkey where the raw cotton bales go in one end of the factory and finished garments come out the other end. In this case the same company is fiber and yarn producer, fabric knitter, **dyer** and **finisher**, and garment maker. Previously, four different companies would probably have been required to perform the same steps.

Why Is Verticalization Happening?

- *Cost.* The fewer middlemen, thus the fewer companies involved in producing and selling garments, the more money that is saved. There is much less overhead (factories, management, labor, etc.) involved in this more efficient process.
- *Clout.* With the big getting bigger, vertical mills tend to be very large. This gives them much greater buying and negotiating power on materials and allows them production savings as well.
- *Control.* This is a less obvious reason, but one growing in importance. If you are K-mart or Sears, you need to be sure that you can get a (huge) steady supply of products to sell. These large chains will seek out vertical suppliers because of their size and dependability. Also, with fewer layers involved, it is easier to make sure that everyone in the process understands the quality required. Within a vertical manufacturer, everyone has the same goals—all employees are striving to accomplish the same objectives.

In this chapter we have given you a feeling for the fashion job market—with a forecast for segments that will see job growth and others that will be contracting. Now that we've talked about you, in Chapter 4 it will be time to move on to the most important person in the entire world of fashion—not Giorgio Armani, not Geoffrey Beene—the most important person in the industry is *your customer.*

SO YOU WANT TO WORK IN THE FASHION BUSINESS?
Here's How to Begin. . . Chapter 3

It is very important to work with actual products as you compare and contrast designer brands with leading private labels and national brand names. The best way to do this is out in the field. You can even keep your notes in your fashion journal. By the end of the course you will have accumulated some terrific research. Here's some advice on how to stay current.

First

Cut out two or three pictures of designer items from leading fashion magazines. Choose only the items that are considered a "must" for the season.

Second

Visit your local mall and try to find these items or something comparable by the designer. Take a look at the quality, the styling details, and the price.

Now Compare

Visit a leading private-label store, the local department store, J.C. Penney or Sears, and a leading discount store such as Wal-Mart. Find a similar item and compare and contrast. Again take a look at the quality, the styling details, and the price. In fact, what styling ideas do you see in the designer-made products that you see in the private-label products? Which do you think the consumer will think is the best value, and why?

A Few Final Thoughts

What fabrications and/or styling ideas do you see in the designer-made products that you feel could be featured in the private-label brands to gain even more customer appeal/acceptance?

CHAPTER 4

The Customer: Different Generations, Different Desires, Different Clothes

So far we've talked mostly about you. You've had a chance to see whether or not you are a good "fit" for this industry, and you've also had a chance to see where the industry is going. But before you start carving out your own special niche, it is important to think about the people you will be working for—no, not your employers, your customers.

In reality your real employers are your customers. If they like your work, you will move successfully through the fashion business. Take a look at Tommy Hilfiger, Donna Karan, and Ralph Lauren. The consumer is the one who made them successful, simply because they have bought and continue to buy their products. It is the customer who has been responsible for the growth of the Limited and GAP organizations. It is the typical consumer who creates the success stories in the fashion industry, not the designer.

Do you remember the typical customer who was profiled in Chapter 1? She wants to look fashionable but not stick out in a crowd. Don't forget her, because you have to satisfy her needs. So before you pick up the sketch pad and start designing, or move into the production market or the merchandising arena, let's take a closer look at the customers to whom you can sell.

GENERATIONAL MARKETING

Generational Marketing Appealing to segmented age groups of customers.

You are living in a world that revolves around **generational marketing**. The first thing you probably want to ask is: What's that, and what does it have to do with fashion? First, generational marketing is a strategy that targets groups of people, defined by age and attitude. Until the 1960s the fashion world was more used to mass marketing. A designer or manufacturer would produce a garment, and based on its acceptance, the garment was knocked off for everyone to wear.

But that is not the way of the 1990s and it certainly won't be the direction that fashion designers take in the twenty-first century. American consumers

THE INSIDE SCOOP

Clara Hancox

Clara spent 50 years in the menswear industry, predominantly at the *Daily News Record*, the menswear trade daily. She retired as vice president and director of publishing. Clara also worked in marketing, advertising, and merchandising for men's firms such as Cricketeer and was codirector of the Boys' Apparel Manufacturers' Association. She is acknowledged to be the first woman to report on the Menswear industry.

On the sociology of fashion:

What does a person need to be successful in this business? It might sound strange but you've got to love people! A job in fashion is not like being an engineer, working in a factory with nuts and bolts. Fashion is a people product. How can you design merchandise, romance and sell it if you don't love your customer? And that means having a wide open mind toward your customer as well.

Once, during an interview with Giorgio Armani, I asked him how he knew which way to lead fashion, since he sets the trend for the entire industry. He said, "There is no such thing as a designer who designs from his head. A designer must observe the people in the streets, their attitudes, their behavior in restaurants, at social occasions, and so on. A true designer is one who can read—who can *feel* his public."

Photo courtesy of Clara Hancox

today demand good value along with innovative styling that satisfies their individual needs and matches their individual lifestyle. Today, designers looking for acceptance must find the "right" segment of society that will become their loyal customers. Once the consumer has responded, it is the designer's job to create a long-term demand by providing products every season that are consistent with this customer's needs.

Needs and attitudes vary, above all, by age. So let's take a quick look next at the generational groups that have formed the marketing strategies for many companies, including the fashion industry. [The following statistics are from *Fortune* June 26, 1995, "Making Generational Marketing Come of Age," Faye Rice.]

The GI Generation (coined from the term "Government Issue")

- Born 1912–1927
- About 13 % of the U.S. population, 24 million people
- Profile: These men and women were raised to save, save, save and to spend very little! This mature generation, living longer than any generation before, wants value for their money. Their attitude is that they deserve their Social Security and government benefits. Give them products that are functional, that last, but are not expensive. National brands are important, designer labels are not.
- Interests: Big Band music, AM radio, group cruises, bingo in the retirement homes.

Remember, these GI-generation folks are still going to be buying clothes when you get into the industry!

The Silencers (the post–World War I generation)

- Born 1928–1945
- About 21% of the U.S. population, 41 million people
- Profile: These men and women save, but they also spend. They were raised during a period of economic growth following World War I when new technology was emerging, such as radios, movies, and refrigerators. But many also went through the Great Depression. The younger members of this group actually feel like a "sandwich" generation, taking care of parents and acting as "second" parents to their grandchildren. A great deal of their spending power is not for themselves but for those they take care of. Quality for the price is very important to this generational group. They want clothes that last without being overpriced.
- Interests: movies, reading, Frank Sinatra and Tony Bennett (for the older silencers), Sam Cooke and Do-Wop (for the younger ones).

The next most talked about generational group is called the baby boomers, yet the baby boomers really are split in two groups. First there are the older boomers, affectionately called the Woodstock generation. Then come the younger, more cynical boomers, influenced by Watergate and the hostages in Iran, called the "zoomers."

The Woodstock Baby Boomers

- Born 1946–1954
- About 17% of the U.S. population, 33 million people
- Profile: These men and women spend, spend, spend—then borrow and spend more! Because of its sheer size, this generation alone is responsible for more changes in lifestyles and values of Americans than any other. When young they produced the youth culture of the 1960s. When they became parents they produced a "baby boomlet." Vietnam, Civil Rights, and the Women's Movement created a lifestyle demanding products on this generation's own terms. Manufacturers and designers were forced to create products, promotions, and selling techniques that spoke directly to this generation. They will not only "leave their mark" on society, but they have flocked together on key fashion statements and brands. They all wore Levi bell bottoms in the 1960s, disco-wear in the 1970s, and the status designers in the 1980s. Now in the 1990s, comfortable dress/casual subbrands such as Slates by Levi are being created just for this group. It won't be long before this "graying" group will be ready for retirement. Again, the sheer size of this group will influence fashion significantly at that time.
- Interests: rock and roll music (Motown, Beatles), dining out, extensive travel, movies, and sports.

The "Zoomer" Baby Boomers

- Born 1955–1965
- About 25% of the U.S. population, 49 million people
- Profile: Like their senior boomers, these men and women also spend, spend, and spend some more! But this younger wing of the boomer generation feels somewhat cheated by their older group members. When the national debt got out of hand, savings and loans scandals rocked the United States, and white-collar unemployment soared to record highs, this generational group felt their seniors had squandered things. It became their responsibility to "fix" society through self-help and New-Age philosophies. Yet just like the older boomers, in clothing, brands do matter, but brands with a hipper attitude (Guess, Tommy Hilfiger, GAP)
- Interests: rock and roll music, dining out, extensive travel, movies, self-help motivators, health food, and personal fitness.

Generation X

- Born 1966–1976
- About 21% of the U.S. population, 41 million people
- Profile: This generational group is probably the most misunderstood and the most complex. Although criticized for their lack of energy, direction, and purpose, they could be the most self-sufficient generation. These young men and women grew up as "latchkey" kids, as their mothers took to the business world. At an early age this generation took care of younger siblings, cooked meals, and took a back seat to their parents' divorces, loss of jobs, and a downsizing economy. As a rebellion against the boomers, the X-ers demanded their own look, one that pushed aside designer labels and focused on finding

a more relaxed, "who cares" lifestyle. They have very little money saved. Brand names are not as important as the fashion statement of antistatement. A very skeptical, pessimistic consumer group, with low consumer confidence and without brand loyalty, they have retailers and designers scrambling to find ways to win their approval. Levi Strauss, an acknowledged leader in fashion marketing, was the first to embrace this group. Its advertising campaigns have moved away from the aging boomers and now feature the Generation X "slackers," plus younger customers still. Bob Caplan, director of sales and retail marketing for Levi's, expresses it this way: "At Levi Strauss & Co., we believe that if you sell and cater to the young, you will own the future. You can't market to all. On the contrary, you have to be extremely focused on who your customer is, and then market to them better than anyone else."

- Interests: rap and retro music, coffeehouses, group dating to clubs, movies, and "just hanging out."

The Baby Buster Generation, or Generation Y

- Born 1977 to ?

Although this consumer group is not yet considered in most purchasing power statistics, their impact on the fashion market is expected to be enormous. In fact, young people in the 12- to 19-year-old range spent $109 billion in 1995, up 38% from 1990. [*U.S. News and World Report*, July 1, 1996, David Fischer and Michele Meyer]. The children of the baby boomers, they are being raised in an economy unlike any before them. This generation has not been affected by major wars or military conflicts. They are technologically advanced, surrounded with interactive toys, talking learning systems, video technology, Nintendo, Sega, cable TV, Disney, the Internet, and computers . Even in their toddler years, they demanded Power Rangers, Nintendo games, McDonald's food, and clothing that challenges with "No Fear," " Bad Boy," "Quicksilver," and "Stussy" logos. Rollerblading and skateboarding are the

THE INSIDE SCOOP

Bob Caplan

As noted earlier, Bob is the director of sales and retail marketing for the Levi's brand of Levi Strauss & Co. He is a 25-year veteran and prior to that, Bob was at Philips–Van Heusen.

> "Irreverent" is a word used to describe our target audience with the Levi's brand, the jean division: 15–19 year olds. How they express their irreverence changes from generation to generation. But we will only express "irreverence" with what ethically fits into our core values. We never want to be distasteful, or go too far. There are things we won't do for commercial success. Morally, each decision needs to withstand the measure of time. If you do what you know is ethically and sustainably right, everything else falls into place.

sports for this generation, and this market has already opened countless opportunities for manufacturers and designers. With TV as a prime source of entertainment, these kids are more name conscious, and they have parents who respond to their demands. In fact, Levi Strauss is using some of these young people as consultants. "Levi Strauss brings in about 500 young people, ages 11–25, who live throughout the United States and Canada. As members of Levi Strauss's three-year-old Trend Advisory Panel, the consultants go shopping with company researchers... and take photographs of young people wearing clothes that intrigue them" [*New York Times*, August 8, 1996, "Consultants with Tender Faces," Margaret Isa].

Levi Strauss is not the only company to recognize this youngest generation, however. JNCO jeans adapted very quickly to teen tastes for very-wide-legged jeans. Executives in the company said the secret of their success is close contact with shoppers. "JNCO has a website featuring surveys that read as if they were written by a 15-year-old, and the company sponsors or attends extreme-sports events that are littered with their target consumer—a 12- to 20-year-old skateboard or surfing enthusiast" [*New York Times*, March 14, 1997, "Squeezing into the Jeans Market," Jennifer Steinhauer].

Dennis Abramczyk, of Ralph Marlin Neckwear, states: "A good friend of mine started a store chain in Dallas called 'Gadzooks.' He's up to 183 stores now and adding more stores daily! The target customer is 'Generation Y'. The stores are eclectic, filled with whatever are the hottest items for this generation (nose rings, irreverent T-shirts). Young store managers get promoted to become young buyers. They are totally in touch with the Generation Y customer. This is why this store has become wildly successful!"

THE INSIDE SCOOP

Dale Nitschke

Dale is the senior vice president and general merchandise manager of men's and children's wear at Dayton, Hudson, Marshall Field. Based in Minneapolis, Dale's skills propelled him from buyer to DMM to GMM in record time.

On the importance of generational marketing:

Every generation wants to have attention paid to it. A retailer definitely wants to know what is really important to their guests [customers], what influences them to buy. So specialized marketing is critical.

It's funny that Tommy Hilfiger is the number one brand for Generation X. His clean, traditional look is counter to everything that Generation X says about itself. But these people still want to be part of a group. Look at Tommy's marketing. It's always a group of people. Generation X says they want to be individuals, but their desire to be part of a group is the same as everyone else's.

(*Note:* "Gadzooks topped $100 million in sales in 1996 for the first time" [*Daily News Record*, March 28, 1997].)

So these are your employers—your real employers, the customers. Each group thinks differently about many things, especially clothes. You can't do one line to appeal to all of them. But you can do a line that meshes with one group's image and needs. If you can really get into that group's head, you can produce the clothing that they will want. This is known as **niche marketing** or **target marketing**. Remember what we said in Chapter 1: This is a business, and to have enough business, you have to have a lot of customers. Each of these generational groups can produce enough customers for success.

> ***Niche Marketing, Target Marketing***
> Selecting a narrowly defined group of potential customers and styling a line to appeal to their needs and preferences.

Now where does this take you? You're still not ready to make the leap into design and manufacturing, because the next step is very important. Once you know who the customers are, you need to find out where they are spending their money and how much they are spending.

SO YOU WANT TO WORK IN THE FASHION BUSINESS?
Here's How to Begin. . . Chapter 4

This chapter has focused on people: getting to know their likes and dislikes. If you know your customer, you certainly have a better chance of producing and promoting products that will be sold successfully. One of the best ways to get to know people is right in your own classroom. Don't think meeting new people is the only thing we are talking about. It is also important to learn something new about people we already know. Designers and manufacturers are always looking for something new that will appeal to their steady customers. In fact, it probably is true that every one of us has turned to a good friend or neighbor and said to them: "I didn't know you liked..." Let's take some time and apply some informational interviewing techniques right in the classroom.

First: Meeting Someone New

Interview someone in your class that you don't know that well. (This is a great way to learn about your instructor.) Prepare your questions and have the person describe for you his or her likes and dislikes about key topics: school, work, cars, and even hot-point topics such as politics, gun control and drugs. Based on this information, develop a shopping profile. In other words, decide:

1. What types of products would this person like to buy?
2. What is important to this person about the products he or she is purchasing? What is not important?
3. Where do you think this person will like to shop? Try to figure out the amount that he or she will spend. (Remember, people don't have to pay top dollar for top names anymore.)

Second: Learning Something New About Someone

Now, here's the real test. Interview someone you think you know pretty well. Prepare a few questions that deal with the future. You might want to ask what the person would like to be doing in five years. Where he or she would like to live? Ask about something that he or she finds to be annoying and something found to be enjoyable. Really focus your questions on the person's lifestyle. Then, based on what you already know, and with this information added, create a customer profile for the types of products that this person would like to buy and identify the key features the person is looking for, including price.

Finally, for a real generational approach, interview someone outside your peer group. This is all very important, because as you move into the next chapter you will learn about fashion taste and price preference and how these factors identify where people shop.

CHAPTER 5

How Much Are Customers Spending, and Where Are They Buying?

PUTTING PEOPLE IN BOXES

With all these customers, it is important to remember that every person has his or her own personal taste. Mass media and other fashion influences have served to standardize taste to a degree. As you have seen, the industry has found that it is possible to break down the generations into definable fashion markets.

The incredibly large and diverse U.S. market becomes easier to understand if it is looked at on a grid with two key differentiators: *price* and **taste level**. First, before you start examining the charts, let's look at each of the two components.

PRICE	How much do people want to pay? Low price, medium, high? Or—as stated in the industry: *budget*, *moderate*, or *better*?
TASTE LEVEL	What "look" are they searching for, one that identifies their personality? How daring are they in fashion: **conservative**, **updated**, or **advanced**?

This represents somewhat of a simplification—the pros can split it much more finely. For example, there is a significant amount of business above these squares in price. In the industry, these levels are called *bridge* and *designer*. We'll get to them later in the chapter.

The best way to understand how customers fit on both scales is to arrange them into boxes forming a grid (Figure 5-1). Most customers will fit into one of the nine squares. Some can also shift between a couple of the squares, depending on time or occasion. But for the sake of simplicity, let's assume that any one person fits into just one box. (By the way, where do you fit?)

Taste Level
A measure of fashion savvy and awareness; the ability to dress stylishly and appropriately.

Conservative
This customer is cautious when it comes to fashion; doesn't want anything too trendy or odd.

Updated
This customer follows fashion, dresses with an eye to fashion, but doesn't want to appear extreme.

Advanced
This customer "lives" for fashion; dresses in the latest style, no matter how it may look to others.

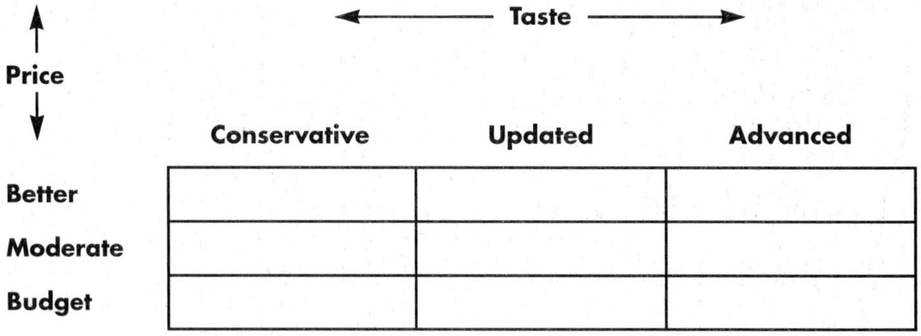

Figure 5-1

As you learned in Chapter 1, more customers are at the lower end of the price scale and the taste scale. In the industry it is felt that the majority of the general populace would probably fit in the four lower left squares. (We bet that wasn't where you put yourself.)

Figure 5-2 shows an approximate visualization of the distribution of numbers of customers. In other words, the bulk of the retail clothing market is either budget or moderate in price and conservative or updated in taste. Both better price customers and advanced taste customers are a distinct minority. (But is this where you are?)

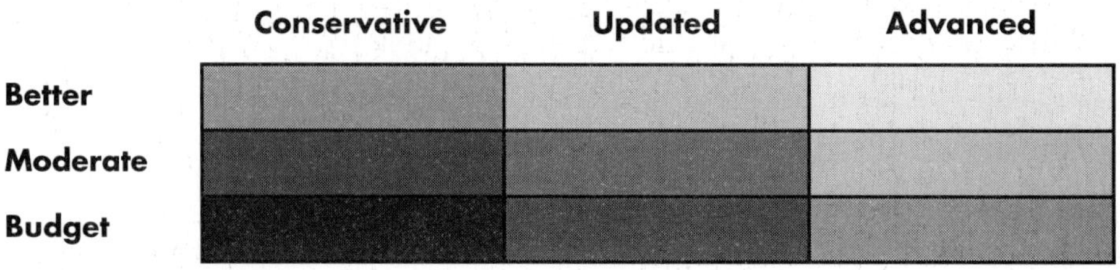

Figure 5-2

These minority customers are highly influential, however. They are the trend setters who will eventually influence even the least sophisticated end of the market. Fashion tends to filter down our grid in the direction shown in Figure 5-3. As fashion moves down and to the left, it becomes more watered down as well, but there will still be some traceable element of that original fashion vision left.

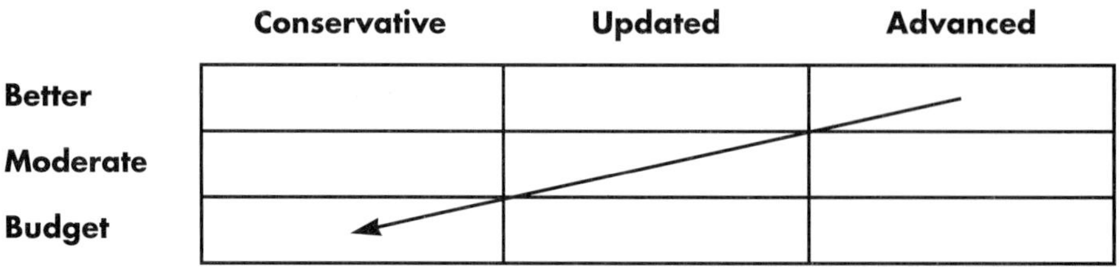

Figure 5-3

Let's take a look at Generation X's favorite wardrobe piece, a crop top. Advanced is the most extreme taste level—if the newest look is tight, advanced is the tightest (Figures 5-4 and 5-5). Or if the newest look is oversized, the advanced look is the most oversized (Figures 5-6 and 5-7). Same with skirt lengths: Advanced is whatever length is newest. If the newest trend is toward short, the advanced customer will probably go short immediately (Figures 5-8 and 5-9).

Figure 5-4

The updated customer will wear a top that is only somewhat tight. Artwork by Mary Lisa Caramico.

Figure 5-5

But the advanced customer will wear a top that is quite tight. Artwork by Mary Lisa Caramico.

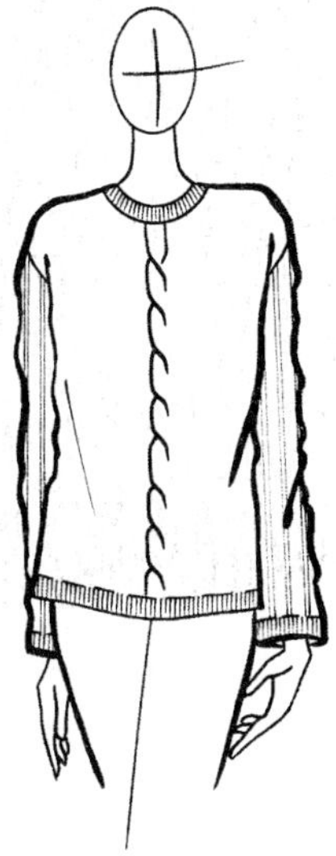

Figure 5-6

Again, the updated customer will only go somewhat oversized. Artwork by Mary Lisa Caramico.

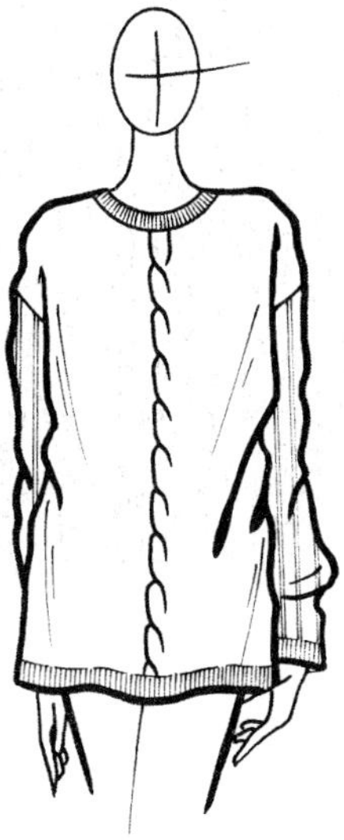

Figure 5-7

But the advanced customer will go more oversized. Artwork by Mary Lisa Caramico.

Figure 5-8

This length is about as daring as a conservative customer will want to go. Artwork by Mary Lisa Caramico.

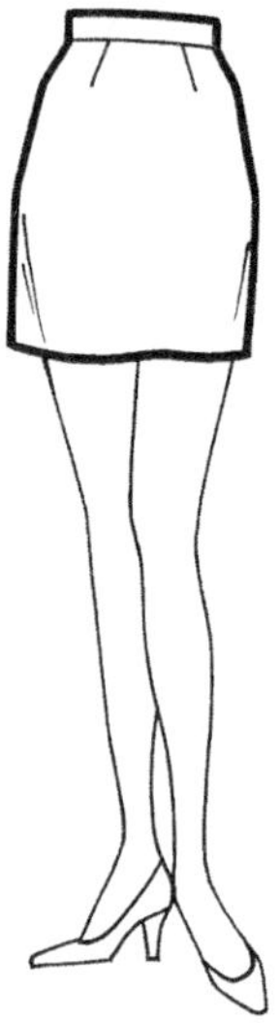

Figure 5-9

But the advanced customer will be comfortable going even shorter. Artwork by Mary Lisa Caramico.

In the spring of 1997, wide-leg jeans were becoming accepted as a young fashion look. But while the department store customers went for the biggest look, discount customers were only comfortable with a watered-down version.

Figure 5-10

Student Josie Miller gives us a current example of conservative. Nothing extreme about this outfit...it looks perfectly appropriate and understated.

Figure 5-11

Student Madelene Semeria could be viewed as updated because of the fit of her outfit (tight-ish), and the fashionable but not extreme styling of her top (cap sleeves, Y neck).

Figure 5-12

Student Mandy Li had this advanced outfit custom-made in Hong Kong. The unusual asymmetrical styling, the very short skirt, and the bold belt could be seen as current hallmarks of advanced.

"Although wide-legs are happening in styles ranging from 18 to 23 inches at department stores, it's the 18-inch bottoms that are the most important style at the discount level" [*Daily News Record*, January 13, 1997, "Wide-Leg Jeans Strut into Mass Market," Stan Gellers].

Just for fun, we found some student versions of conservative, updated, and advanced in Evelyn's class (Figures 5-10, 5-11, and 5-12). How about in your class?

GARMENT CHARACTERISTICS FOR EACH CUSTOMER SEGMENT

Garment construction, or **make**, is probably the most important to a conservative customer. They expect to be able to wear the garment quite a long time, so it has to wash well and stay in shape. The customer most concerned with excellent make and excellent quality fabrics would probably be the better conservative customer. She is looking for beautifully finished, timeless garments that display a certain status, yet can be worn for a considerable time (Figure 5-13). This is how one pictures most U.S. Presidents' wives dressing—but don't include trend-setting Jackie Kennedy here, think more of Nancy Reagan.

> ***Make***
> Refers to the construction of the garment; "full make," for example, has lots of fine details built in.

Conversely, the advanced customer is sometimes more interested in the "look" of the garment rather than the make. (not always, especially at the

Figure 5-13

Cachet
Something carrying prestige and special approval.

better end). The style and trend **cachet** is what she's looking for primarily, which means that she probably will be moving on to an even newer look soon (Figure 5-14). On the grid in Figure 5-15 are some general guidelines for three of the most contrasting customer types.

Figure 5–14

	Conservative	Updated	Advanced
Better			**Look:** could be extreme color, pattern, texture **Fit:** very current, a bit extreme **Performance:** not important, could be handwash or dry clean **Make:** interesting, but less important than the look
Moderate		**Look:** stylish color, pattern, texture **Fit:** stylish but not extreme **Performance:** easy care or somewhat more delicate **Make:** good, serviceable	
Budget	**Look:** totally understandable color, pattern, texture; a look that has been around awhile **Fit:** ample, comfortable **Performance:** wash and wear **Make:** sturdy, simple		

Figure 5-15

HOW WHOLESALERS ADDRESS THE CUSTOMER TYPES

Most brand-name companies have learned that the best way to market their clothing to appropriate customers is to "position" themselves on this same grid. If they keep their merchandise consistently positioned as, say, moderate update or better advanced, retailers will know how to handle the merchandise in their stores, and customers will understand it as well.

A trap that some leading manufacturers and designers fall into is to have a line that tries to appeal to too many different customer types at the same time. Another mistake is to change too quickly over time from one segment to another. The best brands, those that stay consistently popular over the course of years, are generally those that have stayed true to their customer base in both taste and price. There are some exceptions, lines like Ellen Tracy, that have slowly traded up in price or taste, but they are exceptions.

The other tendency is to trade a label down in price and quality, which usually results in an immediate boost in sales as the loyal customer perceives a sudden bargain on their trusted brand. But as soon as the customer becomes disappointed with the cheapening of the garment because of a change in fit or fabric, whatever it may be, they will walk away from that brand in the future. Seventh Avenue is littered with brands that have been ruined in this way.

To help you better understand what each segment on the customer grid is, in Figure 5-16 we put a brand in each box. This will give you the "flavor," based on names with which you are probably very familiar. Actually, if you look more closely at market giants like Liz Claiborne, you could split them even further with their subbrands. The newest division of Liz, Russ, for example, will be distributed in mass merchants for the budget conservative customer. Dana Buchman and Dana B. and Karen would go above our chart into the "bridge" price points, covering bridge updated. (More on bridge in a minute.) The reason for this is that each of these brands can then stay true to its own customer base. In this way, the corporation of all Claiborne brands can cover a diverse market without confusing either their retail stores or their customers.

	Conservative	**Updated**	**Advanced**
Better	Ralph Lauren	Liz Claiborne Collection	BCBG
Moderate	Chaus	Emma James (by Claiborne)	To the Max (by BCBG)
Budget	Sag Harbor	Byer	Necessary Objects

Figure 5-16

THE INSIDE SCOOP

KIM ROY

A graduate of Skidmore College, Kim worked as a buyer at Abraham and Straus and then in various (and constantly ascending) ready-to-wear positions at AMC, culminating in vice president and GMM. In 1995, she joined the Liz Claiborne organization as vice president of merchandising. She became president of special markets (Emma James, First Issue, Russ, Villager, etc.) in March 1996.

On segmentation:

At Liz, we discovered that just one brand name wouldn't do. We needed an extended brand portfolio in order to become the leader in different levels of business. Right now, Liz Claiborne is dominant in the better tier of department store business (from Liz Sport up to Dana Buchman). My challenge in coming to Liz was to establish new brands, such as Emma James. Emma grew out of consumer and retailer research. It has been constructed as a brand that will be responsive to the casualization of the workplace, but in a price zone that won't compete with our existing Liz businesses.

At moderate price points in department stores, there are either private-label **commodities** or brands that are also carried at Penney's or Sears. How can the department store shopper go right from $29.99 price points in moderate, directly up to Jones and Liz? That's too much of a price jump. There's business in between.

We talked to Federated, Dillard's, Dayton-Hudson. As a result, we came up with Emma James, which features better fabrics and looks, but at prices 20 to 25% below Liz Claiborne Collection or Studio. Hitting this **void** has met with such a positive reaction from the stores that some will actually be reorganizing their entire moderate floors to accommodate this new business!

Commodities
These are items in a store's assortment that would be considered day-in day-out large-volume business.

Void
Emptiness; usually used to mean that a business has been overlooked between two existing businesses.

OTHER TYPES OF CUSTOMER SEGMENTATION

Better and Higher in Women's Ready-to-Wear

Women's ready-to-wear is the biggest market in fashion. It's no wonder that it has been sliced, diced, and analyzed to the finest possible nuance. The top top of the market is what you see in the newspapers and on TV, the couture showings in Paris, Milan, and New York. *Couture* is fine designer clothing, custom-made for a particular client. Dresses can cost from $10,000 to

$50,000. What is shown on the runways by these designers does influence the world's fashion trends, but you might never see one of these gowns in person.

Prêt à porter or *designer* fashion is the next step down. These clothes you will see. Make sure your hands are clean, however, if you touch them in a store like Neiman-Marcus or Bergdorf Goodman. They can be up to $5000 each themselves! This is the core of the international fashion world—committed fashion followers worldwide will spend these sums to get fine fabrics and savvy styling from the superstar names in the industry (Armani, Prada, YSL, Geoffrey Beene, Donna Karan). Names can even live on after a designer's death: Christian Dior's did, and Gianni Versace's is expected to.

Bridge collections are the next step down. These are the more "affordably" priced lines, often by the same designers, which are distributed primarily through better department stores. This would include such lines as Donna Karan's DKNY, Calvin Klein's CK, Anne Klein's A-Line, or exclusively bridge lines such as Ellen Tracy. Only after "bridge" do you get down as far as what is called "better" in the industry. Yes, it is confusing.

Size and Fit Segmentation in Women's Ready-to-Wear

People come in all shapes and sizes. That's why clothing has to, as well. The U.S. market, being as ethnically diverse as it is, has an incredibly wide range of body types and sizes to cover. As the industry started to come to terms with this, it quickly realized that there were millions of customers who had been having trouble finding clothes that would fit them. These "special sizes" provided more growth during the 1980s and 1990s than the "regular sizes." Everyone was playing catch-up. One of the latest arrivals is Ellen Tracy. According to *Women's Wear Daily*, July 31, 1996, Ellen Tracy expected to add as much as $20 million in volume by adding petites and large sizes for spring 1997.

A breakdown for women's ready-to-wear sizing follows.

Missy

Missy is the regular fit in ready-to-wear. This is a mature female with an average height of 5 feet 6 to 7 inches. Sizes usually range from 6 to 16.

Petite

The petite customer is similar in build to the missy customer, except that she is generally under 5 feet 4 inches tall.

Women's (or Large Sizes)

Women's sizes are for a larger or more ample customer of more-or-less average height. Sizes range from 14W to 24W. American women, on average, tend to be slightly heavier today than even in the recent past. As a result, this is an increasing part of the market.

Juniors

It can be argued that the junior segmentation is based both on size/fit and on "fashion attitude." This is usually a young, not-fully-developed female with a slightly higher waistline than the missy fit. Junior departments in department stores offer sizes 3 to 13, which fit distinctly differently than the fuller missy fit. In addition, junior departments feature fast, trendy, and usually less expensive clothing.

THE INSIDE SCOOP

NELIA WATTEN

Nelia started in retail at Bloomingdale's. After stops at Bradlee's and the Madison Avenue shop of Dianne Von Furstenberg, Nelia came to AMC and worked with the fashion "guru" Bernie Ozer. She is now doing specialized product development for a Canadian department store chain.

On the changing junior customer:

Today's junior customer is more like the junior of the 1960s and 1970s. She wants to be different, have attitude, be a little funky. In the past 10 years or so, the junior and her mother wanted to be "pals." The mother looked like the daughter; the daughter looked like the mother. They both wore leggings and oversized sweaters.

In the 60s and 70s, juniors had more taste, style, and dressing was fun! Then they became serious and everyone looked like everyone else. But in just the last couple of years, every junior looks different again... They are not all in the same "uniform." They want to make their own mark, have their own "website" of fashion. I predict the junior business will get strong again. We always thought juniors was a "size" thing. No. It's a "head" thing. Juniors should be fun, passionate, and outrageous!

IT'S THE SAME IN MEN'S

In menswear the market is even more heavily concentrated in conservative and updated. Actually, the foundation of U.S. menswear taste is something called **traditional**, which carries pretty much the same fashion credibility as Advanced Designer. Traditional has its own fashion vocabulary and it evolves and updates itself following its own set of rules.

> ***Traditional***
> In menswear, traditional means very specifically the classic button-down, chinos, striped tie look exemplified by Brooks Brothers or Polo.

The number one rule in traditional menswear is that while color and fabric can be quite daring, the model (silhouette) of each garment rarely changes significantly. Think of a button-down shirt: The styling doesn't change, but you've all seen them in surprising colors such as bright purple or coral! This is a typical menswear fashion update.

Brooks Brothers is probably the best-known traditional men's merchant. Figure 5-17 illustrates some well-known brands on the menswear version of the grid.

	Conservative	Updated	Advanced
Better	Polo	Perry Ellis	DKNY
Moderate	Arrow	Dockers	Guess
Budget	Manhattan	Merona	Rush

Figure 5-17

In children's wear, there tend to be fewer taste-level distinctions. Kids clothes tend to be "cute" rather than fashionable. However, all three price ranges are present, with the better end being popular for gift-giving. Kids' brands stack up as shown in Figure 5-18.

When you get up to girl's sizes 7 to 16 and boys' 8 to 20, style does start to become much more of an issue, reflective of the trends in junior's and young men's. Here's how Dennis Abramczyk, former men's and kid's GMM at Carson Pirie Scott, explains it: "Price segmentation also exists in kidswear (budget–moderate–better). But the size of better is very small. In general, price is the key motivator in kid's. There are certain exceptions where a customer is willing to pay a little more, like girl's dresses and special-event dressing. But in general, a customer who wouldn't shop a mass merchant store for herself is very ready to buy her children's clothes there."

Better	Polo Baby Dior Guess
Moderate	Buster Brown Oshkosh
Budget	Hush Puppies

Figure 5-18

OTHER BUSINESSES HAVE THE SAME SEGMENTATION

Even in women's accessories (scarves, jewelry, sunglasses, shoes, bags), and in intimate apparel, there are the same grids with equivalent brands. For example, in shoes, Figure 5-19 plots out brands as shown. You might not be familiar with all these brands (a shoe expert helped us.) But it might be interesting to check out these names (or other shoe brands) in the mall and put them on your own nine-square grid.

	Conservative	Updated	Advanced
Better	Etienne Aigner	Liz Claiborne	Enzo
Moderate	Bass	Unisa	Steve Madden
Budget	Naturalizer	Unlisted	Esprit

Figure 5-19

So now that you know that the two parameters of price and taste level are essential in identifying customers in their buying decisions, we're going to talk about where customers are making these buying decisions.

PUTTING STORES IN THE SAME BOXES

Yes, it is just as important to know not only how much customers want to spend, but where they want to spend it. Successful manufacturers and designers must make sure that their products are represented in shopping districts that reach their "price" customers, in environments that enhance the garment's taste level. The customer needs to feel that they are shopping in "their store."

What Kinds of Stores Are There?

Retailers must know who their customers are and aren't so that their products and customers match. For manufacturers and designers it is critically important to understand the different types of stores, to ensure that the retail store matches the same grid box as their line. So let's take in a quick overview of the major types of stores in the retailing industry. A manufacturer or designer can have a hot line for the right target customer, but if it's in the wrong store, it will be out of balance and will fail.

Department Stores

A department store by definition is one that offers a wide variety of both hard lines and soft lines. This means that the stores carry clothing, accessories, and personal care products under the heading of soft lines. Hard lines are considered businesses such as small appliances, floor coverings, furniture, and toys. Traditionally, the core customers for department stores are the GI generation and the Silencers. Examples are Dillard's Department Store, Robinson-May, Burdine's, and Macy's.

National Department Stores (Originally, Mass Merchants)

J.C. Penney and Sears used to be strictly lower-priced mass merchants, known more for dishwashers than for dresses. Both have **traded up** so effectively that they are now considered national department stores. The GI generation made these stores what they are today, and they taught their children and grandchildren to find the same values. In these industry giants you will discover Boomers, Silencers, and GIs standing next to each other in the checkout line.

> ***Trade up***
> To increase in price; if a store drops its lower-priced merchandise and adds expensive merchandise, it is said to be "trading up."

Specialty Stores

Specialty stores generally carry a narrower range of merchandise. What makes these stores unique is that they typically offer personalized service and a very strong assortment of their specific category of merchandise. The store buyers tend to be very knowledgeable, making sure that the garments appeal to a specific and narrow customer group. Generation X and many of the Zoomers find specialty store buying appealing, since they find (only) merchandise that is just for them. Examples are: Structure, Express, Gap, and Contempo Casuals.

Boutiques

Boutique operations focus on a particular classification of merchandise and are often known for their unique one-of-a-kind styles. Shopping in individual boutiques is mostly for either fashion-savvy or better conservative customers who want something different from everyone else. Each generational group has some consumers that fit into this category of store.

Discount Stores

Discount stores offer low prices with no-frills service. There was a time when only lower-income customers shopped there. No more! These giants have done such a powerful job in the last 20 years that all the generational groups depend on them for certain categories of merchandise, especially basics and staples such as underwear, hosiery, and activewear. Examples are: Wal-Mart, K-mart, and Target.

Off-Price Stores

Off-price stores carry designer labels and leading manufacturers' brands at lower prices than are typically found in the department stores. They are no-frills operations, lacking the customer service of a department store. Examples are: Loehman's, TJ Maxx, and Marshalls.

Manufacturer Outlet Stores

Manufacturer outlet stores sell only one brand. They are set up by the manufacturer or designer themselves, as a vehicle in which to sell the garments that they did not sell to the department or specialty stores. Typically, they are located in the northeastern part of the United States or in the large outlet malls that have been built across the country. They have found a life because of the "power shopping" demands of the Boomers: designer goods, deeply discounted. Examples are: DKNY, Ann Taylor, Van Heusen, Polo, and J. Crew.

Designer-Owned Specialty Stores

Designer-owned specialty stores are regular-priced stores that carry only the labels of one designer—owned, operated, and promoted by the design house. These stores enhance a designer's image and generally reflect the most accurate representation of the designer's "vision." Examples are: Jessica McClintock, Ralph Lauren, Armani, and St. John. Of course, the Boomers established this marketplace, but more than the Boomers, this store type survives because of the advanced/better image, and there are (a few) customers for this merchandise in all generational groups.

Cyber Stores?

With less and less free time, consumers are finding less time to shop. Home shopping networks on television have catered to this need, albeit with mixed success. However, catalogs, the more traditional time-savers, have exploded in the past decade. There are already some fledgling electronic Internet versions. Stay tuned on this one!

Does this mean that one store falls exactly into one and only one definition? Nothing is ever that clear cut. For example, Saks Fifth Avenue and Neiman Marcus are department stores, but they are also specialty stores. They both cater to a very specific target market, with high levels of customer service, but are much bigger than most specialty stores. They could be considered specialty department stores or "limited line" department stores. The smaller specialty stores tend to appeal to the narrowest customer base. For

example, Barney's could be viewed as exclusively better advanced, at least on the women's side. National specialty chains such as Limited's Men's Structure would be considered moderate update.

The larger the store, the more squares on the grid it will probably cover. However, even in such a case, and much like the wholesaler's subbrands, stores usually segment into departments that appeal more or less to one box. Department stores have found that putting merchandise of various price ranges and taste levels side by side on the selling floor is almost always a mistake. Customers get confused and walk away.

As we noted, department store retailing is getting more and more challenging because of the increased competition. However, like any other business,

THE INSIDE SCOOP

DENNIS ABRAMCZYK

As you have seen earlier, Dennis has a long history at the famous midwestern department store, Carson Pirie Scott. He is now on the wholesale side at Ralph Marlin Neckwear.

> Segmentation is critical to the success of a department store. It creates focus. If you don't have focus in your business, you won't be successful... you can't be all things to all people.
>
> A customer looks for "clarity of offer." If your offering is not clear, you end up with a confusing mix of merchandise that isn't appealing. In addition, you won't have a big enough or broad enough selection at the price level your customer is willing to pay.
>
> Department stores also need to segment by category of merchandise. For example, designer sportswear lines (where the name and label are very important) are distributed to fewer competitors. That means the department store carrying it will achieve differentiation, which sometimes allows for more price "flexibility." However, on a generic staple category such as turtlenecks or T-shirts, the label is not important to the customer. What they want is their size, reasonable quality, good colors, at a sharp price. And here department stores struggle, because other stores (Target, Kohl's) are better known for sharp prices and good values.

there are some basic timeless principles that can help. The industry veterans were the total pros, but many of these techniques, unfortunately, are being forgotten. Here are some fundamental retailing pointers from an expert:

THE INSIDE SCOOP

TED SHAPIRO

Another of those famous Abraham and Straus trainees, Ted's career rose to merchandise manager in the Budget Store. A&S in those days was known as the best-run store in its aggressively competitive marketplace. After A&S, he went to Gertz Department Stores and then to AMC as divisional vice president of menswear.

On having the right inventory:

"Day-to-day rightness" is what a good buyer should aim for. At every point in time, you need to have the "customer preference" items, in all sizes and colors. A "customer preference" item is hot, timely, and semi-fashion; and it's also usually seasonal in nature. The "Member's Only" jacket was a perfect example. Customer preference items usually have their day... and then they either become a basic or they get phased out completely. They are different from basic-basics such as socks and underwear, for example.

Overbuy and overemphasize these customer preference items. If you think you can sell 50, buy 75. You'll figure out how to sell them! Put these customer preference items out at a reasonable price every day. They'll sell. And hopefully you can find one in each classification to lead the department.

Next: you've got to learn to buy "narrow and deep." Some buyers overassort [buy little bits of lots of styles] because they think it is safer to have a little of everything. This is wrong. It just leads to markdowns. One style of 100 pieces is easier to sell than 10 styles of 10 pieces—because on the one style, you will at least have a full color and size assortment to offer. And the more times you reorder, the more correct your inventory will be.

Taking a step back at this point, let's see in Figure 5-20 where examples of the various retailers would fit onto our grid.

	Conservative	**Updated**	**Advanced**
Better	Nordstrom	Bloomingdale's Claiborne Retail	Bergdorf Goodman Saks Fifth Avenue Armani
Moderate	Penney's	Macy's Robinson-May Loehman's	Limited Express
Budget	Wal-mart	Target	Wet Seal

Figure 5-20

Of course, broader retailers such as Macy's are involved in almost all nine squares, depending on department and branch store. But for easy reference, Figure 5-20 gives you a "feeling" for the segmentation of retailers.

OK, SO WHAT DOES ALL THIS MEAN TO ME?

Let's take a look at where you are now. In the chapters of Unit I, you have learned that a career in the fashion field is filled with multiple avenues and opportunities. Now you know that the industry is taking a new focus into the twenty-first century, a focus on customers' needs and wants rather than a designer's whim. By looking at the customers out there, you have also had a snapshot of the generations, price points, and taste levels that will be controlling fashion in the future.

Here's the bottom line:

- Yes, you do like clothes.
- You follow the fashion reports in the newspaper.
- You are a good dresser.
- And now you know that designers can find success creating garments for a wide variety of design firms, national labels, and private labels, big and small.
- You also know that your real employer is the customer, who either buys your ideas and makes you a success—or rejects your ideas and shoots you down.

You also know that you've still got lots to learn before you go out and take the world by storm. In Unit II you will learn exactly how designers and wholesalers create products that appeal to the target customer, at the right price, at the right time, and in the right store. And hold on, because it isn't as easy as you might think.

SO YOU WANT TO WORK IN THE FASHION BUSINESS?

Here's How to Begin. . . Chapter 5

It is time to have some fun and build your own boxes. Write down your favorite TV character on a piece of paper. Based on the character being portrayed, briefly list as much of the following information as possible:

Age: ______________________________

Occupation (on the show): ______________________________

Favorite hobbies: ______________________________

Favorite music: ______________________________

Type of car: ______________________________

Three words to describe the character: ______________________________

Now fit the character into one of the boxes on our nine-square grid. Go back and identify the clothing brands the person would probably purchase and then the types of stores in which he or she would shop. As a class, see if you can fill up all nine squares of the grid with different TV characters. Then choose both lines and locations that each character would select to fulfill his or her shopping needs.

UNIT 2

The Wholesale Timing and Action Calendar or, What Month *Is* This?

Lost in the Subway!

"After a long day of reviewing the retail performance of my current line, troubleshooting the pending deliveries, plus projecting colors two seasons out, I dragged down the subway steps to go home. People around me were wearing light jackets and sweaters, but I suddenly realized that I couldn't remember what season it was. Was it spring? Fall? The weather was cool—but that's as much as I could come up with! Just what month was this?"

Working in fashion means working on different stages of multiple seasons at the same time. It's easy to lose track of the real world. Sticking to a schedule is critical in garment production: Time marches on and so does the garment production line. If you are one day late in making a key decision, your goods might be taken off the line and someone else's put on. Now your one day late has mushroomed into a week's delay of delivery!

Critical decisions get made at dozens of points in the product development calendar. In the industry, they are known as *trigger dates.* This sounds a bit severe, and it is! It's time to roll up our sleeves and start working on that line.

CHAPTER 6

Research: Putting Out Fashion "Feelers"

It really doesn't matter where you are working in the fashion industry, you must have a vision for the future but one that is firmly rooted in the past. Everyone in the industry starts with some type of research. Research can help you with past, present, and future: an evaluation of past successes and failures, measured against current customers' wants and needs, balanced by future challenges and changes.

ECONOMIC TRENDS

The fashion business is affected as much as any other business by the larger economic and consumer trends—maybe more. In uncertain economic times, new clothes become a purchase that can be postponed. In the industry, some say that women stop buying for their husbands immediately when the economy falters; only if the economy turns really bad do they stop buying for themselves!

When the economy is good, opulent fashion often sells. The 1980s saw the explosion of the high-end **Italian designer business**, for instance. People had a lot of money to spend, and the expensive fabrics and fine tailoring used by Italian designers provided a new and glamorous fashion look for U.S. customers.

Italian Designer Business
High-end designers such as Armani, Missoni, and Krizia.

When the economy is difficult, everyone in the business works to reduce prices. Sharp-value merchants such as Gap, particularly with their Old Navy stores, often flourish under such circumstances. The unemployment and inflation rates affect consumer confidence, which in turn, affects clothing sales. "One reason Old Navy is making money in this competitive market is that its stores are not in malls. One of the more obvious ways Old Navy keeps prices down is using less expensive fabrics and fewer details. Old Navy is also less strict when it comes to consistency in colors and sizes of its merchandise. Because Old Navy merchandise does not carry the same hefty markups as Gap and Banana Republic clothing, robust sales volume is the name of the game" [*Fortune*, March 18, 1996, "Will Old Navy Fill the Gap?" Susan Caminiti].

You have also learned that with powerful national chains setting up more and more retail stores, consumers have an actual overabundance of places where they can buy clothes. This means that retail purchases are spread out over many comparable players. As a result, in the past 10 years or so, we have rarely seen the big positive increases in business during the "good times" that were common previously.

As recently as the 1970s, department stores could "hit on" a hot item and sell tens of thousands of units in a matter of weeks, because they were the only ones to have this item. Now the same item can probably be found in any department store and there might be other versions of it in the national specialty chains and mass merchants as well. There might still be tens of thousands of units sold, but no longer just in the one lucky store that discovered it!

LIFESTYLE TRENDS

Lifestyle
Catch-all word used to denote taste, style, and look.

There are many good books and articles written on **lifestyle** changes in the United States. These changes influence clothing like everything else. For example, the trend "guru" Faith Popcorn, author of the *Popcorn Report* and *Clicking*, coined the phrase *cocooning* for the tendency of people to stay comfortably at home and pamper themselves. A whole industry of very casual, comfortable loungewear emerged to play to that need, such as Calvin Klein's loungewear and A Month Of Sundays.

Even more obvious has been the change in corporate America toward casual dressing in the workplace. Both women's and men's sportswear firms have cashed in on this. Retail stores such as Dayton/Hudson/Marshall Fields and Target have as well by issuing books and holding customer seminars on how to dress casually (but appropriately) for those "dress down" Fridays.

CONSUMER RESEARCH

Most large-scale industries with products that have longevity (detergents, foods, cars, for example) do official research to determine consumer likes and dislikes. The garment business, on the other hand, is one of very rapid change. Each item tends to have a rather short **selling life**. Therefore, it usually doesn't pay for garment companies to spend lots of money to find out if a specific style is going to be popular. By the time the research is finished, the fashion trend could be over.

> ***Selling Life***
> The length of time an item is desired by the public.

THE INSIDE SCOOP

KIM ROY

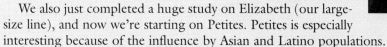

The president for special markets at Liz Claiborne, Kim was introduced to you earlier with her thoughts on segmentation. But Liz is also one of the few garment companies that does a great deal of research. So here's Kim again on customer research:

When Paul Charron [chairman and chief executive officer] joined Liz Claiborne, he had come from Procter and Gamble. P&G, of course, does lots of customer research to find the current needs of the marketplace. So, in 1995, we at Liz Claiborne spoke to over 6000 consumers: in malls, in special focus groups, and in question-and-answer sessions. This research laid the foundation for the new product evolution which is in the stores now.

We also just completed a huge study on Elizabeth (our large-size line), and now we're starting on Petites. Petites is especially interesting because of the influence by Asian and Latino populations.

We use our research to guide our strategic and tactical decisions in many different areas:

Internally:

- To define our consumers and their needs.
- To design products that better address the lifestyles of our consumers in terms of versatility, care, quality, and style considerations.
- To position our various brands in terms of their value and end use to consumers, both emotionally and functionally.

Externally:

- To partner with our retailers in presenting our product to best advantage in the shopping environment (for example, showing outfits that suggest versatility and enhance stylishness).
- To most effectively communicate with our consumers in various forms of advertising, promotion, and point-of-sale materials.

At Liz Claiborne Inc. we believe that more than ever knowledge is power and that a true understanding of the consumer gives us a strong competitive edge."

More often, wholesalers and retailers will do general research of their customer's preferences. They will try to figure out such things as. What is the most someone will pay? Why do customers prefer one brand over another? As Bob Caplan, director of sales at Levi Strauss says: "In consumer research, gathering data is less critical than interpreting data."

Decisions about individual styles become much more a case of trial and error. Some companies are starting to preview with actual customers, however. "Reebok expects to visit some cities several times a month to show revisions in the product or in potential ad campaigns, since teenagers' suggestions could become corporate strategy." [*Women's Wear Daily*, January 30, 1997, "Taking It from the Streets," Rosemary Feitelberg]. Through experience, designers learn what has worked in the past and what hasn't. Retailers learn what has sold and what has not. Here's the really tricky part: What sold yesterday in fashion is no guarantee that it will sell tomorrow!

Here's a perspective from Federated: "Retailers must learn more about their customers through research and more sophisticated data technology. It's a difficult task, Allen Questrom former CEO said, given the nation's rapidly changing demographics, including growing Asian and Hispanic populations and aging baby boomers." [*Women's Wear Daily*, January 7, 1997, "Questrom: Make Your Stores Entertaining and Lower the Prices"]. Still, there are general trends that help you define what will tend to sell and not sell. It's driven more by the consumer's wants and needs than by any one designer's "unique vision."

DEMOGRAPHIC TRENDS

You learned about the different generational groups in Chapter 4. But it is also important to note that the needs of each generation change as its members grow older. The same baby boomers who squeezed into hip-huggers and poor-boy rib knits in the early 1970s (Figure 6-1) had put on enough weight by the late 1980s that they fueled the demand for oversized clothes (Figure 6-2). When you're in the industry, these graying boomers will want comfortable and casual clothes for lounging in their new retirement condos.

Even ethnic heritage can influence clothing purchases. The influx of Asian immigrants into California, for example, has led stores to skew their size scales more toward the smaller sizes. As an illustration; In the midwest (Ohio, Illinois, Indiana, Michigan, Minnesota, Wisconsin), a typical size-scale assortment breakdown on a dozen garments might run:

Small	–	Medium	–	Large	–	Extra large		
0	–	3	–	6	–	3	=	12 pieces (1 dozen)

In California, a size scale might be:

Small	–	Medium	–	Large	–	Extra large		
2	–	5	–	4	–	1	=	12 pieces (1 dozen)

Figure 6–1

Artwork by Michael Carnegie.

Figure 6–2

Artwork by Michael Carnegie.

WHAT WORKED? WHAT DIDN'T?

Producing a wholesale line is a little like waking up in the middle of the night in a pitch-black house. You carefully walk with your arms extended in front of you to touch walls and doors so you don't bump your head on them. In wholesale, it is very hard to know where to direct your line. You must tentatively reach out in different directions until you bump into a "wall." At that point, you course-correct and aim in a slightly different direction. With your "fingertips" you try to check and gather as much information as possible so that you don't make a big mistake.

Past Line's Successes and Failures

To know what to design for the next season, the place to start is with your most recent line. What booked big? What flopped? What was the feedback from the sales staff? The last line needs to be examined carefully for performance and profitability. What was the overall financial plan for the season—what was the actual result? Which items turned out to be profitable for us (the manufacturer)? Which were profitable for the stores? Did we lose money on something that sold well that we had underpriced? If we raise the price next season, will it still sell?

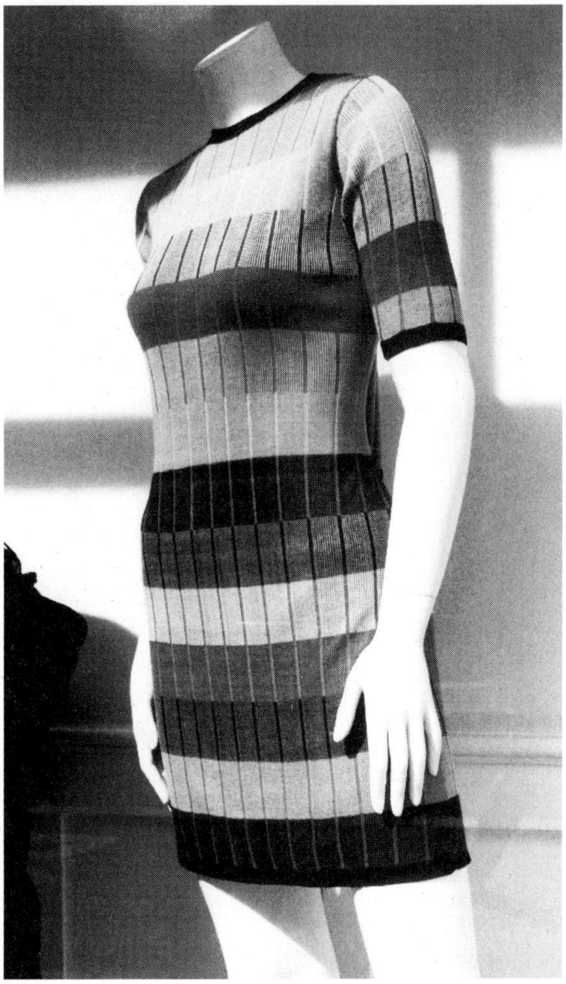

If this dress is a best seller, you can be sure a version of it will be on next season's line.

Good designers and merchandisers sit in with their showroom sales people during appointments with their largest or most insightful retail buyers. The buyers' reaction to the line is the first feedback from outside the wholesale company. Wholesalers will probe the most savvy buyers to find out why they like one style and dislike another. Unfortunately, there are fewer and fewer really in-touch buyers these days. They are often far removed from the customers on the selling floor and can only guess why they have sold one thing well and not another. (Maybe knowing this, you can become a really great buyer.)

As part of this probing, wholesalers often ask buyers how competitors (other wholesalers) look. Have they done anything that is especially good? How do prices compare? They also usually ask about current retail performance of their competitors' lines. Is anything selling really well? Is anything a "**dog**"? (Here you can see these wholesalers with "arms extended in the darkness, bumping for clues!")

A "Dog"
A really bad seller.

Wholesalers must stay right on top of their competition because everyone works hard in the garment business. "Well priced" one season might be "too expensive" the next season because a competitor happened to move its garment production from North Carolina to Indonesia in the meantime. A line can also get too "unique" or "special" for retailers and customers to understand. Conversely, it can also get "tired" or "stale," so that buyers pass on it as well.

Being a wholesaler means that you must stay on constant alert. There are still too many lines trying to sell to fewer and fewer retailers. (Don't let this confuse you: There are more individual store units, but they are owned by fewer and fewer conglomerates. More store buildings, but fewer store chains. As a result, there are many fewer buyers.) Only the most appropriately designed, constructed, and well-priced lines get bought by retail buyers. These lines then have to sell well to the masses—and then you've got to repeat this "double success" three, four, or five times a year! Now do you see why it's called work?

ONE OF OUR FAVORITE THINGS: SHOPPING!

Here's something that you probably like to do—that you will be able to do in your new job—shopping! One of the most important ways that a wholesaler keeps in touch with the retail market and with competitors is to get out into the stores and look closely at actual garments. Timing is an issue, since what the designer has to create is probably two seasons later than what is on the selling floor. But still, it is another reality check.

Photo by student Jason VanBlaricum.

Samples are bought of garments that could be used as "inspiration" for styling, fit, fabric, color, trim, or print. Most fashion evolves as **knock-offs** or interpretations of someone else's good idea. So these samples will be modified such that they will become appropriate for the wholesaler's target customer.

Knock-offs
Copies or imitations.

Visionary designers and merchandisers are able to see inspiration in the most unlikely places. An infant's designer might spot a great fabric in a men's knit shirt. A woman's outerwear maker might see a sensational fabric in a drapery department. Color trends could come from stationery or from cosmetic packaging. Home trends, even flower trends (for example, the popularity of sunflowers in the mid-1990s), can influence fashion. Don't get "tunnel vision" and look only at women's departments if you are designing womenswear, for example.

THE INSIDE SCOOP

Cheryl Pollard

Cheryl got her start in this business at Bloomingdale's NY. After that she moved to G.H. Bass and Coach, where she added experience in distribution and specialty retailing. From there she moved to AMC, where her design/product development career blossomed as a product manager.

On design inspiration:

Where does inspiration come from? It's a matter of exposure: reading, theater, opera, magazines, museums. I find myself constantly looking for design inspiration. A painting might inspire a color idea. Or it could come from graffiti spotted along the West Side Highway!

I look closely at people on the street. (I've learned to look someone up and down, discretely.) I try out outfits on myself.

The toughest part is staying fresh. For that, you must be constantly looking. But you also need to trust your gut. You can't do any of this until you have a comfort level with your own personal style. That style becomes one ingredient in the recipe. Then you must incorporate that into your client's needs. You put all this into a pot, stir it, and see what comes out. Hopefully, it will be a fabulous mix!

Mavins
Experts.

Bernie Ozer, a fashion consultant to top department stores, was one of the great New York fashion experts (called **mavins** in the business). For trend inspiration meetings with store buyers, he would bring in foods that were just the right color, street dancers that were wearing some "extreme but directional" style of pants, or a snake charmer to reinforce a reptile print message. It's always been a visual business, and that's how he made his point. As you can tell, his dramatic visual message stuck with those of us in the audience.

Within the United States, New York is the most directional shopping market, primarily because of the huge range of retail outlets. Bernie Ozer would say that you can't just shop Bloomingdale's, you've got to shop the *barrio* as well! California is also great for sample shopping, especially for young, hip, surf looks. Montreal is a kind of "trade secret." Styling there is somewhere between the styling in the United States and that in Europe. It's especially good for outerwear styling and tailored women's apparel.

Now, as much fun as shopping New York, Los Angeles, and Montreal is, if you really want to get the most up-to-date fashion information and shop for the purest high-fashion styles, you've got to fly to Europe. (OK, we admit it. This part of the job is exactly as glamorous as it sounds! Sure, you have to spend long days traipsing in and out of shops—but oh, those shops! And oh, those restaurants!)

Designers shop "upmarket"...

...but they also shop "downmarket" as well.

European customers are the most fashion-savvy in the world. They place a high priority on dressing stylishly and will pay a high price for beautiful clothes. Often, Americans are appalled by the prices and wonder, "How do these people afford such expensive clothes?" We have been told that they tend to buy fewer garments, but they are comfortable wearing them more frequently while they are at the peak of style. Then they buy another exquisite item or two the next season. The high-fashion runway shows in Europe represent the pinnacle of fashion. Influences from these lines will be felt for seasons.

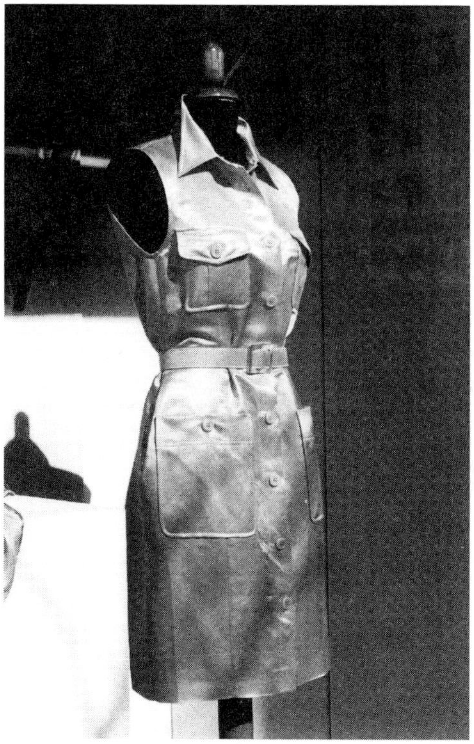

THE INSIDE SCOOP

J. Stan Tucker

A native of Charlotte, North Carolina, Stan was another of those famous trainees at Abraham and Straus. Afterward, he was with AMC for many years, including five years in San Francisco. In 1982, Stan became chief operating officer of Geoffrey Beene, Inc.; this was followed by a stint as managing director of Gieves and Hawkes. Stan is now a vice president and fashion director of Saks Fifth Avenue. He knows everyone in the industry!

On the Paris fashion show scene:

Fashion shows in Paris are glamorous, serious, and big business. If you want to observe fashion and its glitterati, lodging in the "glamor" hotel is a good start. (Today, it's the Hotel Costes on the Right Bank.) It's where fashion is visible; where the press takes note.

Shows never start on time, which is unfortunate, as it becomes a domino effect. It only takes one to be late, and, you can be assured, the rest will follow suit. But everyone knows this, and it seems that 10:00 A.M. is always 11:00 A.M., and so on—it just becomes an accepted fact.

Getting into a Paris show is sometimes no easy feat. It is always a mob scene at the door, photographers rushing in early to establish their position—press, retailers, and, many times, the social set all arriving at the same time, and all wanting individual attention. Inside is what counts: where you are seated, who is next to you, whether store X has as many front row seats as store Y, what celebrities are there, and so on. It is all about posturing. However, the seating is well planned by professional public relations firms overseen by the designer or VP of the company.

Nowadays, the fashion business is likened to Hollywood. It's closely related to TV, music, and movies. It's important to many to see famous people in the audience, as well as superstar models on the runway. All of this can cost hundreds of thousands of dollars.

Fashion shows give the audience the design concept or fashion statement the designer wishes to convey. It is how he or she sees the collection as a whole. I make copious notes during a show and try to spot a look that best exemplifies the collection. Many times this look will be chosen for advertising (therefore, we would want it to be "**exclusive**"), so it is important to speak to the business partner immediately following the show to secure it. At the same time there is a frenzied rush by others, including the press, to get backstage and congratulate the designer, whether the collection was good or not. It is what I call "fashion protocol," in other words, just fashion good manners.

In a single day I will attend six to eight shows with business meetings in between—and many times, no lunch. The day starts at 7:30 A.M. and usually ends at midnight, Saturdays and Sundays turn into Mondays and Wednesdays—in other words, every day is a workday in Paris. Everyone comes home exhausted but must jump into the New York [fashion show] market right away, as it usually follows the European shows.

Photo courtesy of Stan Tucker.

An Exclusive
Sales are limited to just one company.

Again it must be remembered that much of what is shown on these runways is exaggerated for shock value. "When fashion people look at collections on the runway, they look for creativity and newness. But the rest of the world is often turned off by anything that looks too different, finding it strange and even scary. Which is one reason that high fashion is worn by a microscopically small percentage of women, while the vast majority wait until new styles have been adapted and modified to look more familiar" [*New York Times*, September 24, 1996, "When Designers Hone Ideas for the Mainstream," Anne-Marie Schiro].

Fashion usually filters down from its purest form in Europe to the United States within 6 to 18 months. Some say it is getting faster. In the process, however, it usually gets somewhat watered down. This is particularly true in menswear: European men are much more comfortable dressing "fashionably" than are American men.

Certain cities in Europe tend to be the best for fashion shopping. Some seasons they look great, some not so good. In general, the most consistently strong fashion leaders are:

Cash-and-Carry Wholesale
Wholesale showrooms where small retailers can go through and literally pick up their inventory to resell.

Paris	The all-around best. There is even a **cash-and-carry wholesale** district called "Le Sentier."
St. Tropez	French Riviera resort, for spring/summer casual wear.
London	For either very classic or very funky styling.
Milan	High-style, understated chic.
Florence	This is the menswear capital of the world.
Amsterdam	Strictly young and funky.

Other stops that are sometimes included: Munich, Barcelona, Brussels, and Rome.

FASHION AND COLOR SERVICES

Other than traveling to Europe, where else can designers get their inspiration? Fortunately, there are excellent services that designers can buy to help steer them in the right fashion direction. There are fashion design companies that will provide booklets full of styling, fabric, and color ideas that are appropriate for an upcoming season. Among the largest are Promostyl (Figures 6-3 and 6-4), Nigel French, and Here and There. The designer needs to remember, however, that these designs could in some cases be a bit too European or advanced for their own market. But by combining the past successes of their own line with the direction and feeling of the design service sketches, the designer can evolve the line in the right overall fashion direction. Full fashion services can cost $2000 to $6000 per year or more.

Often, designers will buy color services. These companies predict the important fashion colors by business (women's, men's, kids) about 18 months in advance. Huepoint, Color Box, Design Intelligence, Pat Tunsky, and Promostyl are several of many in New York. Designers will often buy two or three services each season ($600 to $1500) and look for commonalties and specific shades that will work for their market. Again, the designer might not end up using the colors exactly as proposed but would modify some or most shades, depending on the customer. Still, the general direction has been identified by the service.

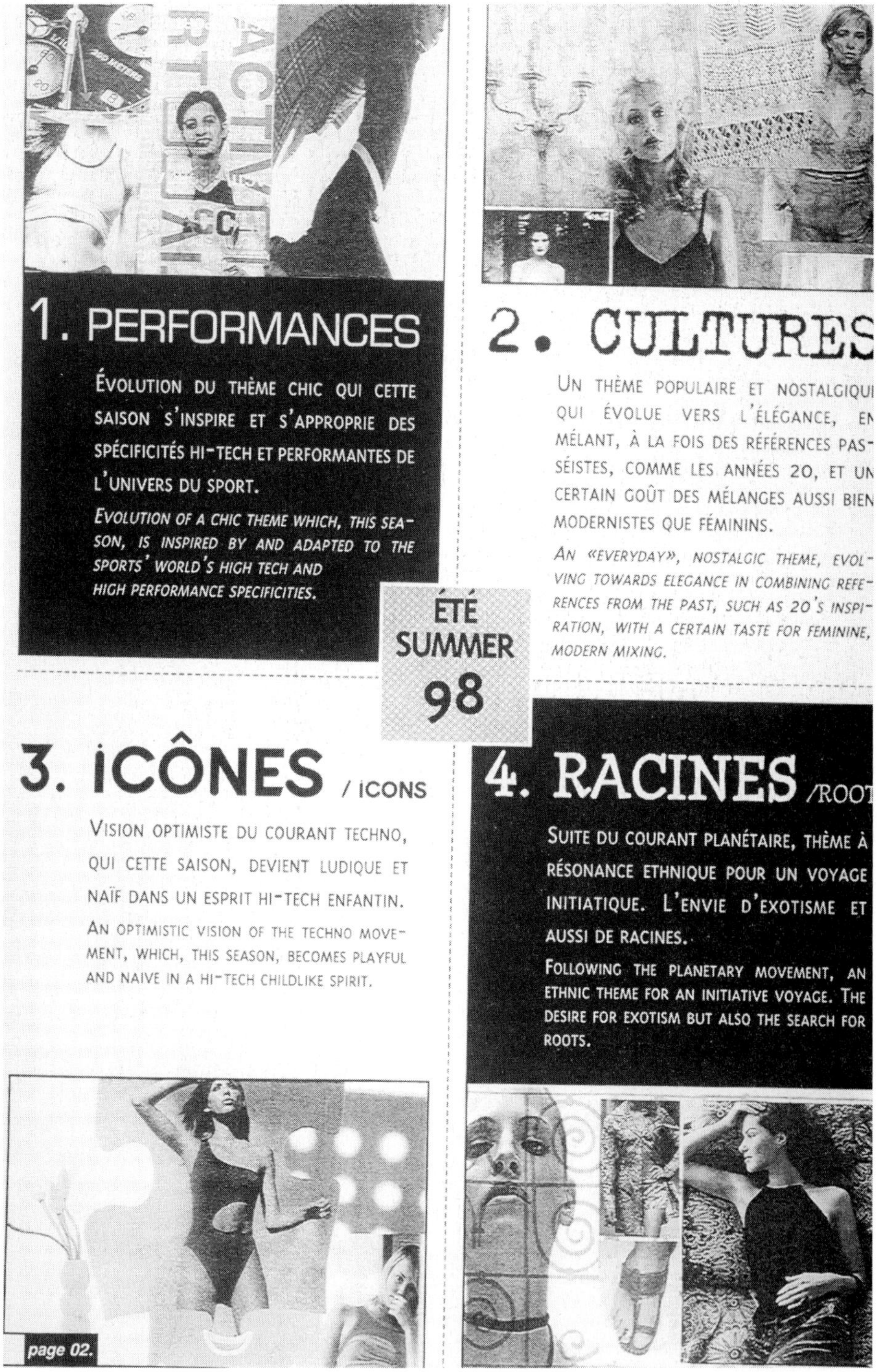

Figure 6–3
Pages from Promostyl's "Women's Fashion Planner." Courtesy of Promostyl.

FIBER AND FABRIC RESEARCH

"There is no understanding of fashion without an understanding of fabric," says Clara Hancox. She's absolutely right! Fabric both drives trends and follows trends. In the early 1990s, for example, there was an explosion of new

Figure 6–4
More from the "Women's Fashion Planner." Courtesy of Promostyl.

synthetic fiber and fabric development, the most famous being the **microfiber** fabrics. This stimulated drapey outerwear designs that showed the soft, flowing fabric to an advantage. In this case, the new fabric brought about a change in styling.

> ***Microfibers***
> Very fine yarns that are less than 1 denier thick (that's less than half the thickness of silk).

In the opposite direction, in the later 1990s, there was a movement toward tighter-fitting clothes. This renewed an interest in spandex, which had been around for a long time. But what became new was the blending of spandex with unusual fibers. In this case, the change in fit brought about changes in fabric.

Figure 6–5

Yarn-making process in Italy. The "finisher": the last stage for bulk combed yarn. Photo by Sergio Sani.

Figure 6–6

Turning the semi-bulk yarn into single-ply yarn. Photo by Sergio Sani.

THE INSIDE SCOOP

Sergio Sani

Sergio has been a marketing consultant for an Italian yarn mill, *Lanificio e Tessitura di Tollegno (Lana Gatto)*, since 1993. Prior to that, he worked for 30 years in international product design and development for U.S. stores. Based in Florence, Italy, Sergio is known worldwide for his design creativity, manufacturing know-how, and his "ice to Eskimos" salesmanship.

On competing in a congested market:

Our mill production has increased more than fourfold in the past five years. Italy now dominates the world market in fashion and fashion/volume **fine-gauge yarns** such as **super 100's merino**. This didn't happen by accident.

To approach a market like the United States you need a special niche; something to open the door; something that is different from the competition. Each time I go to American wholesalers like Dana Buchman and Ralph Lauren, I make sure I have something brand new: **superwash merino** with a new formula to keep it very soft, for example. Or merino stretch yarns made without lycra.

You need to talk directly and often with the designers and manufacturers. Don't be vague, get specific. And don't just talk... feel the goods! Fashion evolution happens on a daily basis. Either a mill keeps up with this pace of innovation, or forget it!

Italian mills have constantly invested in new machinery to keep them competitive in spite of the high labor costs in Italy. But aside from cost, the number one goal has always been to keep or improve quality. The minute you let quality slip, you lose your business. Without quality, you jump into the *calderone* (big pot). And then you don't know where you will end up!

The fiber and fabric mills that are considered the world fashion leaders are (not surprisingly) in France and Italy (Figures 6-5 and 6-6). Their fabrics are new, exciting, innovative—and expensive.

Most wholesalers, designers, and retailers come in contact with these leading mills at the European fabric shows, such as **Premier Vision** (Paris) and **Interstoff** (Frankfurt, Germany). Some actually buy these beautiful fabrics and have them shipped to their garment factories. Chains like Banana Republic and wholesalers like Liz Claiborne have done this extensively. Other wholesalers might buy 40 to 50 meters of European fabric to have their sample lines made up, and then "knock off" the fabric in the Orient for their bulk production. Still others just shop the show for direction (kiosks are set up with fabric and color stories swatched) and then with their "eye" educated, they travel to the lower-priced mills in the Far East to seek out affordable "look-alikes."

Many big buyers who can order large quantities of fabric also have the alternative of working directly with the fabric mills to develop something exclusively for them. For European fabrics, a normal production run of one

Fine-Gauge Yarns
Yarn size is measured by a number of different (and confusing) systems; fine gauge means a thin yarn.

Super 100's Merino
An exceptionally thin and fine woolen yarn.

Superwash Merino
A woolen yarn that can be laundered.

Premier Vision
A semiannual fabric trade show held in Paris.

THE INSIDE SCOOP

MAURICE ZUCKER

Maurice's career has been in the New York buying offices: Consolidated Clothiers, Arkwright, and since 1968, the Associated Merchandising Corporation. His areas of specialization have been boyswear and men's dress furnishings. He is widely acknowledged in the industry as perhaps the top authority on men's dress shirts and neckwear.

The most important fabric fair in the world is now Premier Vision in Paris. But don't expect to just wander in. You need prearranged appointments with fabric mills just to get in the door. Usually this means, at the beginning, that you should go with someone who has actually bought from these mills before. And if you want to come back, you'd better place some orders yourself!

At the appointment, they will ask you what category of fabric you are interested in (what quality, what general look, i.e., men's classic—dress shirts, or casual—sport). For the next 45 minutes or so, they will flip hundreds and hundreds of swatches in front of you. At the end, you are expected to say "OK, I'll take fabrics numbered *x*, *y*, and *z*." **Clippings** for reference are very rare because these are usually trial looms woven by hand and because the mills fear getting "knocked off."

References are sent after orders have been placed. Once a level of confidence has been established, they will send cards to you for additional review. The best approach is to come in knowing what you are looking for, but then having an open mind if something unexpected impresses you. And these innovative mills always come up with something new and exciting in textures, patterns, and colors! It's really an inspirational experience for the creative mind!

Photo courtesy of Maurice Zucker.

pattern (called a **full warp**) is about 900 to 1200 meters (approximately 980 to 1300 yards). In the Orient, for standard fabrics, minimums typically range from 3000 to 10,000 yards (yes, that's a lot).

Interstoff
A semiannual fabric trade show held in Frankfurt.

PRINT STUDIOS

Clippings
Small fabric pieces clipped off a swatch.

Full Warp
The minimum quantity for a regular production run of fabric.

Knitdowns
A trial knitting piece knitted as a flat panel rather than as a full garment.

In Chapter 2 you learned a little about the fashion and color services. Companies that are set up as print studios are typically run by one or two people who commission and/or collect original pieces of art from various artists, which they then sell to designers, merchandisers, or retailers. There are also studios that specialize in knit swatches or sweater **knitdowns** as well. Costs generally range from $75 to $400 per print or pattern. Print studios often meet their buyers at large print fairs held in New York's Garment District several times a year.

It is often necessary to adapt this original work so that it can be used technically. Most prints need to be **put into a repeat** so that they can be printed by a roller onto fabric. Knit swatches sometimes need adjusting to fit the knitting machinery available.

Student Menjeer Upadhya designing fabric prints.

Put into a Repeat
Patterns generally have to repeat over and over so that they can be printed automatically, such as by a roller. If a pattern does not show where it would start over again, the design must be completed or altered to achieve this.

Converter
A fabric middleman who contracts with fabric mills to make specialized fabrics for individual customers.

Open Market
Available to everyone.

THE INSIDE SCOOP

MELISSA NIEDERMAN

Melissa is a graduate of FIT New York, where she studied buying and merchandising. She is now an account executive for Style Council, a large fashion service organization in New York.

On discovering a great corner of the industry:

When I started out at FIT, I thought I would probably end up as a buyer. But I really wasn't sure what I wanted. Before graduation, I started working part-time for a textile **converter**, and they wouldn't let me go after graduation. I stayed there six years!

But converter business is much harder today. Business is tough. While at the converter, I had worked with some textile and art design studios. I educated myself about this new end of the industry—by asking around and by grilling the people who interviewed me!

I didn't realize how important this service was. One part is original design (artwork for garments, prints). Manufacturers need to be original; they can no longer use **open-market** goods because their competition could end up with the same prints. The second part of the service is redesign and recoloring of prints and patterns. We have 40 in-house artists.

This is a great section of the business to be in. You're a step ahead, directing designers and manufacturers on what themes, prints, and colors they should use. We work 1½ years in advance of the season.

My advice to students would be to find out about textile design studios—this is the future! If I had known about this branch of the industry, I would have gone into it right away!

HOW DO YOU START?

Probably the most common questions we hear from students and other newcomers to the business are: How do I learn all of this? Where do I go? Who do I talk to? The first source for research is as close as your school or public library. There are several standard reference books that can start you on your way.

Economic and Consumer Trends

You will want to start with the "big picture." These books are in your library, and they can provide the general background.

What: Standard and Poor's	*Why:* To learn the direction of the economy. Each year a report is published identifying key consumer and economic trends for the United States. The report then breaks down the direction of the retail, manufacturing, and textile industries.
What: Moody's	*Why:* For a statistical look at economic trends.
What: U.S. Global Trade Outlook	*Why:* To get a view of how the United States is positioned in the global market place.
What: Survey of Buying Power	*Why:* To see where consumers are spending their money.
What: Business Week *Money* *Time* *Newsweek*	*Why:* To find timely articles about the global economy and consumer behavior.

Industry and Business Trends

Next, it is important to move into the industry trends. This information is also available in libraries, or through the internet using sites such as www.ceo-express.com and www.pathfinder.com.

What: Hoover's	*Why:* Hoover's publishes a variety of books each year that include: Top 500 companies in the United States Top 100 private companies A capsule version is available through "pathfinder" on the internet. Hoover's will tell you the corporate financial status, the operational structure, and the principal competition.

What: *Ward's*	*Why:* The Ward's directories list the companies and their product lines and produces cross-directional directories that identify brands and their companies. This can be helpful for designers and business owners, due to the growth of product development and private labeling.
What: *Sheldon's*	*Why:* A list of retail stores throughout the United States, by state.
What: All companies' annual report and press kit	*Why:* Any company that is on a public stock exchange is required by law to provide materials to the public. Simply phone the public relations office and ask for an annual report and the information will be sent to you. This information is extraordinary because you can learn about the direction of a company easily. Don't limit yourself to just manufacturing or retailing firms. Call and ask for information about leading textile/fiber companies—the information is invaluable. (Also, check their Web sites!)
What: *Stores*	*Why:* Leading retailing magazine featuring the growth and changes of many retail operations.
What: *WWD Buyer's Guide* Fairchild Publications 7 West 34th Street New York, NY 10001	*Why:* Information on manufacturers including market weeks, apparel marts, trade associations, and individual wholesalers' profiles.

Fashion Trends

OK, after all that "dry" research, we know this is where you really wanted to start! Remember in Chapter 1 when we said, " Do you follow fashion reports in magazines and on TV?" When we asked you that question, we were asking you as a consumer. Now that you have entered the fashion world, you will have to look at trends two ways: as a consumer and as a trade member. So let's take a look at fashion in both ways.

Trade Publications	Consumer Publications
Women's Wear Daily (WWD) Considered the backbone of the industry. Covers U.S. Women's and Children's, European markets; Top retail news. *Published by* Fairchild Publications 7 West 34th Street New York, NY 10001	*W* *Vogue* *Harper's Bazaar* *Elle*

Daily News Record (DNR)
The major source for the men's industry, with an exceptionally good job done on the textile market. Also published by Fairchild.

Gentleman's Quarterly
Esquire

MR Magazine
The magazine of menswear retailing
Published by Business Journals
185 Madison Avenue
New York, NY 10016

California Apparel News
This is an excellent publication on the west coast market. They also publish Men's Apparel News.
Published by California Fashion Publications
110 East 9th Street,
Los Angeles, CA 90079

The Licensing Book
Latest news on hot licensing properties.
Adventure Publishing Group
1501 Broadway
New York, NY 10018

Earnshaw's Review
The monthly kids fashion trade magazine.
225 West 34th Street
New York, NY 10001

Bobbin Magazine
Textile industry coverage.
1110 Old Shop Road
Columbia, SC 29202

Are there more? Absolutely! But remember that you are starting out right now, and sometimes too much research can put you into overload. But we promise you, finding the fashion trends and staying aware of the industry timing will come through clearly in the publications cited above.

Now, as you move on and get more familiar with the designs and collections, you'll want to know about some services that can help as well.

Reporting/Consulting Services/Trade Associations

What: Tobe
500 5th Avenue
New York, NY 10036

Why: This is an analysis of the retailing trends and fashion trends.

What: Promostyl
80 West 40th Street
New York, NY 10018

Why: Projects trends.

What:	Cotton Incorporated 1370 Avenue of the Americas New York, NY 10019	*Why:*	Information center for cotton and cotton-blend fibers and textiles. Provides information to designers, manufacturers, retailers, and consumers.
What:	Color Association of the United States 409 West 44th Street New York, NY 10036	*Why:*	Predicts colors.
What:	The Wool Bureau 330 Madison Avenue New York, NY 10017	*Why:*	Up-to-date information on wool yarns and products.
What:	Fashion Group International, Inc. 597 Fifth Avenue New York, NY 10017	*Why:*	Nonprofit professional organization. Maintains information on the fashion industry; promotes networking.

Now for the twenty-first century! With cable TV and the Internet, brand new opportunities are beginning to open up! There's something new on the net every day. Here are some of the newest (all around) sources.

What:	*firstVIEW* http://www.firstview.com 175 Fifth Avenue New York, NY 10010	*Why:*	This is a site on the World Wide Web that provides access to tens of thousands of photos of the world's top designers' most recent collections.
What:	*The Look On-Line* http://www.lookonline.com	*Why:*	Site with phone numbers and addresses for fashion companies and other retail professionals.
What:	*New York's Fashion Center* http://www.fashioncenter.com	*Why:*	Updates on the New York market.

Other web sites are developing. Make the Internet one of your research vehicles, because you can see what is happening across the world instantaneously. Make sure you set your screen saver to the latest trend color!

Don't forget, good research doesn't stop here—it keeps you going. Watch some TV, do some people watching, go to the movies. Yes, go to the movies! Watch the classics, see the elegance of designers like Edith Head, who created for stars such as Carole Lombard, Mae West, Grace Kelly, and Shirley McLaine. Look at the styling, look at the flow. Then watch the "fun" movies. You can get a great 30-year overview of fashion in a movie such as *Forrest Gump* or a slice of the 1950s in *Back to the Future.*

And yes, it is OK to watch TV. Let's face it, every teenage girl has one character on the screen who wears all the looks that she would like to wear herself! Teenage boys won't admit it, but they too follow TV and (above all) sports shows, imitating this "look." In the 1990s, sports stars are setting more menswear fashion trends than anyone else! "Doug Levine, president of Crunch, a five-unit health club operation that markets activewear, suggests that the street style of male athletes on the courts—from tattoos to earrings—is what appeals to urban markets" [*Women's Wear Daily*, January 30, 1997, "Taking It from the Streets," Rosemary Feitelberg].

Other Options

If you happen to be lucky enough to live near a local art or costume museum, please visit! If not, maybe a vacation will find you near some of the famous costume museums:

Costume Institute, The Metropolitan Museum of Art in New York
The Costume Gallery, The Los Angeles County Museum of Art
The Smithsonian Institute in Washington, D.C.

and if you are traveling to Canada or Europe:

Costume Institute, McCord Museum in Montreal
Le Centre du Documentation de la Mode Parisienne in Paris
Victoria and Albert Museum in London
Centro Internazionale Arti e del Costume in Venice

The collections, which are magnificent, are referenced with detailed information about the creation of these garments. If you can't get to one of these museums, there are other ways. First, many have produced books about their historic costume collections. Second, there are costume exhibits that tour the country on a regular basis. For example, the Fellini exhibition, featuring extraordinary costumes from the Fellini films, spent six months at the Bass Museum of Art in Miami in 1996. That collection, like many others, will move around the United States for everyone to see.

NOW, THE FASHION FEELERS ARE OUT!

With all this information, you really are ready to move forward. Don't think that this is all too much, and can I remember it all? You will. Using these sources, thinking in these patterns, will all become a part of your daily working life. If you do make research the foundation for your business, you will be successful because you will be meeting your (well-researched) customer's expectations. Next, we move on to the fun stuff—the actual designing process.

SO YOU WANT TO WORK IN THE FASHION BUSINESS?

Here's How to Begin. . . Chapter 6

It's important for you to research trends, lifestyles, fabrics, stores, manufacturers, and designers. Each plays an important role in the consumer buying habits of today. Here are a few suggestions that we think you might try.

TO FIND OUT ABOUT THE PHILOSOPHY OF A DESIGNER OR MANUFACTURER

First: Ask for the Information

Using the Women's Wear Daily *Buyers' Guide*, the *Fashion Guide Index*, or even the phone books at the public library, locate the corporate headquarters for key designers or manufacturers that you admire. Some fascinating companies include:

Ellen Tracy	Levi Strauss	Betsey Johnson
Oscar de la Renta	Oshkosh	Calvin Klein
Nautica	Tommy Hilfiger	Dana Buchman
Donna Karan	Olga	Perry Ellis
Carole Little	Karen Kane	Mossimo
Timberland	Anne Klein	Chanel
Versace	Lagerfeld	St. John
Ike Behar	Ralph Lauren	Liz Claiborne
Yaga	No Fear	Gotcha!
Hanes	Coach	Ferragamo

Most designers have offices in New York City, so if search time is tight, simply call information at 212-555-1212 and ask the information system for the corporate phone number. Once you've made the phone call, ask for the public relations department. Ask the PR director to send you a press kit and/or annual report.

Second: Go "On-line"

Using the computer systems at the public and school libraries, (if you don't have your own home computer), find out what the business and trade publications are reporting about the designers and manufacturers. Complete a search on the two designers or manufacturers you have asked for press kits and see how they are being viewed in the marketplace. By the way, you can see each day's headlines from *Women's Wear Daily* at http://www.wwd.com.

Third: See What the Consumer Thinks

Gather up consumer publications; *Vogue*, *Glamour*, *Elle*, and *Town and Country*, and don't forget to look for men's information in *GQ*! Find advertisements or articles about the designer or manufacturer that you are researching. Does the designer's vision coincide with what the industry is saying and what the consumer is seeing?

Finally: What Do You Think?

Were you surprised to find out how a designer or manufacturer started? If everyone in the classroom chooses two different firms, the amount of information to share will be wonderfully rich.

TO FIND OUT ABOUT THE DIRECTION OF THE TEXTILE MARKET

Calling or writing textile companies will provide you with a good outlook on how the textile market is moving as to texture and colors. Follow the same procedure as you did when asking for press kits and annual reports for the designers or manufacturers. Once you've found the phone number, either by using the WWD *Buyer's Guide* or information, make the phone call and ask the public relations department to send you a press kit and/or annual report.

Don't focus only on textile mills; it is important to review the information and reflect on the direction provided by the Cotton Council, Burlington, Monsanto, and DuPont. And don't forget the knitting mills and the fur industry. In fact, here are a few places to check that will provide some good industry trends:

Cotton Incorporated
1370 Avenue of the Americas
New York, NY 10019

Wool Bureau, Inc.
330 Madison Avenue
New York, NY 10017

Knitted Textile Association
386 Park Avenue
New York, NY 10016

Fur Information Council of America
655 15th Street, NW
No. 320
Washington, DC 20036

International Silk Association
200 Madison Avenue
New York, NY 10017

National Cotton Council
P.O. Box 12285
Memphis, TN 38182

By this time you should be building your own library of information, so don't stop.

TO FIND OUT ABOUT STORES: THEIR CONSUMER PHILOSOPHY AND THE PLACE THEY HOLD IN THE MARKETPLACE

Using *Hoover's*, *Sheldon's*, and even local store information, locate the corporate headquarters for leading stores. Again, with just a phone call you will learn how stores were started, by whom, and even why. In addition, you can learn firsthand where stores are planning to expand under the current corporate structure. Again, simply call the corporate headquarters and ask!

There are dozens of fascinating companies. Learn how they started, where they are now, and what are their visions of the future. Here are a few suggestions:

Bloomingdale's
Gap
Laura Ashley
County Seat
L.L. Bean
K-mart
Burdine's
Lord & Taylor
J.C. Penney
Bergdorf Goodman
Saks Fifth Avenue
Limited (all divisions)
Brooks Brothers
Episode
Nordstrom
Wal-mart
Dillard's
Robinson-May
Sears
Loehman's
Macy's
Coach
Neiman-Marcus
Spiegel
Target
Marshall's
Jacobson's
Marshall Field
Wet Seal
Bebe

Don't forget to check with the

National Retail Federation
325 7th Street NW
Washington, DC 20004

Remember, these are the stores you will be working for either as a designer on the design team, selling products to them, or on the product development design team, making products for them. Simply put, what is important is knowing where they are positioned with consumers in the marketplace. Don't stop with gathering press kits and annual reports when you call a textile firm or a store. Get back on-line and see what you can find through the computer. The trade publications in both hard copy or on-line will be a wonderful source of information. Use the trade and business journals to focus on your questions, and then always look to the consumer publications to reflect on their image.

CHAPTER 7

Fashion's Triangle of Balance: You Can't Sell Granny Bloomers to Baby Boomers!

Sometimes when you exaggerate, as the chapter title does, the point seems obvious and maybe a little funny. But the point is this: Three elements need to be in balance to produce fashion success. The right designer needs to be providing the right clothes to the right store for these clothes to sell well. Every designer has his or her own vision, design philosophy, and personal sense of taste, and you do, too! Here's a test to help you identify yours:

- Close your eyes for a few moments, and relax—really relax.
- Imagine that there are no barriers, no restrictions and that you are living in your dream home. Keep your eyes closed.
- Can you hear the noises; can you smell the air? Describe your home and the area.
- Now describe how your home looks, feels, and smells.
- Now consider the furnishings: the touch, the colors, the look.
- At what types of stores did you shop for these furnishings?
- Oh yes, one last thing: Do you see yourself in your home? What are you wearing?

This exercise helps you picture yourself in the surroundings in which you are most comfortable. When comfortable, you can picture what clothes you naturally lean toward. If the setting was casual, chances are that you pictured yourself in casual, stylish clothes. If the setting was more formal, chances are that your clothes were as well. The most successful designers are clear not only about their own taste but can also actually visualize their customers, where those customers live, and where those customers shop. The *triangle of balance* must be struck:

- The right designer
- Designing the right clothes
- Which are shown in the right store

It all has to be in balance, like an equilateral triangle (Figure 7-1).

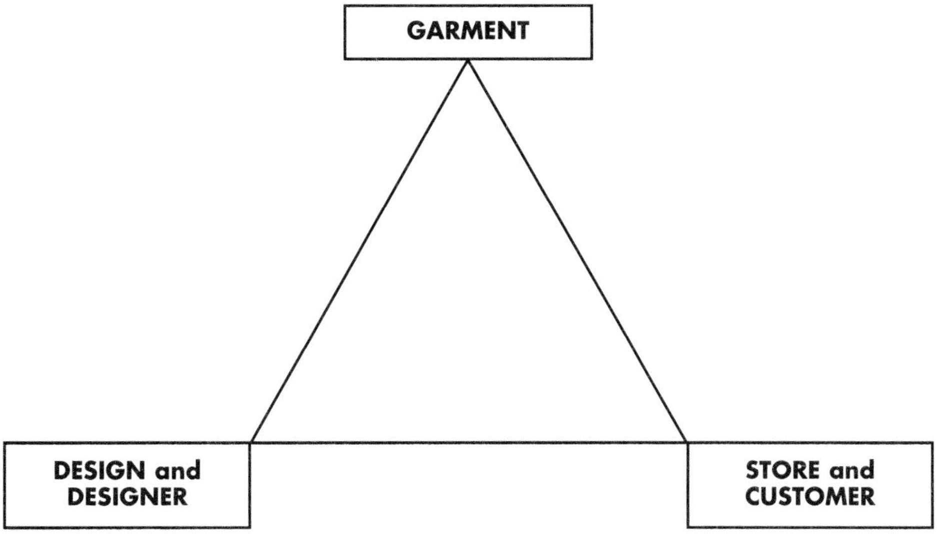

Figure 7-1

THE INSIDE SCOOP

PAMELA DENNIS

Pamela is president and designer of Pamela Dennis, a line that stands for glamor, taste, and sexy "wow" gowns. Winner of the Gold Coast Fashion Award, Pamela has shown her collection on the *Oprah Winfrey Show*, *E! Entertainment*, and *HBO n Style*. The line can be found in Bergdorf Goodman, Neiman-Marcus, Saks Fifth Avenue, Barney's NY, and Harvey Nichols, London. Her clientele includes Jamie Lee Curtis, Bette Midler, and Hillary Clinton.

On knowing your customer and store:

I know my customer because I do lots of trunk shows and really like them! I'm a hands-on, roll-up-the-sleeves person. I work right in the dressing room with them. Without knowing what my customers' needs are, I couldn't do this.

In designing, fabrics are key. I also love antique shopping. At times we've duplicated antique fabrics for the collection. The fabric sometimes "says" what to make out of it.

How could I tell which stores would be best for my merchandise? I'm at the same price points as Armani and Chanel. That's an indicator. So I'm in Bergdorf's and Neiman's.

Then it became word of mouth from customers. They told me which stores they shopped in!

Photo courtesy of Pamela Dennis.

Remember, this is not new! In Chapters 4 and 5 you learned how customers buy according to their lifestyle, their perception of value, and their taste level. If one element is off, success can't follow. Picture this:

- The right designer (young, streetwise, urban)
- Designing the right clothes (fast street fashion)
- But shown in the wrong store (a promotional department store with mostly elderly customers)

These clothes won't sell (Figure 7-2).

Here's another example of the store being wrong: We've all seen expensive items, beautifully made, but marked way, way down, because everything

Figure 7–2

Right clothes maybe—but wrong store for sure! *Artwork by Michael Carnegie.*

else in this particular store was much less expensive. This store's customers couldn't recognize the incredible value of the (marked-down) better items. These items were in the wrong store, thus out of balance. And it can work the other way, as well: Something that doesn't sell because it is too cheap—when surrounded by high-end, well-made garments—again, out of balance.

A customer evaluates a garment to see if it is in balance for them by:

- Eye appeal (color, pattern, texture): Do I like the overall look of the garment?
- Touch (the **hand** of the garment): Does it feel appealing to me?
- Price and value: Is it an affordable price? Is it a good value for my money?
- Fit and wearability: How does it look on me?

Hand
The feel or touch of a fabric.

This next example might be a bit obvious but may make the point: Picture two customers, one a 65-year-old grandmother and the other a 17-year-old high school senior. Ask them the four questions posed in Figure 7-3.

	Grandmother	**High School Senior**
What is the overall look of the garment that you want?	Not too flashy.	Attention getting.
How should it feel?	Soft, comfortable.	Fashionable—It doesn't matter how it feels!
Is it affordable?	As low a price as possible.	Price needs to be within reach; maybe a splurge for the right look or designer name.
How does it look on me?	Does it cover me up?	Does it show me off?

Figure 7-3

Let's quickly look at three successfully balanced triangles: Figures 7-4, 7-5, and 7-6.

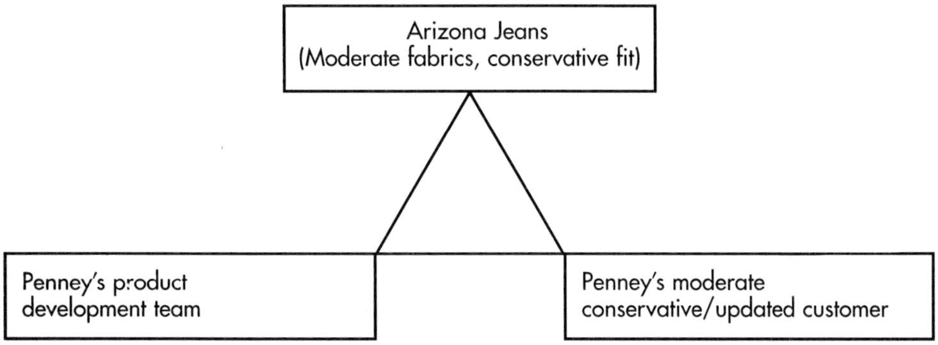

Figure 7-4

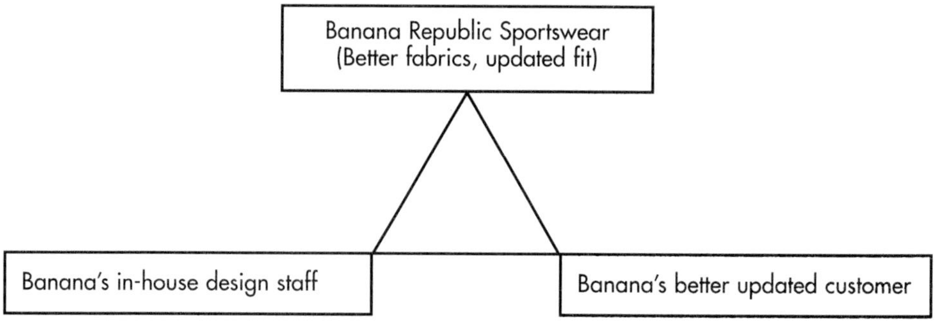

Figure 7-5

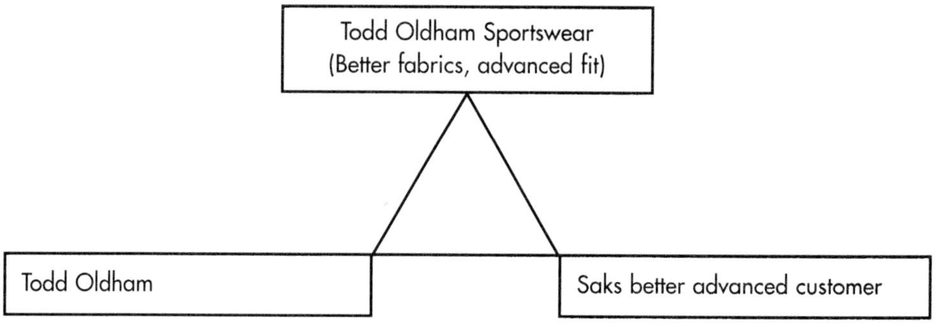

Figure 7-6

Here's another interesting triangle-of-balance example: Halston was one of the classic designers of the 1960s. (Jackie Kennedy was a fan.) His merchandise was shown in better stores and it sold successfully. In the 1980s, as J.C. Penney was pushing hard to get designer names represented in the store to enhance its fashion credibility, the Halston company agreed to design a Halston line for Penney's exclusively, which was then sourced by the Penney's staff or by licensees. It didn't work because the triangle was out of balance (Figure 7-7). The Penney's customer didn't "get" Halston; and as a result, Halston was "tainted" by being in Penney's at that time.

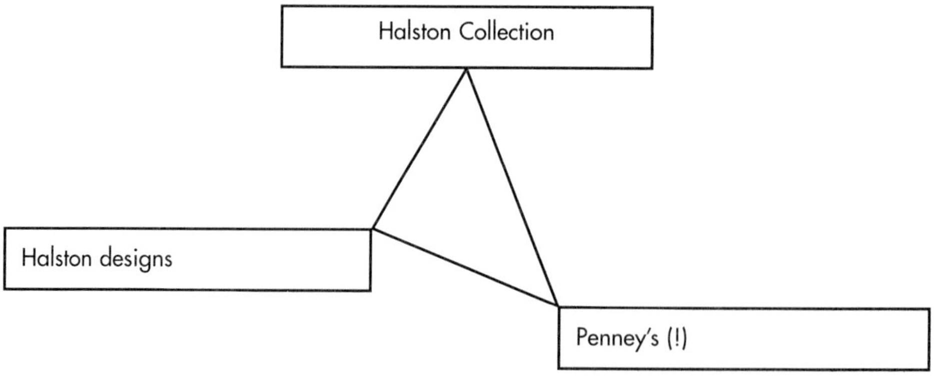

Figure 7-7

But no story is ever completely over. In 1997, TTI International launched a new Halston line, designed by cutting-edge designer Randolph Duke. The merchandise was priced at core department store price points, and it was purchased by Federated, Dayton's, Belk's, and Carson's. [*Women's Wear Daily*, December 31, 1996, "Halston Revisited"].

Now, the triangle is back in balance (Figure 7-8). In fact, this Halston line has performed much better. So a men's Halston line is now being planned for 1998 [*Daily News Record*, May 23, 1997].

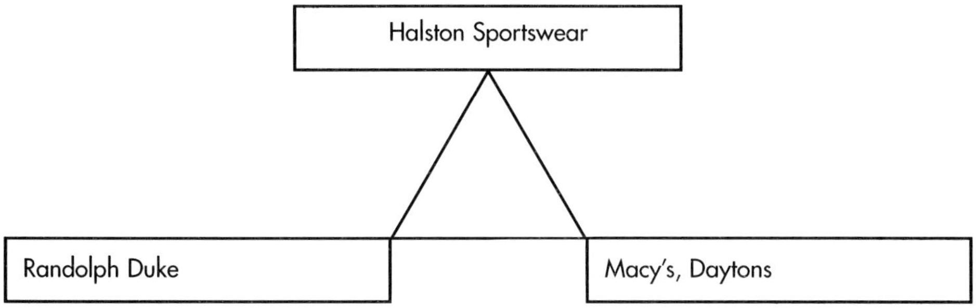

Figure 7-8

Each customer has a different point of view and different needs. The designer who understands the particular customer, designs the right clothes for that customer, and places them in the right retail store will have achieved the triangle of balance that is necessary for success.

Building lines that are salable starts by being in balance because the object is to develop a profitable business. Where do you start? You start in the next chapter with concept and mood boards, which will be your first visual tools for building a successful line.

THE INSIDE SCOOP

MICHAEL MCKEITHAN

Michael is a textile CAD designer for Tommy Hilfiger. He studied at both Parsons and FIT.

On the difference between school and business:

In school I was still looking at clothes as an end-user (what did I like?), not as someone who has to manufacture these clothes. A design can be fabulous, but if the buyer doesn't like it, you might have to scrap that whole line and start over. That's where the *real* creativity comes in!

On my first job, I was doing very expressive designs—until my boss came over and said "Simple sells!" I said, "Simple? Who wants to do simple?" When you're designing in business, you've got to start asking yourself such questions as: What store is this going in? What fabrics can't we use? How much will it cost to make?

SO YOU WANT TO WORK IN THE FASHION BUSINESS?
Here's How to Begin. . . Chapter 7

You did a lot of research for Chapter 6. Take some time to analyze the information and make your own forecasting predictions on the designers and manufacturers headed for continued growth and success in the twenty-first century.

TO DETERMINE IF A DESIGNER OR MANUFACTURER IS IN BALANCE

First: Gather the Information

Put together a team of three or four students and make a list of six manufacturers or designers that you feel are leading the industry right now, based on the information you have gathered on industry leaders, the fashion trends, fabrics, stores, and consumer lifestyles.

Second: Analyze the Facts and Build Your Own Triangle of Balance

Based on the information your team has gathered, answer the following questions:

a. What do you think is the designer's vision? What statement is the designer trying to make?
b. Who is the customer? Use Chapter 5 to help you find the niche.
c. Does the customer share the vision of the designer?
d. Where are the garments being sold? In what type of store? Again let the information in Chapter 5 guide you.
e. Now, go shop the line. Yes, go shopping. Take a look at the garments. Do you think the eye appeal, wearability, and price are all in line with the store, its customers and the designer's philosophy? In other words, is the triangle balanced, or is something missing?

Third: What Is Your Opinion?

Interestingly enough, you are providing opinions on two different levels: one, as a member of the industry, analyzing and interpreting trends, and on the other hand, as a consumer. It is OK to combine the two. Remember that focus groups are one vehicle used to determine consumer needs. It is now time for your team to deliver your opinions as a focus group.

a. Which designer or manufacturer does the team feel is most successful and will continue to grow? Why?
b. Which designer or manufacturer does the group feel is struggling, and in what area? Is it in the product, or is it in the wrong store, or is it missing the target market?

DISCUSSING A DESIGNER OR MANUFACTURER THAT IS NOT IN BALANCE

a. While you were shopping, did you see a well-made, creatively designed product that was priced right but in the wrong store? As a group, discuss where you feel these products should be shown to sell successfully.

b. Look through old fashion magazines and find designers or manufacturers that have faded. Find out why! A bit of research may be required, but many of the answers will be easy to see, such as:

   Good product–wrong store?
   Good product–too expensive?
   Great idea–great store–poor quality?

Designers and manufacturers can make mistakes. The key is correct them and get back on track! How many companies did you see in ads that you no longer see in the marketplace? How many companies do you think have had to make significant changes to become successful in today's marketplace? Discuss these topics in your group, and then each team should share the information with the entire class.

CHAPTER 8

Building the First Design Ideas: Don't Lose That Thought!

IN GREATER DEPTH

THE BASIC PRINCIPLES OF DESIGN

Before we go further, we need to cover quickly some basic design principles. There are complete (and excellent) books on this topic. But since a designer cannot begin to sketch without taking these principles into consideration, we thought we would touch on this topic very briefly. Although this is not a book on high-fashion design, it is important for anyone involved in manufacturing and product development to have at least a grasp of design principles. If you're at the cutting table and need to move a zipper, you want to move to the aesthetically most pleasing place.

Proportion

Proportion is simply how the individual parts of a garment relate to the whole shape. The human body has many different contours, and a designer has to modify parts of the garment to flatter the body. Sometimes this is done by emphasizing the natural body shape, or sometimes by creating a new shape. A designer will look at the space, dividing it by height and width to create a pleasing look (proportion). The classic natural waist proportion is a ratio of 3 (the top) to 5 (the skirt) equals 8 (Figure 8-1).

But other proportions work as well. The junior market in the mid 1990s featured a "babydoll" look for dresses. By making the bodice a shorter part of the design and the dress a longer part, the junior dress took on a younger, perhaps even a taller, look. The empire waist exaggerates a young girl's proportions (Figure 8-2).

Finally, broader shoulders creating a wedge proportion can help to play down a heavy-set build (Figure 8-3).

Balance

A designer divides a garment both horizontally and vertically. For the garment to appear appealing, the right amount of detail and emphasis must be distributed to

Figure 8-1
Proportion: Natural waist. Artwork by Mary Lisa Caramico.

Figure 8-2
Proportion: Empire waist. Artwork by Mary Lisa Caramico.

Figure 8-3
Proportion: Wedge shape. Artwork by Mary Lisa Caramico.

each of the horizontal and vertical parts. Too much or too little in one area of the garment makes it appear unbalanced. Look at Figures 8-4, 8-5, and 8-6.

Unity

Unity means that all the elements included in the design work together and don't fight each other. For example, if a jacket has an off-center opening, the skirt underneath it should not have an on-center opening (Figures 8-7 and 8-8). Elements should look like they were planned, not a mistake. In Figures 8-9 and 8-10, notice how a slight shift in the seaming makes a huge difference in the unity of the garment.

Emphasis

Simply put, emphasis is the focal point, the center of interest on the garment, much as there is always a center of interest in a painting. It might be a fabric, a color, a detail, or trim—but it is the main reason your customers look at the garment! Look at Figures 8-11 and 8-12 and decide what makes each of these samples eye-catching.

Silhouette

Silhouette is the overall outside shape of a garment, and it is the most common element among all garments at a given point in time. When you see the padded shoulders and severe military suit silhouettes in a movie, you know that it was made in the 1940s.

(Continued on next page)

Figure 8-4

Balance: Simple, equal left-to-right balance. Artwork by Mary Lisa Caramico.

Figure 8-5

Balance: Vertical and horizontal balance. Note how the cuffs balance the bodice stripe. Artwork by Mary Lisa Caramico.

Figure 8-6

Balance: Asymmetrical. Artwork by Mary Lisa Caramico.

Figure 8-7

Unity: Bad example—jacket and skirt seams don't line up. Artwork by Mary Lisa Caramico.

Figure 8-8

Unity: Good example—jacket opening and skirt seams are both off-center. Artwork by Mary Lisa Caramico.

Figure 8-9

Unity: Bad example—bodice and skirt fight each other. Artwork by Mary Lisa Caramico.

Figure 8-10
Unity: Good example—vertical seams meet at the waist. Artwork by Mary Lisa Caramico.

Figure 8-11
Emphasis: What is the center of interest on this dress? Artwork by Mary Lisa Caramico.

Figure 8-12
Emphasis: Why is the yoke on this dress white? Artwork by Mary Lisa Caramico.

The tight-waisted full skirt, paired with a clinging knit top, is pure 1950s. Silhouette tends to change rather slowly, and it is one of the few features that will probably be alike from designer to designer. When the silhouette trend is oversized, for example, almost everyone will be doing oversized. The 1990s, for example, will probably be remembered for a return to tighter fits. Figures 8-13 and 8-14 illustrate the two different silhouettes.

Line

The lines of a garment include the seams and edges of the garment that divide it (Figure 8-15). What lines in a garment usually do is to create a kind of "visual illusion": longer, taller, or maybe slimmer. For example, princess seams create a slimming effect. But sometimes, lines are used to create the illusion of weight. For example, a strapless look can be especially good for a thin woman because the shoulders appear wider (Figure 8-16). Strong asymmetrical lines tend to make a bold statement (Figure 8-17).

Color

It has been found that the first thing to grab the customer's eye is the color of a garment. Color is the most fundamental fashion element; it is usually the first thing a designer decides on each season. Color is a study all by itself. Most schools have full courses on color theory. But for our purposes it is most important for you to remember the three ways color is measured:

(Continued on next page)

Figure 8-13
Silhouette: Oversized. Artwork by Mary Lisa Caramico.

Figure 8-14
Silhouette: Slim. Artwork by Mary Lisa Caramico.

HUE: the difference between one color (red, blue) and another (say, yellow).

CHROMA: the saturation or intensity of a particular color, the difference between brightness and dullness. Stated another way, it is the amount of gray in the color. For example, a dusty blue and a very dusty gray-blue can have the same hue and the same value but differ only in the amount of gray (chroma) in each color.

VALUE: the difference between a light color (say, light green) and a dark color (say, dark green) of the same hue and chroma.

This may seem abstract to you now, but when you're sweating over a light box trying to judge whether or not a proposed sweater yarn is going to be a "close enough" match to a "matching" wool skirt, you will need to instruct the Hong Kong sweater maker in technical terms, as, for example, that the color should be 10% brighter (chroma) and 20% lighter (value). This specific direction is the only way to achieve the appropriate match. There are machines that analyze these colors (Macbeth), but it almost always requires the human eye as well. (By the way, there is no such thing as a perfect match, especially between two different fabrics. The question becomes—how close is close enough?) To keep things interesting, there are some colors like khaki which can match under daylight, but not under store (fluorescent) light, and vice versa! Colors like these are called *metameric* and they can cause you to start to have nightmares in (metameric) color!

Pattern and Texture

Patterns also follow fashion trends (animal prints are in, then they're out, for example). But even more basic is the designer's knowledge of what size patterns work (or

Figure 8-15

Line: The seams and edges of a garment create the "line." Artwork by Mary Lisa Caramico.

Figure 8-16

Line: Strapless. Artwork by Mary Lisa Caramico.

Figure 8-17

Line: Asymmetrical. Artwork by Mary Lisa Caramico.

don't work) on a given garment. It is very tricky to find a large pattern that can be used effectively, for example.

Texture is almost always referred to as the *hand* of a fabric. Does it feel soft, harsh, smooth, rough? Again the challenge is to pair a fabric of a particular hand with the right color in the right silhouette. This skill usually comes after making a few mistakes.

WHICH ONE IS THE BUSINESSPERSON?

In most design and garment-manufacturing books, one concept seems to be universal. The manufacturing process in the fashion industry is viewed in three parts:

Design Production Sales

Hearing this, your first impression might be that sales sounds like the only part that is really "business." Surely designers are, above all, expected to be fashion visionaries. And production is run by engineering types who don't really care about either the design or the salability of the garments. *Wrong!*

Each of the three areas needs to be run as a business. Each needs to search for efficiencies and savings. Each needs to think about the requirements and challenges of the other two areas:

- *Design* should be sure that its concepts can be produced efficiently and sold easily. (Designers are often accused of wanting the impossible!)

- *Production* needs to preserve the design integrity of each garment, but in the most cost-efficient manner.
- *Sales* needs to understand the designer's vision plus the technical quality features that the production team has been able to build in. Salespeople are also the link to the retail buyer. They must be able to communicate the buyer's needs back to both design and production personnel.

The goal of any business is to produce a product or service that sells well and thus earns profits for that company. Each of the three parts of our business (design, production, and sales) must share this goal, and each must make its own businesslike contribution toward it. Communication between the three segments is key throughout. Midstream changes that aren't clearly communicated to everyone are a frequent source of production problems. Where do you, a businesslike profit-oriented designer, start?

What's the First Step?

Mood Boards
Presentation boards that show pictures and other visuals to create a general fashion "feeling."

The first step is the development of something called **mood boards**. (In these early stages, just collecting stimulating images is more important than organizing them. First you need to find the overall "mood" of your collection.) This being a visual business, designers and merchandisers often build their lines on corkboard walls or something similar. They start by pinning up anything that strikes their fancy. (This is the creative "right brain" process: If it pops into your head, pin it to the wall!) Then, gradually, they edit, move, reconfigure, and refine the ideas until they come together into a cohesive and practical line. (This is the organizing "left brain" part of the process.) It is very helpful to be able to stare at the entire line often, if even for a minute or two at a time. Chances are that each time, you will see something that could be improved.

First you have to know what season you are designing for. In the fashion industry you are usually designing a year in advance. When the major European fabric shows are held in February, they are featuring fabrics to be used for spring and summer of the following year. When the fabric shows are held in October, they feature fabrics to be used for the following fall and holiday seasons. So when you are starting out, you have to think about what has just happened in the previous season and what you want to happen next year.

Swipe
A picture cut out of a magazine.

The best way to show you how this is done is with pictures, which illustrate how the mood boards progress month by month during the process. Designers will start compiling pictures, **swipes**, words, fabric swatches, colors, trims—anything that might inspire them. They must also keep firmly in mind who their customer is. Into what square does this customer fit on the price/taste grid? A fall season plan, which covers shipping apparel from August through October, might go through a six-month planning phase before any samples are made.

Figure 8-18 shows your blank bulletin board, ready to receive any and all ideas. To start, in July you will begin pinning up anything that you think could be directional or helpful in building next fall's line (Figure 8-19). In August, the board captures much of the inspiration, but in greater detail (Figure 8-20).

THE INSIDE SCOOP

Blair Crane

Blair is a unique combination of designer, product developer, and sourcer. She has used these talents at Ruff Hewn, Banana Republic, and AMC (for Dayton/Hudson/Marshall Field's highly acclaimed Field Gear program).

On using workboards:

The reason I like to have everything up on boards is so that it's constantly in front of me. I like to have them right in my office. This is important because when you're out in the streets, in the market, shopping piece goods, in shows and stores—it hits you automatically if your work is trend right—also if your line is consistent with the rest of the market.

The first step is with the trend services. If you can see three to five of them, you'll get a good indication of color, color flow, and some degree of fabric and silhouette. For me, the game plan starts with color. I've been fortunate that the companies I've worked for always had colors relating to trend themes ("Havana", "Varsity"). Once you establish your themes and colors, they will be a natural lead-in for specific fabrics and silhouettes.

Designers want to be able to build on all good thoughts, not lose them. That's why they will pin up anything that hits them, when it hits them. Not all ideas might get used, but it is easier to eliminate ideas than to come up with them.

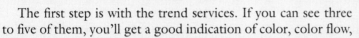

Figure 8-18

The blank mood board in June, before the planning begins.

> **Work Boards**
> Visual working tools used by designers and merchandisers to picture entire lines, style by style.

Now the boards start taking on a different slant and become real **work boards**. First, everything you just reviewed was from the creative right-brain side. This was when you were collecting ideas, and anything at that stage was possible. But now take a look at the board development from September on. The business of design takes over and the left brain starts editing and redefining ideas into a cohesive and salable line. This is when you will start remembering to stay in balance. Don't go off the deep end of design! These clothes have to sell.

In September the business projections also start seeping in. Just what are the goals of your firm? How many pieces do you project to make and sell? What styles can you create from your ideas: what colors, what patterns? The details by style must be pinned down. The board will begin to reflect these decisions.

Ratios

This is an important measuring stick that is used by wholesalers and retailers alike. Retail store buyers work to keep their inventories balanced to hit the correct proportion of basic merchandise, fashion merchandise, and promotional merchandise.

Basic Merchandise

Basic merchandise, sometimes called *staple merchandise*, includes items that are wanted day in and day out. They tend to have a long selling life. Basic solid-color cotton turtlenecks (through the fall and winter seasons) and basic khaki shorts (in spring and summer) would be two basics that a moderate missy department would want to be fully stocked in throughout the given season. Men's and kid's tend to have a relatively high proportion of basics; missy and especially juniors, somewhat less so.

Fashion Merchandise

Fashion merchandise includes styles that are very current, or are in demand for a limited period, but then fall way off in popularity. This is one of the trickiest parts of a buyer's job: how to know which fashion styles the customer will want, when she is ready to accept the look, and when she has moved past this look. When fashion items are new and hot, they can often command extrahigh markup. But when the look is over, they require an extralarge markdown!

Promotional merchandise

Actually, it was much more common in the past to bring in special groups of merchandise at reduced prices (perhaps a vendor's overstock, perhaps a closeout) and sell this special merchandise at reduced (promotional) prices. Today, it is more common for stores to promote their in-stock basic items (even their fashion items) in order to drive sales volume. Customers won't put up with second-best just to get something on sale. They want the regular merchandise (including brands and designers) to be on sale. This has taken a significant toll on overall profitability, but since all the competition is doing it, no store can avoid it.

There is one more small category of merchandise that you'll hear about: *impulse items.* These are usually inexpensive items, often shown near the register, which a customer might pick up on a whim or "impulse." A cute little novelty stuffed animal, a funny hat, a catchy printed T-shirt, or any number of eye-catching items are often stocked for this reason.

You, as a wholesaler, need to understand that a buyer is going to evaluate your line by looking at ratios. You need to examine (above all) the ratio of basic to fashion items as the line develops. In addition, you might think about the need to be involved in promotional items or impulse items. Each type of retail store will probably require different ratios of basics to fashion to promotional. Again, the wholesaler must know his or her customer (the retail buyer), and the buyer must know his or her customer (the consumer).

Still More Ratios

Other ratios will also need to be taken into consideration, usually measured against past selling history:

1. Ratio of number of tops styles to number of bottoms styles.
2. Ratio of hard pieces (tailored items such as jackets) to soft pieces (less constructed items such as sweaters and blouses).
3. Ratio of knit styles to woven styles.
4. Ratio of long sleeves to short sleeves.

There are many more, depending on your line. Each ratio takes on more or less importance based on the season, the store, and the customer. (Does this sound like the triangle of balance again?)

Now, on to our work boards in September (Figure 8-21). You need to create two groups, each of which has its own design theme, with a cohesive presence on the selling floor. By October the two deliveries are becoming clearer (Figure 8-22). Then in November, you need to make final decisions. The board in Figure 8-23 reflects:

- Work sketches of each item, incorporating the principles and elements of design. (Keep in mind that some wholesalers' lines could be 200 to 300 styles per season.)
- Color stories that project a fashion-forward image, yet will be understood by the target customer.
- Fabric stories that will capture the fashion message, yet are affordable.
- Cost sheets that will project the cost of each style.

This was just for two deliveries! Some lines can have as many as 10 or 20 deliveries per year.

It is at this point that the merchandiser takes over. It becomes the merchandiser's role to find a way to turn the designer's line into a feasible, practical, and affordable line of actual garments. If the designer has been a true businessperson as noted in the introduction, the merchandiser's job becomes that much easier!

SO YOU WANT TO WORK IN THE FASHION BUSINESS?
Here's How to Begin. . . Chapter 8

It's time to start designing, so let's take some time and get the on-the-job training that we talked about before!

First: Gathering Information

We're going to ask you to start thinking about what you might be designing one year from now for a particular consumer group of your choice. Working with a team of three or four students, decide what category of merchandise you would like to design. Some suggestions are:

Men's casual sportswear or activewear
Women's casual sportswear or activewear
Contemporary women's sportswear
Women's bridge/better sportswear
Children's, boys 4–7 or 8–20, girls 4–14
Juniors

If you cannot decide, look back at Chapter 5 to give you some ideas.

Based on the information you have gathered on industry leaders, fashion trends, fabrics, stores, and consumer lifestyles, identify the category, look, price points, fabrics, and colors that you would like to present to your consumer.

Second: Gathering and Analyzing Information to Build Your Own Line

As a team, you are all staring at a blank board! Using photos from magazines, industry publications, press kits, or newspapers, pin pictures of garments on a class bulletin board or corkboard (or even tape them to the class board) that were top sellers for this past season. Add to the board swipes reflecting trends that you like, along with color swatches or fabric samples. Add to your board words that capture the feeling of the line you are developing. Words can often create a mood—and that mood can help you get started. Continue to add to the boards anything that you feel interprets the ideas you are looking to create. Trims, buttons, zippers, or even a paint swatch from a hardware store might be important to your line.

Third: Start Designing!

As you look over the information you have collected, some practical reasoning has to apply, and it is time to start developing styles that you feel will sell, along with color and fabric stories that reflect the vision of your design team and will appeal to your target market. Now, have someone on your team sketch samples that reflect the principles of design and will appeal to your consumer market. Don't forget: Stay in balance!

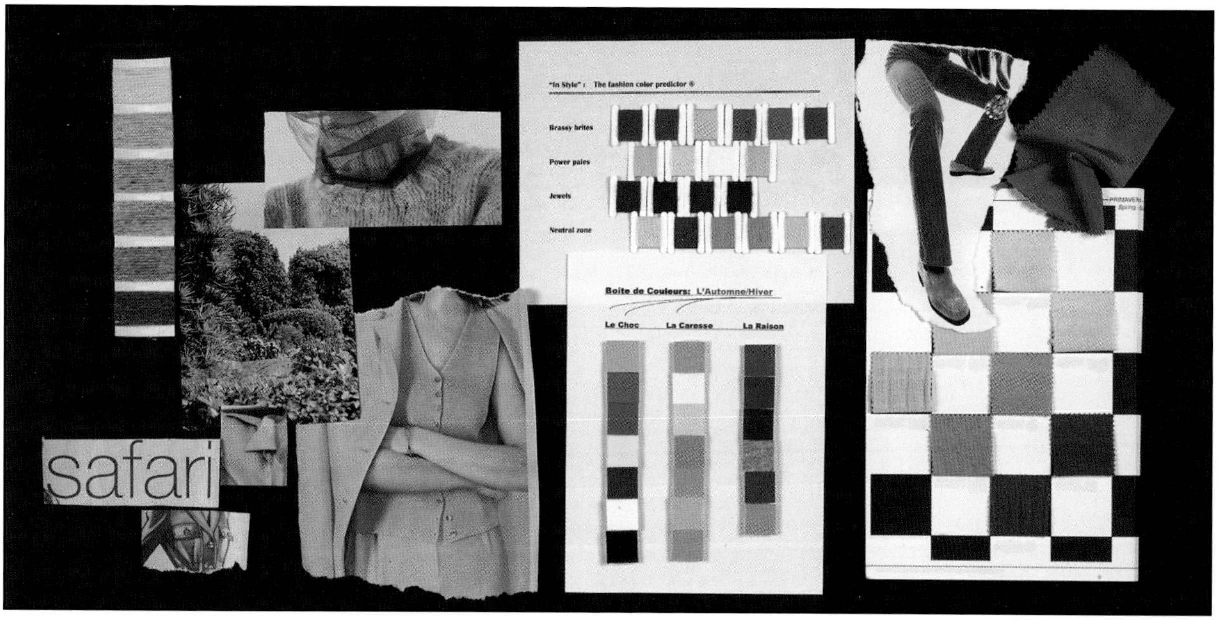

Figure 8-19

This is the mood board in July. The first things to go up are color services and early yarn cards. "Swipes" are pictures that are torn from magazines or newspapers that capture a look or feel. They could be just for a color feeling, such as the landscape picture. Photo by David Coulter.

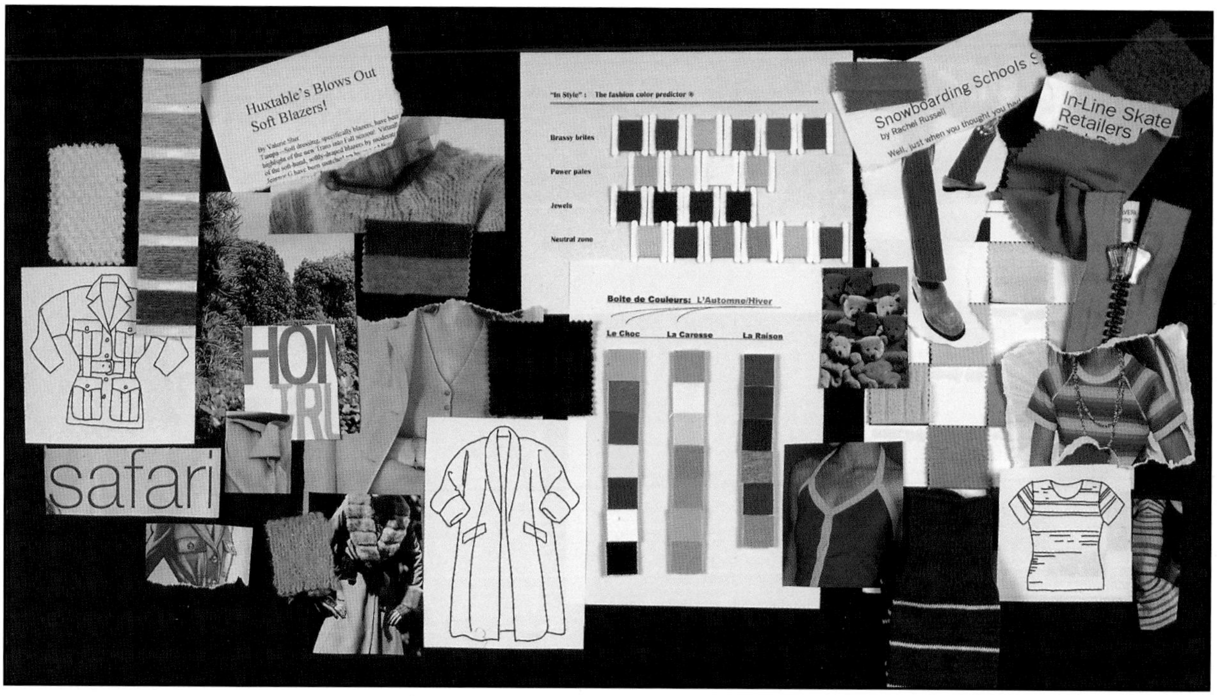

Figure 8-20

August: More specifics are added: fabrics, trims, zips. Trade newspaper headlines about retail successes; contrasting green colors in a magazine typeface; perhaps a couple of line drawings of silhouettes spotted at retail. The teddy bear swipe captures the bright color feeling of one of the color services. The green sock and long gold dress swipe are for stripe ideas. Photo by David Coulter.

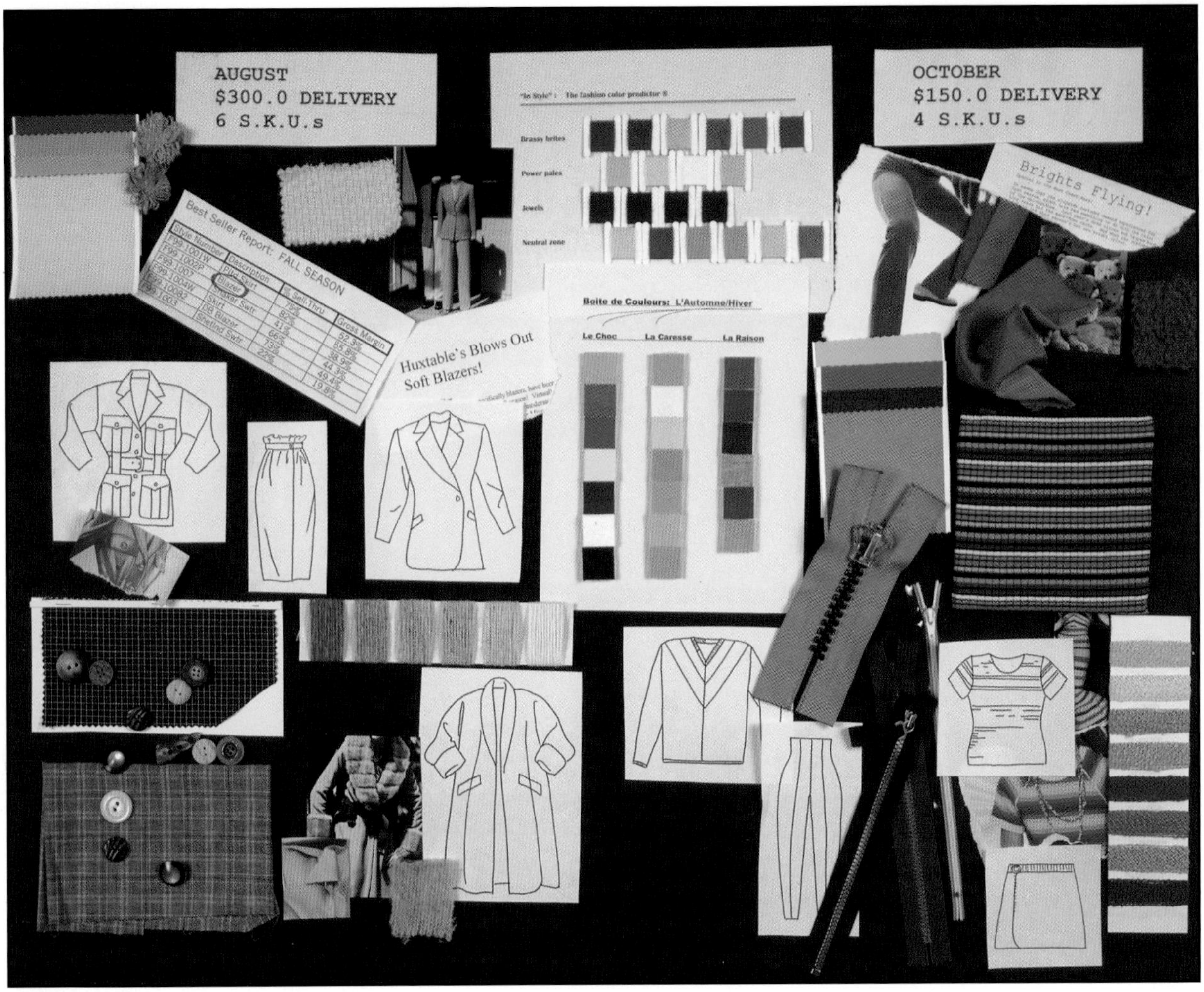

Figure 8-21

September: Two separate deliveries are starting to take shape: one for next August and one for next October. Right now the August "buy plan" is budgeted at $300,000 (written $300.0) with six stock keeping units (six styles). October will be a smaller delivery, at $150.0 and four SKUs.

For the August delivery: A neutral-plus-blue/green color story has been extracted from the two color services. The soft blazer has become the key style, based on two different retail selling successes. A picture of a soft blazer in a store window captures the perfect proportion. More fabric swatches and trims are added. The fisherman sweater swipe disappears—too casual for this delivery.

For the October delivery: Four bright colors have been selected—influenced by the French color service direction. Brights are selling! A great multicolored bright striped swatch is found, perfect for the T-shirt body. A slim pant and ski-inspired sweater are added. A novelty yarn card in brights is found—but maybe it is too expensive? Have to check the price. Photo by David Coulter.

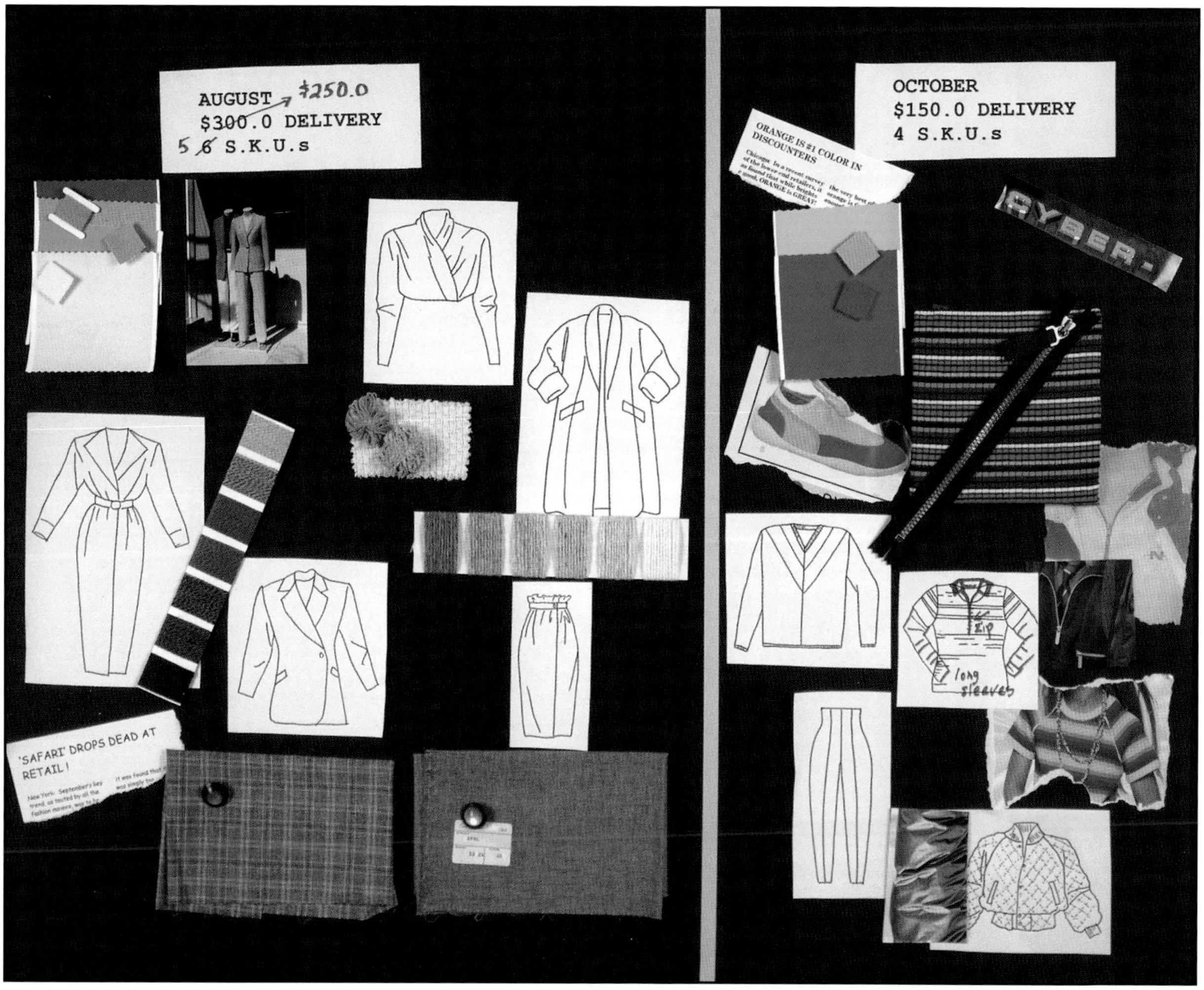

Figure 8-22

October: The two distinct deliveries are firming up. Actual bodies are being matched with actual fabrics.
For the August delivery: The budget has been cut, so one SKU is dropped. The color story is becoming dominantly neutral (gray with cream). However, the knitted top in two color combinations will keep a trace of the blue/green story. Smoky pearl buttons are selected to complement the heather gray fabrics. "Safari drops dead at retail!" Drop the safari jacket, quick!
For the October delivery: Another shock! "Orange is the #1 color in discounters." Downplay the orange—use only as an accent. We don't want to look like the low end of the market. This shifts the brights into a blue/green/black story, as exemplified by the sneaker. Zip collars suddenly take off, so the striped T-shirt is converted to a zip collar with long sleeves (October is still a bit too early for short sleeves). A shiny quilted jacket is added (in small quantities) as a show stopper. Photo by David Coulter.

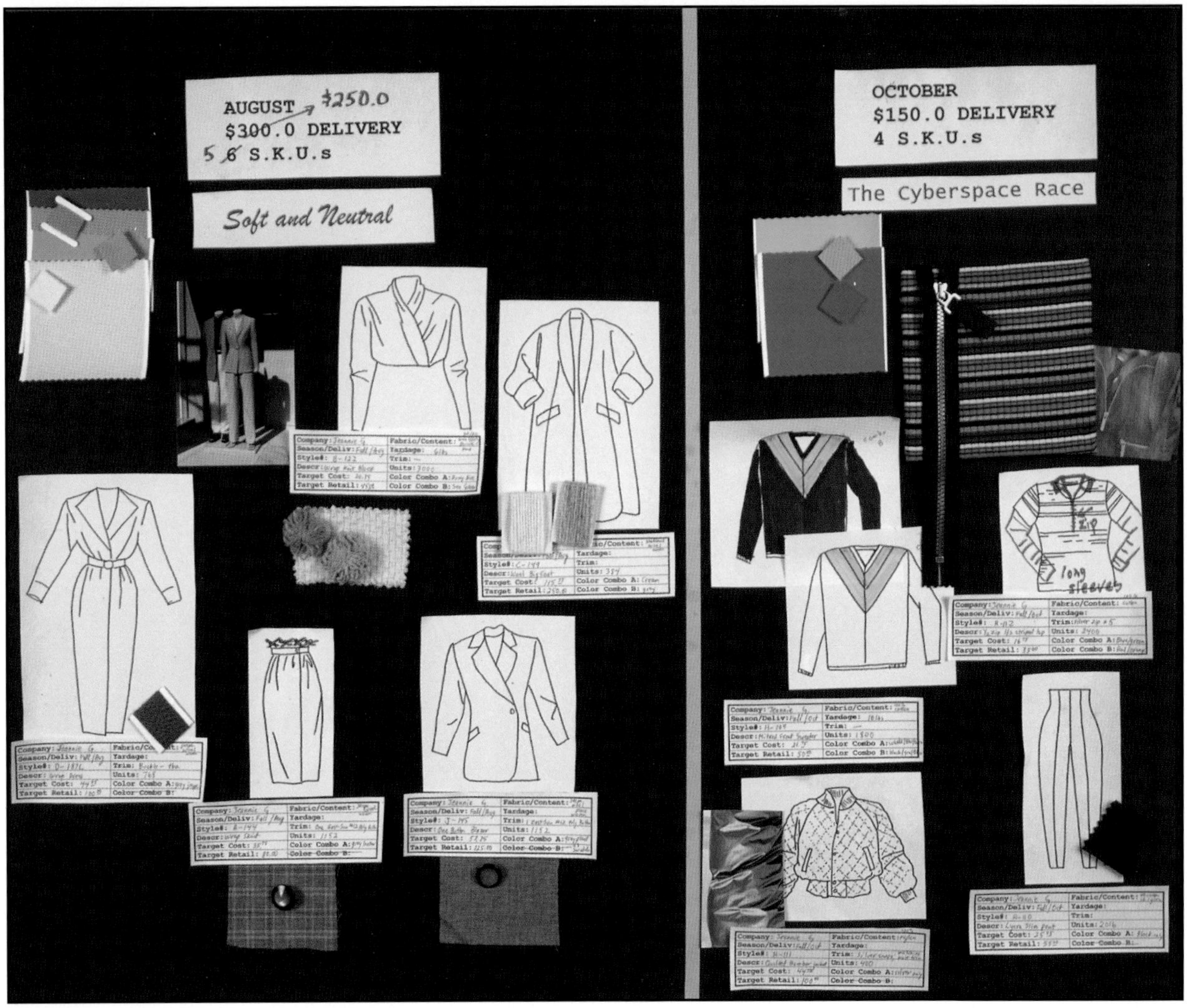

Figure 8-23

November: This is the final "line planner." The line is now set, item by item, with target prices, fabrics, colors, and color combinations per item, as well as projected units and dollars for each delivery.

For the August delivery: Now called "Soft and Neutral," August stays with five SKUs. The ratios are two tops (blouse, jacket) to one skirt, plus the dress and the topper coat. At the last minute, a small styling change: The paperbag waist on the skirt doesn't work with the blouse, so a regular waist is substituted.

For the October delivery: "The Cyberspace Race" is a fun, active group that actually looks better now that the colors have been narrowed down. The ski sweater is shown in two color combinations. An appropriate and affordable spandex-blend fabric is (finally) found for the slim pant. Photo by David Coulter.

Fourth: Time to Fine Tune

It's time for everyone to stand back now and take a look at the styles that are developing, along with the color and fabric stories, and identify specific groups. You may decide if you are working in the spring/summer season to have two major deliveries, one for January and the other for March. If you are looking at fall/holiday, you may decide to have three deliveries: one in August, one in October, and then a small group for holiday delivery in November. Start to get rid of the excess: Pull off the pictures that don't work, remove the color stories that don't reflect the moods, and begin fine tuning your boards so they don't get overpowering. You may have two lines with 10 to 20 pieces in each for two different deliveries. Make sure to narrow the work field and keep the items that are strongest for your consumers based on your research!

Fifth: Time to Decide

At this point your board should reflect work sketches of each piece in your line, the color stories that you want to project, and the fabric stories. It is also time to decide how many pieces you think you would need to manufacture based on the number of stores you are selling to. In your case you don't have actual numbers, but from your past research on stores, you can determine how many branch operations a company has and how many pieces you would need in each store. The numbers can get staggering, so it is important to be focused on what your customers want!

The next step will be crucial, because now it is time for you to develop cost sheets and to determine if the line is affordable. In Chapter 9 we provide ways to do that, so you might want to leave the boards in your classroom so you can go back and prepare an item-by-item cost analysis, just as you would do on the job!

A Final Note

It may take your team a few classes to complete these work boards, each week bringing in more pictures, ideas, and sketches. Remember that it takes a designer about six months to put boards together! Keep pinning things on the board, look at them for awhile, go back and see if they still interest you—take items off, put them back. Trust us, this is the same thing you will be doing on the job! And don't forget to have some fun and let your creativity take over. This is the time, so go for it!

CHAPTER 9

Going from Planning to Costing: Squeezing Out Those Pennies

THE KEY IS ALWAYS "COST"

Now that we have our designs, we need to make sure that they can be made at a workable cost. There are three major components of cost in a garment:

1. The cost of the material (fabrics)
2. The cost of trims and findings
3. The costs of labor and shipping

Those who have gone before you in the fashion industry have already squeezed and shaved each of these components in an effort to save money. As a newcomer, you will need to squeeze and shave with the best of them! Otherwise, you're going to be too expensive. According to retail veteran Ted Shapiro, "If you sold 500 dozen at $5.00 retail, ask yourself how many more you could sell at $3.00."

The best values are produced with close attention to every detail. For example, you might ask yourself:

- I love this fancy button, but is it absolutely critical or is there a cheaper version that will do?
- The imported fabric is gorgeous but the shipping costs are high. Is there a domestic alternative?
- Factory X in Pennsylvania charges more for labor (**cut-make-and-trim**), but it is much closer than the one in North Carolina and we need these goods fast! Is the faster turnaround more important than the higher cost?
- Can I negotiate more favorable payment terms so that my money will stretch until I am paid by my customers for the completed garments?

Cut-make-and-trim
Refers to the production part of the garment-making process (only). Does not include the fabric buying, pattern-making at the beginning, or the shipping at the end.

Each component and process must be efficient and cost-effective. To achieve this, you will need to start with the foundation of every deal in the fashion business: negotiating.

NEGOTIATING

On her very first trip to the Orient when she had to stand in at the last minute for her boss, Hope Cohen got to the airport and realized that there were things she should have discussed before leaving. So she got her boss on the phone and said, "I'm not supposed to just take the price the vendor offers, am I? I'm supposed to negotiate or something, right?"

Right. Negotiating is the old push-pull. As the designer, merchandiser, or product manager, you need to get your items made with the best possible fabrics and trims, constructed in the best possible way, for the lowest price and earliest delivery. The manufacturer or contractor on the other side of the table wants to use the cheapest possible fabrics and trims, constructed in the fastest (cheapest) possible way, for the highest price and (probably) the longest delivery. Somehow the two of you have to find a workable compromise. It's often possible, but not always. You may have to walk out because you simply can't reach a middle ground that works for both parties. Both have to be able to make a profit; neither is doing this for charity.

Negotiating techniques could fill another book. But in our years of experience, one overall approach has always worked: Be firm, but polite. Ted Shapiro reminds us, "If you don't ask, you don't get!" Tough but cordial negotiations allow everyone to keep their dignity. As you win some points, find a way for the other guy to win some, too. Don't scream and rave. You'd be shocked to know how many people take this approach. It's almost always a mistake.

But one word of caution as you are outlining your requirements with the manufacturer, called *specification buying*. It is the buyer's responsibility to specify the quality required in fabric, trim, construction, and performance. As long as these standards are articulated by the buyer (always in writing) to the manufacturer, he or she will be obliged to meet these standards (or to make good if something falls short). But *caveat emptor*. (Buyer, beware!) If a buyer fails to specify a single detail, the manufacturer could view it as something that could be skimped on later if needed to protect his or her own **profit margin**.

> ***Profit Margin***
> Percentage of sales that is profit.

How Do You Negotiate the Best Terms of Sale?

First: Discounts

You need to start by negotiating the best price on the raw materials. This is done by working for the best discount, a deduction from the original price. Let's take a look at a few of the most common discounts that might be available on materials, trims, and findings:

1. *Trade discount*: a discount deducted from either the cost or price. It is a discount given for being a consistent and sizable customer, working in the same field.

2. *Quantity discount*: a discount given for large quantities purchased.
3. *Seasonal discount*: a discount given for merchandise purchased prior to a normal buying season or well after the traditional selling season. (In both cases, when the demand is low, and the vendor has plenty of available production.)

Second: Shipping Charges

After you negotiate the lowest possible price on the materials, the next step is to discuss who pays the shipping charges. Don't forget, you've learned that fabric mills and manufacturing centers are located everywhere on the globe. Moving materials around the world costs money. Manufacturers, designers, and retailers all identify the shipping expenses with specific terms. Take a moment to learn what they are.

FOB means *freight on board* or *free on board*. This designation determines when the change of ownership of goods takes place. Once that exchange occurs, it must be determined which party is responsible for the shipping charges up to that point and from that point.

IN GREATER DEPTH

SHIPPING TERMS

FOB Store or Destination: The manufacturer owns the merchandise and pays all freight charges until the merchandise reaches its destination.

FOB Factory or Shipping Point: The buyer pays all the freight charges, and the transportation charges are added to the invoice.

FOB (city name) or FOB 50/50 (or some other split): With foreign goods the transportation charges are often split. Sometimes the manufacturer or mill will pay from their shipping point to a designated city and then the importer or store will pick up the shipping expense from that point to the final destination. For example, if the terms agreed on were FOB New York, the manufacturer has agreed to pay the shipping charges from their location to New York and the store picks up the shipping charges from New York to the next destination. Another way to negotiate high shipping charges is to agree to split the charges.

Prepaid: The shipping charges are paid when the shipping company picks up the merchandise, and the seller is billed accordingly.

Third: Dating and Payment Terms

Although the dating and payment terms are not usually calculated at the time that cost sheets are developed, you should know that when you pay your bill is very important. You can lower the final cost if you keep a sharp eye on due dates and thus earn extra discounts for prompt payment. Let's take a look at cash discounts and dating terms.

Cash Discounts: Cash discounts are incentives to pay bills promptly. They usually involve an additional percentage that is deducted from the net amount of the invoice if the bill is paid within a specified period. Here are some important features about cash discounts:

1. Cash discounts are calculated after all other discounts have been deducted.
2. Cash discounts are given only if the bill is paid within the specified number of days.
3. If the letter "n" or the word "net" is written next to the terms, it means no discount.
4. Cash discount terms never stand alone but are combined with specific dating terms.
5. When written out, cash discounts look like fractions with each number or letter representing one aspect of how much the discount amount is and how many days the buyer has to earn that discount.
6. Cash discounts are an important way to earn more profit!

Dating: Dating is the practice of setting a specific time for paying the bill. There are several types of dating and they work hand in hand with the cash discounts. Sometimes bills have to be paid all at once; sometimes a mill or manufacturer will allow payment at a future date. The most important thing you have to negotiate is exactly what day the invoice has to be paid.

IN GREATER DEPTH

DATING TERMS

COD: *collect on delivery*. This is often used with new accounts.

Example: $300.00 COD. Collect $300.00 when the goods are delivered.

DOI (Regular): called *ordinary dating*. The payment window begins by identifying the date of the invoice (DOI) and calculating the payment days allowed from that date. This is frequently used for supplies.

Example: 2/10, n/30.

This means a company will earn a 2% discount if the bill is paid within 10 days of the date of the invoice. If the payment is made between 11 and 30 days, the company must pay the amount in full.

ROG Dating: *receipt of goods*. When using ROG dating you do not calculate the days to pay until the merchandise has been received. This is used primarily for merchandise bought overseas. It is too difficult to calculate when merchandise will be received, due to duties and customs in the worldwide ports.

Example: An invoice is dated May 5; the terms read 8/20, n/30 ROG. The merchandise was received on July 3. To receive the extra 8% cash discount, payment must be made by July 23.

(Continued on next page)

IN GREATER DEPTH *(Continued)*

EOM Dating: *end of the month*, which means that the invoice will be paid within a specified number of days from the end of the month. This is the most popular type of payment terms used in the fashion industry.

Example: An invoice is dated August 15. The terms read: 8/10 n/30 EOM. The merchandise was shipped on August 22. To receive the eight percent cash discount, payment must be made on September 10.

But what is really the end of a month? Some months have 30 days, some have 31, and then we are always faced with the 28/29-day dilemma of February. Companies need to have a common cutoff date, and in the fashion industry, businesses have assigned the twenty-fifth of each month as the standard cutoff date for the end of the month (Figure 9-1). What this means is: If an invoice is dated from the first to the twenty-fifth of the month, payment is made from the end of that month.

Example: An invoice is dated January 18, terms are 8/10 EOM. Payment is due February 10.

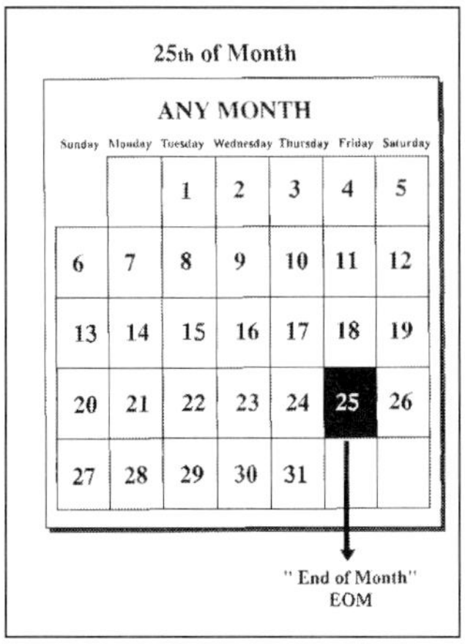

FIGURE 9-1

Artwork by Michael Carnegie.

If an invoice is dated from the twenty-sixth to the thirty-first of the month, payment is made from the end of the next month.

Example: An invoice is dated January 28, terms are 8/10 EOM. Payment is due on March 10. These are often the terms that many manufacturers and buyers strive for because a business can have a six-week period (float) before the invoice has to be paid. They will still earn the extra eight percent discount. (Does this sound a little like your own checking account?)

Now, with this overview of terms and conditions you might negotiate when purchasing materials and supplies to make a garment, let's take a look at an important work tool that you will be using: a *cost sheet.*

IN GREATER DEPTH

STEP-BY-STEP GUIDE TO COST SHEETS

How do you know if it is affordable to produce a particular garment? Wholesalers use a tool called a cost sheet that helps make this decision. Each ingredient and its cost is itemized. Each cost is the result of negotiating to get the best price. The cost sheet not only adds up these individual costs to project the actual total cost of goods, but it also helps to pinpoint if one or two ingredients are inflating the price inappropriately. After all, the lower the cost of the garment, the sharper the wholesale and retail prices.

Let's see what a cost sheet looks like. (Don't panic: It looks a bit overwhelming, but we will explain it, line by line.)

COST SHEET

Sketch and Materials Swatch

C

Date **A** Style Number **B**
Description **D**
Fabric Mill **E**
Manufacturer **F**
Size Range **G**
Size Scale **G**
Fabric Width **H**
Estimated Marker Yardage **I**
Actual Marker Yardage **J**

MATERIALS	**Yardage**	**Price per Yard**	**Total Amount**
Fabric	K	L	M
Fabric			
Lining			

Total Cost of Materials **N**

TRIMS	**Amounts**	**Cost Each**	**Total Amount**
Buttons	O	P	Q
Zippers			
Belts			
Other			

Total Cost of Trims/Findings **R**

LABOR

Marking Costs **S** Grading Costs **T** Cutting Costs **U**
Construction **V**

Total Labor Costs **W**

SHIPPING AND DUTY EXPENSES

Import Duties **X** Shipping Expenses **Y**

Total Shipping and Duty Costs **Z**
Total Cost of Goods to Be Sold **AA**
Suggested Wholesale Price **BB**
Suggested Retail Price **CC**

It is important to note that a cost sheet determines the price of only *one* garment, so let us review how the components work together.

A. *Date:* signifies that the prices are firm for an order placed *as of this date*. The negotiation and terms of sale have been determined with the textile mills and the findings companies. Generally, these prices are good for about 30 days.

(Continued on next page)

B. *Style number:* numerical identifier of this garment.

C. *Sketch and material swatch:* actual look and feel of the garment.

D. *Description:* written description of the garment.

E. *Fabric mill:* where the fabric is being purchased. This is important for shipping, timing, duties, import/export quotas, and fees.

F. *Manufacturer:* Where the garment is being produced (contractor/country). This is important because of duties, import/export fees, and quotas.

G. *Size range/scale: size range* are the sizes to be cut (for example; small, medium, large) *size scale* is the number (proportion) of each size.

H. *Fabric width:* used by the marker makers to calculate the minimum yardage use.

I. *Estimated marker yardage:* fabric needed for most effective placement of pattern pieces for a full size run. This is a *critical* number: When all the pattern pieces have been laid out for a complete size run, this is the amount of fabric that is required. The less fabric used, the lower the cost.

J. *Actual marker yardage:* companies often go back and review cost sheets and spec sheets to determine the actual yardage used: to see if their calculations were accurate or if something has changed, such as fabric width, which altered the amount of yardage used.

K. *Material/yardage:* specific yardage for one garment. This is determined by dividing the total marker yardage by the number of sizes being made. For example, S,M,L,XL—21 yards for our size scale, which is 12 pieces; we're doubling up on mediums and larges (2 smalls, 4 mediums, 4 larges, 2 extra larges). Although a small size will certainly take less fabric than an XL, 21 yards ÷ 12 =1.75 yards; 1.75 would be the *average* yardage identified on the cost sheet.

L. *Price per yard of material:* price that was negotiated after all the trade discounts were discussed and shipping terms and payment arrangements made.

M. *Total amount of material:* total cost of material (yardage x price per yard).

N. *Total cost of all materials:* for one garment.

O. *Number of trim pieces:* for one garment.

P. *Cost of each trim:* for one garment.

Q. *Total cost of trims:* number of trims x cost—for one garment.

R. *Total cost of all trims and findings:* for one garment.

S. *Marking costs:* marking is laying out all the pattern pieces necessary to make a full size range of a garment or group of garments. Due to advances in technology, much of this work is done on CAD/CAM systems (Computer-aided design systems are discussed in Chapter 14.) Generally, a total price is quoted and the designer or manufacturer will take the cost and divide it by the number of pieces being produced to determine the price for *one* garment. This expense is generally incurred once and will not show up on a reorder.

T. *Grading costs:* cost incurred for developing a full size range of products. Often, this cost is combined with marking costs.

U. *Cutting costs:* manufacturer's price based on a minimum cut to determine cost per unit. For example, a $100 fee for a 200-piece minimum cut = 50 cents per garment.

V. *Construction:* labor costs, including bundling, sewing, pressing, trimming, and inspection. Generally determined as piecework (per piece) costs. This is discussed further in Unit III.

W. *Total labor costs:* for one garment.

X. *Import Duties (See below)*

Y. *Shipping expenses:* both import duties and shipping expenses are based on fiber content, weight of shipment, and location of manufacture and shipping. Freight companies and brokers calculate the cost of freight and advise on import duties and taxes. These figures are given as a total and must be divided out per piece.

Z. *Total shipping and duty costs:* for one garment.

AA. *Total cost of goods to be sold:* materials (N) + trims (R) + labor (W) + Shipping/Duty (Z)

BB. *Suggested wholesale price:* price the buyer would pay, determined as: cost of goods to be sold + markup = wholesale price. *Markup* is the amount of money added on, which must be high enough for the designer or manufacturer to cover expenses and make a profit but low enough to keep the price competitive.

CC. *Suggested retail price:* price the retail consumer will pay, determined as: wholesale price + markup = retail price.

Now, take a look at a cost sheet on the next page that is filled in and see how the values were determined. The information on this cost sheet tells the design team that:

1. On June 12, xxxx, these were the prices negotiated.
2. This is a women's two-piece knit style No. 510, to be manufactured in the United States, with the fabric coming from a mill in North Carolina.
3. Four sizes are being made, but out of every 12 pieces, there will be two sixes, four eights, four tens, and two twelves.
4. The fabric runs 60 inches wide. The markers have determined that 21 yards are needed for one full-scale run to be made. Therefore; 21 ÷ 12 = 1.75 yards per average piece, based on the size scale.
5. The material costs $6.40 per yard. This is the amount per yard that was determined after all the trade, quantity, and seasonal discounts were deducted. Sometimes even the shipping charges are calculated into this figure if the shipping charges are high. Therefore; 1.75 yards x $6.40 = $11.20.
6. 0.25 yard of collar fabric (costing $1.25 per yard) is needed for a collar trim: 0.25 x $1.25 = $0.31
7. Total cost of materials: $11.51.

(Continued on next page)

COST SHEET

Sketch and Materials Swatch

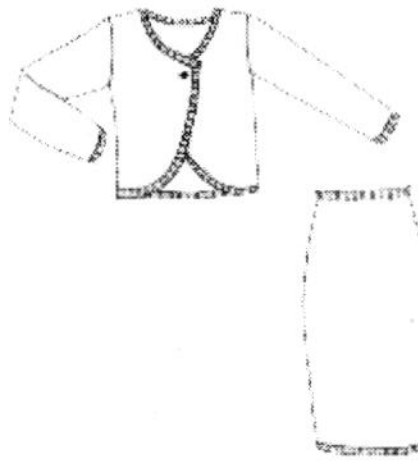

Artwork by Trudi Trudeau-Lopez.

Date June 12, 19— Style Number 510
Description Women's two-piece knit
Fabric Mill North Carolina
Manufacturer U.S.A.
Size Range 6, 8, 10, 12
Size Scale 2-4-4-2
Fabric Width 60 in.
Estimated Marker Yardage 21 yds.
Actual Marker Yardage ______

MATERIALS	Yardage	Price per Yard	Total Amount
Fabric	1.75 yds.	$6.40	$11.20
Fabric (collar)	0.25 yd.	$1.25	$ 0.31
Lining			

Total Cost of Materials $11.51

TRIMS	Amounts	Cost Each	Total Amount
Buttons	1 button	$0.04	$0.04
Zippers	none		
Belts	none		
Other	0.50 yd.	$1.50/yd.	$0.75

Total Cost of Trims/Findings $0.79

LABOR

Marking Costs $0.50 Grading Costs $0.50 Cutting Costs $0.72
Construction $4.48 each

Total Labor Costs $6.20

SHIPPING AND DUTY EXPENSES

Import Duties none Shipping Expenses none

Total Shipping and Duty Costs none
Total Cost of Goods to Be Sold $18.50
Suggested Wholesale Price $33.75
Suggested Retail Price $75.00

8. The trims include one button at $0.04 each, for a total of $0.04, and 0.5 yard of elastic tape at $1.50 per yard, for a total of $0.75. The total cost of the trims is: $0.79

9. Labor expenses are determined as follows:

Marking costs (these charges are usually quoted for minimum cuts; in this case we are saying that the minimum is a 100-piece cut): For every 100 pieces the marking charge is $50.00; therefore, the marking expense would be $0.50. ($50.00 ÷ 100 pieces = $0.50).

Grading costs: For every 100 pieces the grading charge is $50.00 ($50.00 ÷ 100 pieces = $0.50).

Cutting costs: For every 100 pieces the cutting charge is $72.00 ($72.00 ÷ 100 pieces = $0.72).

Construction costs: The designer or manufacturer has negotiated a construction cost of $4.48 per garment. The manufacturing company has presented this offer based on the amount of work in each garment. Again, this is an area that can be competitive, as we review in Unit III.

10. The total labor costs are $6.20. This was determined by adding

$$\begin{array}{r} \$0.50 \\ +\ \$0.50 \\ +\ \$0.72 \\ +\ \underline{\$4.48} \\ \$6.20 \end{array}$$

Now, let's take a step further. The total *cost of goods to be sold* is

$11.51 (materials) + $0.79 (trims) + $6.20 (labor) = $18.50

This is what you, the designer/wholesaler, will actually pay for each garment.

CALCULATING MARKUPS

The designer/wholesaler then has to calculate the selling price: what the wholesale price will be when this garment is sold to a store buyer. It is important to remember that the selling price will be a combination of two parts.

1. The actual cost of goods to be sold, in this case $18.50.
2. **Markup**, the amount of money planned to cover expenses and make a profit.

> ***Markup***
> Difference between the retail price and the wholesale cost; always expressed as a percentage of the retail price.

In the wholesale industry the markup is generally 30 to 50% of the total selling price. Let's take a look and see how to calculate.

The selling price (which is always the total price) is equal to 100%.

If the desired markup is 45%, the cost of goods to be sold would be 55%.

This means that the final selling price (100%) is a combination of 45% and 55%.

If you put this information in *T-chart format*, it is very easy to see.

	Dollars		**Percents**
Selling price		=	100%
Markup	-	=	45%
Cost of goods to be sold	$18.50	=	55%

Now what do you do? Simple: Always remember that you are looking at the parts in relationship to the whole, and you know that $18.50 = 55%. If you divide those two amounts, it will give you the selling price. Try it!

$18.50 ÷ 55% = $33.64

That's right, $33.64. Typically, a designer or manufacturer would round that amount off to the closest quarter, so let's round it up to $33.75. If you'd like, fill in that amount in the chart below, and using some basic math training, check your work.

	Dollars	**Percents**
Selling price	$33.75	100%
Markup	-	= 45.2%
Cost of goods to be sold	$18.50	= 54.8%

	Dollars	**Percents**
Selling Price	$33.75	100%
Markup	-$15.25	= 45.2%
Cost of goods to be sold	$18.50	= 54.8%

Check your work:

1. $33.75 – $18.50 = $15.25
2. $33.75 x 0.452 = $15.25
3. $33.75 x 0.548 = $18.50

The $15.25 the designer/wholesaler earns has to be enough to pay the salaries and expenses of the design team and the rest of the operation. In addition, each company is in business to make a profit, and there must be money left after all the expenses have been paid. As you can see, the price is now inching its way up, because the wholesale price is just the price at which the designer/wholesaler will sell the merchandise to the store. Now the wholesaler must determine what the suggested retail price will be to the consumer. (It is the store buyer's job to make the final determination of the retail price, but a good wholesaler will have a pretty clear idea of what that price will have to be.)

When the designer is looking at the work board, filled with sketches, fabrics, and colors, and then at the cost sheet, the most important thing to ask is: How much will the customer pay for this garment? Alan Glist, president of Alan Stuart (a men's wholesale line), on "merchandising" prices: "Pricing a garment must also be done by eye appeal. If (using our normal markup) a shirt prices out at $20.00, but it looks like more, we might mark it $22.00. The opposite also happens: A $20.00 top might only look like $17.75." Stanley Kreinik, president of the Sockyard (a hosiery wholesaler), puts it this way: "Picture the profitable items in your line as bricks. Picture the 'loss leaders' in your line (items sold slightly below cost) as mortar. If you build a house of all bricks, it falls down. If you build a house of all mortar, it cracks and falls. You need a good mixture of both bricks and mortar. The key is the profitable proportion of bricks to mortar."

THE STORE HAS TO GET ITS MARKUP, TOO

In the retailing industry it is expensive to run a company, and sellers are competing for everyone's business. The garment must be quite exciting to command enough markup. There are markup standards in the industry that can be researched in the financial operating reports filed by the National Retailing Federation. The rule of thumb is that retailers need to earn between 45 and 60% **initial markup** to be profitable. The same rules apply: Retail markup has to be enough to cover the store's expenses and make a profit (yet the item must be competitively priced so that the consumer will buy it).

Initial Markup
This is the first markup amount that a buyer adds to the cost price of a garment. If the cost price is $4 and the retail price is $10, the initial markup is $6, or 60% (of the retail price). Later, the price (and thus the markup) may be reduced to clear the goods. That's why 60% in our example is called the initial markup. The "maintained" markup will be lower.

Mathematically, the same concept applies when calculating retail prices. The wholesale or cost price plus a markup will determine the actual retail price, the total price which is always equal to 100%. Let's take a look at the T-chart below, which shows the cost at $33.75, since that is what the store paid.

	Dollars		Percents
Retail selling price		=	100%
Markup	-	=	
Cost/wholesale	$33.75	=	

In this case the designer has decided that the sales team will propose a $75.00 suggested retail price to buyers. Let's see what kind of markup can be earned.

	Dollars		Percents
Retail selling price	$75.00	=	100%
Markup	-	=	
Cost/wholesale	$33.75	=	

Again, you are only going to be working with parts of the total and looking for the relationship, but this time you are going to work with the numbers. Let's find out what the markup percentage really is.

1. $75.00 – $33.75 = $41.25
2. $41.25 ÷ $75.00 = 55.0% (the markup the store will get)
3. $33.75 ÷ $75.00 = 45.0%

Once again, check your work. You have two parts, the markup and the cost, which have to equal the total amount, which is always equal to 100%.

$41.25 + $33.75 = $75.00
55.0% + 45.0% = 100%

The math formulas for all markup problems are the same:

Selling price always = 100%
Cost dollars ÷ cost % = selling price
Markup dollars ÷ markup % = selling price
Selling price x markup % = markup dollars
Selling price x cost % = cost dollars

Once you have made all the calculations, you finally know if the financial numbers will support the illustrations, the colors, the fabrics, and the shipping plans.

COSTING AND PRICING: WHOLESALE VERSUS PRIVATE LABEL

You just costed out a two-piece knit for $18.50 that will sell in the department store for $75.00. The reason for the large difference in price goes back to what you learned in Chapter 3. Designers must sell their products to stores, and the stores in turn sell the products to the consumer. There are lots of middlemen in that process: Fashion shows are held, major publicity and public relations events are staged, and there are dozens of people along the selling/customer service ladder who have to be paid. The designer still is only going to make $15.25 in markup, and that has to be enough to cover the company expenses and make a profit.

But what if you were a product development specialist for a major department store? You would go to the same fabric shows, and probably visit the same factories to make your products. But the difference now is that you don't have to sell it to a store. You are making it for your own store. Sure, you will incur some advertising expenses to promote the product, but let's take a look at this:

	Dollars		**Percents**
Retail selling price	$75.00	=	100%
Markup	-	=	
Cost of goods to be sold	$18.50	=	

If you marked the two-piece knit at the same price as the designer prices, look at how much margin/markup you could make:

$75.00 - $18.50 = $56.50

That's a lot more profit than the designer would earn!

If you fill in the numbers and percentages on the T-chart, it will look like this:

	Dollars		**Percents**
Retail selling price	$75.00	=	100.0%
Markup	- $56.50	=	75.3%
Cost/wholesale	$18.50	=	24.7%

Remember, you did not change the cost of the goods to be sold at all. However, you must also realize that customers will usually pay more for a well-recognized national brand. Private labels tend not to command as much loyalty. So what if you reduced your selling price? You would still be giving the consumer the same product, but now at a sharper price. That might get the customer to buy!

Let's see what your profit will look like if you mark the two-piece knit at $60.00:

	Dollars		Percents
Retail selling price	$60.00	=	100.0%
Markup	- $41.50	=	69.2%
Cost/wholesale	$18.50	=	30.8%

$60.00 - 18.50 = $41.50 and then $41.50 ÷ $60.00 = 69.2%. Just follow the math process you just reviewed.

At $60.00 you are still providing a high markup for your company (69.2%) to cover expenses and make a profit; suddenly you are cutting into the designer's business and giving the consumer a much better price! The challenge a product development/private-label buyer faces is to build strong and consistent name recognition. Private-label stores such as Banana Republic, Express, Structure, Laura Ashley, and Gap have reached this goal, and now the department stores are joining them. Consumers are seeking out the Charter Club, INC, Field Gear, and Arizona Jeans brands of products and the department store organizations are pleased.

In the chapter exercises, calculate some garments on the cost sheets and then determine the wholesale and retail selling prices. Trust us when we tell you that a lot of products never make it past this point. They just don't cost out because the cost is too high and/or the profits are too low. But all designers will tell you that it is much better to be disappointed now than to proceed further and invest a great deal of money in products that won't sell.

Is it time to produce this line? No, not quite yet. First you need to get some friendly free advice.

TALK OUT

At this stage, most wholesalers bring everyone (sales, design, merchandising, production) together to talk through the line as it is. Some call it a *line review*. Each area brings a different perspective, and each is important if the line is to be successful. Questions such as these will be raised:

Sales	What will the major store buyers love? Hate? Will the prices fly, compared to those of the competition? Does anything look too conservative or too advanced?
Design	Does the line look cohesive? Is it consistent with the brand? Designs have been altered for price reasons. Can we live with these changes?
Merchandising	Are there one or two items where we will have to take a shorter (lower) markup as loss leaders? If so, where can we make up that lost markup on other items?
Production	Can these garments be made? Are there any potential pitfalls? Do we have them planned for the appropriate sewing plants?

From the back-and-forth friction of this process, the compromise that is reached usually produces a line that will get placed by buyers, be easily handled in production, and be profitable for the wholesaler. (Not always! We said, usually.)

Sometimes a very trusted key retail store buyer is brought in at this time for his or her opinion. Again, here's that key concept: The wholesaler is making sure that his or her customer (the store buyer) is going to be satisfied. The wholesaler knows who his or her customer is and wants to make sure that what is produced will be met with approval. Each item in a group is approached in the same way. (Yes, just like we've said before, this is work.)

So, one season is planned, and thought through. Now we need to move into the next phase of the process: going from size specs to samples.

SO YOU WANT TO WORK IN THE FASHION BUSINESS?
Here's How to Begin. . . Chapter 9

Now that you have gone through the process of costing out garments, let's take a look at three different problems. Relax, it's a lot easier than you realize. Let's go through the steps.

First: Determine the Cost of Goods to be Sold

Using the cost sheets, fill in all the information that is given to you. Make sure that all the numbers are in decimal forms. Often, the cost sheets are done through computer programs and a computer can't read ½; it has to read 0.50. Once the information is entered on the cost sheet, extend out the values. Add up all the materials, trims, labor, and shipping costs and find out just how much it costs to make a garment.

Second: Determine the Wholesale Selling Price

The next step is very important. Just follow the formulas and fill in the T-charts with the information you have in the problem and determine the cost or wholesale price—that which a store buyer will pay for the merchandise.

Third: Determine the Retail Selling Price

Remember that the consumer pays retail price, so find out what that should be, using the information you have in the problem. Just follow the formulas in the chapter and fill in the T-charts. The answers will be easy to find.

Fourth: Talk Out

With all the math out of the way, you are now facing the most important question. Will the consumer be willing to pay the price? Have everyone give his or her opinion—think of all the pros and cons. Remember, a designer cannot afford to make a product that the consumer does not want to buy! If the consensus is that the item is great but a little too pricey, go back to the work sketch and the cost sheet to see if you can figure out a way to cut some corners and get the price down. It might be something as simple as eliminating a belt or changing a zipper. Don't be afraid to change (that's where the "creativity within limitations" comes in). Design teams face these decisions daily, and it is important for you to know how to do this, too!

PROBLEM 1

Using the following information:

First: Determine the Cost of Goods to be Sold

Description: girls full-skirted Victorian-style "party" dress with collar and sash trim

Date: April 23, ____

Style: 962

Size range: 7,8,10,12,14

Size scale: 1–2–3–3–3

Fabric mill: located in Taiwan

Manufacturer: located in Hong Kong

Fabric width: 36 inches

Estimated marker yardage: 24 yards

Material: Victorian print broadcloth, 2 yards, cost $1.48 per yard after shipping from Taiwan to Hong Kong. This yardage for one garment was determined by estimating the total yardage for a one-dozen run and then dividing by 12. Take a look: 24 total yards ÷ 12 pieces = 2 yards for one garment. That is what will be entered on the cost sheet.

Collar facing: ¼ yard at $1.19 per yard

COST SHEET

Sketch and Materials Swatch

Artwork by Trudi Trudeau-Lopez.

Date ________ Style Number ________

Description ________

Fabric Mill ________

Manufacturer ________

Size Range ________

Size Scale ________

Fabric Width ________

Estimated Marker Yardage ________

Actual Marker Yardage ________

MATERIALS	**Yardage**	**Price per Yard**	**Total Amount**
Fabric	________	________	________
Fabric (collar)	________	________	________
Lining	________	________	________

Total Cost of Materials ________

TRIMS	**Amounts**	**Cost Each**	**Total Amount**
Buttons	________	________	________
Zippers	________	________	________
Belts	________	________	________
Other	________	________	________

Total Cost of Trims/Findings ________

LABOR

Marking Costs ________ Grading Costs ________ Cutting Costs ________

Construction ________

Total Labor Costs ________

SHIPPING AND DUTY EXPENSES

Import Duties ________ Shipping Expenses ________

Total Shipping and Duty Costs ________

Total Cost of Goods to Be Sold ________

Suggested Wholesale Price ________

Suggested Retail Price ________

Trim: 2½ yards at $0.54 per yard

Zipper: $0.12 each

Marking and grading costs: $285.00 based on a 500-piece minimum order (combined cost). Don't forget: That would mean $285.00 ÷ 500 to determine the cost for one piece.

Cutting costs: $175.00 based on a 500-piece minimum order

Construction costs: $48.00 per dozen (this is for all 12; what is it for one?)

Duties/shipping costs: $1.05 each garment

Second: Determine the Wholesale Selling Price

Using a 50% markup, determine the wholesale selling price. Fill in the T-chart below to help you out.

	Dollars		Percents
Wholesale price		=	100%
Markup	-	=	50%
Cost of goods to be sold		=	50%

Remember to go back and look at your formulas. The selling percentage will always be 100%, and in this case since you want the markup percentage to be 50%, the cost percentage will also be 50%. Simply divide the cost of goods sold by the cost percentage and you will arrive at the wholesale selling price, after rounding the final dollar value to $0.00, $0.25, $0.50, or $0.75.

Third: Determine the Retail Selling Price

Use the wholesale price you reached in the T-chart below. Then, applying a 50% retail markup, determine the retail selling price for this garment. Round this price to the dearest dollar.

	Dollars		Percents
Retail selling price		=	100%
Markup	-	=	50%
Cost/Wholesale Price		=	50%

Fourth: Talk Out

Now it is time to discuss if you think this will be a strong-selling item, or if you need to go back and look for a better price on some element of the cost sheet.

And Now, the Private-Label Version

If you are working in a resident buying office in the product development division, or if you are working with a major chain designing garments that will carry a private label, calculate the retail selling price, earning exactly the same number of dollars in retail markup as you calculated in step 3. Let's take a look. The cost of goods to be sold for this problem is $10.70. A designer/manufacturer will divide 10.70 by 50% and determine that the wholesale/cost price would be $21.40. The designer would round this up to $21.50 to show to the store buyers. At this point, when store buyers purchase the garment, they too will mark up the dress by 50% and the retail selling price would be $43.00, which means that the retail markup dollars that you show in your T-chart is $21.50. Now, let's take a look at what happens when we squeeze out the middle and have the product manufactured and shipped directly to the selling store, just as do the major department stores and private-label companies.

	Dollars		**Percents**
Retail selling price		=	100%
Markup	- $21.50	=	
Cost of goods to be sold	$10.70		

Calculate the retail price, rounding it off to the nearest $00.00 ending. Also calculate the retail markup percentage. Now, if you are a designer or manufacturer, what would you do with your product line to compete with this price point? The designer label sells for $43.00 and the private label for $32.00. Same dress, same store profit!

PROBLEM 2

Using the following information:

First: Determine the Cost of Goods to Be Sold

Description: men's Henley shirt, a collarless three-button placket-front cotton knit shirt

Date: May 14, ____

Style : 402

Size range: S, M, L, XL

Size scale: 1–4–5–2

Fabric mill: located in North Carolina

Manufacturer: located in Miami, Florida

Fabric width: 60 inches

Estimated marker yardage: 24 yards for 12 pieces

Material: solid-colored cotton knit jersey at $1.60 per yard

Buttons: 3 buttons at $0.03 each.

Marking and grading costs: $185.00 based on a 500-piece minimum (combined cost)

Cutting costs: $175.00 based on a 500-piece minimum

Construction costs: $42.00 per dozen

Shipping costs: FOB factory (Shipping charges to the store will be paid by the store, and thus are not calculated in the manufacturer's cost.)

COST SHEET

Sketch and Materials Swatch

Date ____________ Style Number ________

Description ____________________________

Fabric Mill ____________________________

Manufacturer ___________________________

Size Range _____________________________

Size Scale _____________________________

Fabric Width ___________________________

Estimated Marker Yardage _______________

Actual Marker Yardage __________________

Artwork by Trudi Trudeau-Lopez.

MATERIALS	**Yardage**	**Price per Yard**	**Total Amount**
Fabric	________	________	________
Fabric (collar)	________	________	________
Lining	________	________	________

Total Cost of Materials ________

TRIMS	**Amounts**	**Cost Each**	**Total Amount**
Buttons	________	________	________
Zippers	________	________	________
Belts	________	________	________
Other	________	________	________

Total Cost of Trims/Findings ________

LABOR

Marking Costs ________ Grading Costs ________ Cutting Costs ________

Construction ________

Total Labor Costs ________

SHIPPING AND DUTY EXPENSES

Import Duties ________ Shipping Expenses ________

Total Shipping and Duty Costs ________

Total Cost of Goods to Be Sold ________

Suggested Wholesale Price ________

Suggested Retail Price ________

Second: Determine the Wholesale Selling Price

Using a 40% markup, determine the wholesale selling price. Fill in the T-chart below to help you out.

	Dollars		**Percents**
Wholesale price		=	100%
Markup	-	=	40%
Cost of goods to be sold		=	60%

Remember to go back and look at your formulas. The selling percentage will always be 100%, and in this case since you want the markup percentage to be 40%, the cost percentage will be 60%. Simply divide the cost of goods sold by the cost percentage and you will arrive at the wholesale selling price, after rounding the final dollar value to $0.00, $0.25, $0.50, or $0.75.

Third: Determine the Retail Selling Price

Use the wholesale price you reached in the T-chart below. Then, applying a 55% retail markup, determine the retail selling price for this garment. Round this price to the nearest dollar.

	Dollars		Percents
Retail selling price		=	100%
Markup	-	=	55%
Cost/wholesale price		=	45%

Fourth: Talk Out

Now it is time to discuss if you think this will be a strong-selling item or if you need to go back and look for a better price on some element of the cost sheet.

And Now, the Private-Label Version

If you are working in a resident buying office in the product development division, or if you are working with a major chain designing garments that will carry a private label, calculate the retail selling price, earning exactly the same number of dollars in retail markup as you calculated in step 3. If you are a designer or manufacturer, what would you do with your product line to compete with this price point?

PROBLEM 3

Using the following information:

First: Determine the Cost of Goods to be Sold

Description: women's better sportswear: walk shorts
Date: Feb. 25, ____
Style: 1605
Sizes: 6,8,10,12,14,16
Size scale: 1–2–3–3–2–1
Fabric mill: located in Honduras
Manufacturer: located in Honduras
Fabric width: 45 inches
Estimated marker yardage: 18 yards
Material: khaki twill at $2.45 per yard
Zipper: $0.15
Belt: $1.00

Buttons: 2 buttons at $0.04 each.

Marking and grading costs: $50.00 based on a 200-piece minimum (combined cost)

Cutting costs: $90.00 based on a 200-piece minimum

Construction costs: $5.00 each

Duties/shipping costs: $0.82 each garment

COST SHEET

Sketch and Materials Swatch

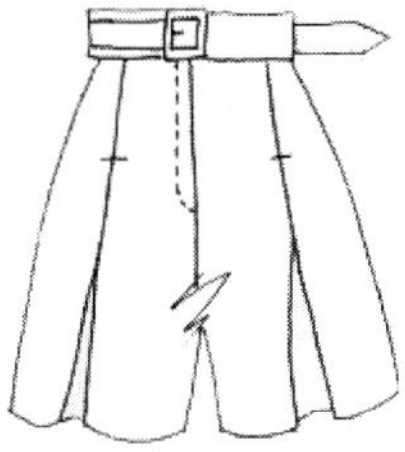

Artwork by Trudi Trudeau-Lopez.

Date ________ Style Number ________

Description ________

Fabric Mill ________

Manufacturer ________

Size Range ________

Size Scale ________

Fabric Width ________

Estimated Marker Yardage ________

Actual Marker Yardage ________

MATERIALS	**Yardage**	**Price per Yard**	**Total Amount**
Fabric	________	________	________
Fabric (collar)	________	________	________
Lining	________	________	________

Total Cost of Materials ________

TRIMS	**Amounts**	**Cost Each**	**Total Amount**
Buttons	________	________	________
Zippers	________	________	________
Belts	________	________	________
Other	________	________	________

Total Cost of Trims/Findings ________

LABOR

Marking Costs ________ Grading Costs ________ Cutting Costs ________

Construction ________

Total Labor Costs ________

SHIPPING AND DUTY EXPENSES

Import Duties ________ Shipping Expenses ________

Total Shipping and Duty Costs ________

Total Cost of Goods to Be Sold ________

Suggested Wholesale Price ________

Suggested Retail Price ________

Second: Determine the Wholesale Selling Price

Using a 30% markup, determine the wholesale selling price. Fill in the T-chart that follows to help you out.

	Dollars		Percents
Wholesale price		=	100%
Markup	-	=	30%
Cost of goods to be sold		=	70%

Remember to go back and look at your formulas. The selling percentage will always be 100%, and in this case since you want the markup percentage to be 30%, the cost percentage will be 70%. Simply divide the cost of goods sold by the cost percentage and you will arrive at the wholesale selling price, after rounding the final dollar value to $0.00, $0.25, $0.50, or $0.75.

Third: Determine the Retail Selling Price

Use the wholesale price you reached in the T-chart below. Then, applying a 55% retail markup, determine the retail selling price for this garment. Round this price to the nearest dollar.

	Dollars		Percents
Retail selling price		=	100%
Markup	-	=	55%
Cost/wholesale price		=	45%

Fourth: Talk Out

Now it is time to discuss if you think this will be a strong-selling item or if you need to go back and look for a better price on some element of the cost sheet.

And Now, the Private-Label Version

If you are working in a resident buying office in the product development division, or if you are working with a major chain designing garments that will carry a private label, calculate the retail selling price, earning exactly the same number of dollars in retail markup as you calculated in step 3. If you are a designer or manufacturer, what would you do with your product line to compete with this price point?

CHAPTER 10

Line Building: From Specs to Samples

MAKING THOSE STYLES A REALITY

You now have a complete profile of each item that you want on the line:

Item, style number
Sketch (silhouette)
Proposed (target) fabric
Target cost
Planned delivery

Target cost
Desired cost.

Wanting an item in your line, however, doesn't necessarily mean that you will produce it exactly as you planned. After reviewing the cost sheet, you might decide that it's just too expensive for the customer. That does not mean that you have to eliminate the item; it might mean that you must rethink how to produce it less expensively. Two major components determine cost: fabric and manufacturing. Let's discuss fabric first.

Each item takes on a completely different character depending on the fabric that is selected for it. Some basic items require very little guesswork on fabric. For example, a basic T-shirt would probably be made up in 100% cotton jersey, 180 grams per square meter (180 grams per square meter means the weight is about 5.3 ounces per square yard, a typical light fabric weight).

But other styles might require a more unusual fabric. Textile shows such as Premier Vision often provide actual new fabrics. But for some designers, these expensive mills can only provide the inspiration. Sometimes a designer will find a garment at retail or a swatch of a fabric that would be nice for a style being planned. The designer would then research various fabric mills to see what could capture this look at a workable price. There are many fabric mills that can develop a fabric that has a similar "look," but they change a few features of the fabric to keep the price down. Let's look at a typical design problem.

Maybe the designer loves a complex, multicolored paisley print (Figure 10-1) but it costs $7.00 per yard. At $7.00 per yard, the garment would be too expensive for the customer. The designer's job is to find an alternative. In checking with various mills, it is found that other options (although not identical) exist at a more affordable price, because they use fewer colors and are less complex (Figures 10-2 and 10-3).

The designer has to be able to visualize how this fabric would work in the planned silhouette. (How soft/stiff? How drapey/rigid? How limp/crisp?) Even experienced designers get both pleasant and unpleasant surprises when the first sample is made up. Then, if there is a problem, they scramble and change the model to better suit the fabric, or they change the fabric to better suit the model. Once the right fabrics are found, most wholesalers order sample yardage (often about 15 to 60 yards) to be knitted or woven up immediately so they can have sets of samples made up in the correct fabrics in time for the opening of the line.

The technicalities of yarns, fabrics, and dying are another one of those areas that fills (other) books. But we're going to give you a few of the "big picture" definitions so that you can show off on your first job. Almost everyone else (like us) had to look totally blank when this came up the first time! But all joking aside, this knowledge is critical.

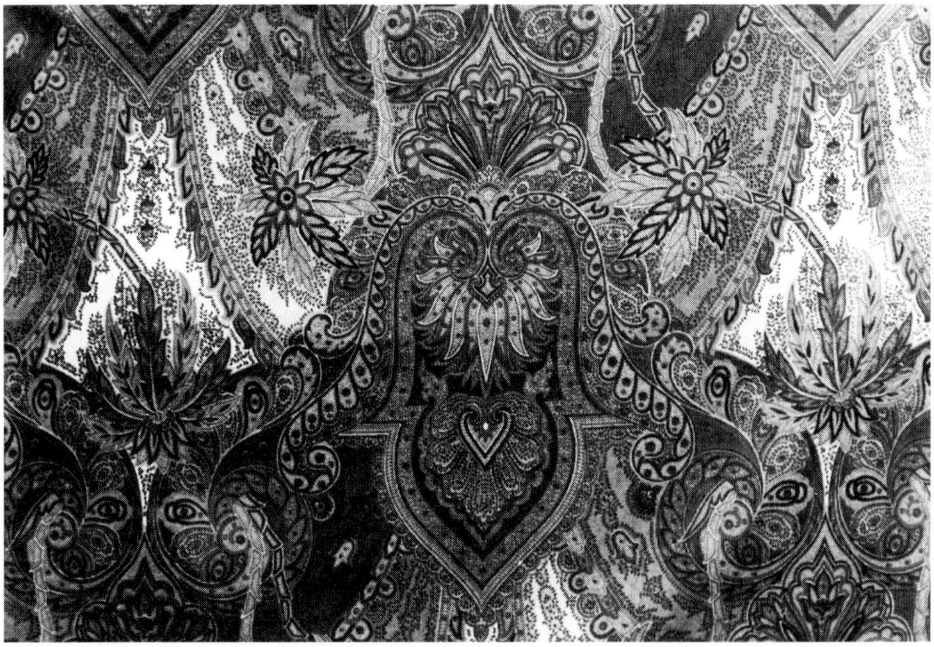

Figure 10–1
Complex, multicolored paisley print at $7.00 per yard.

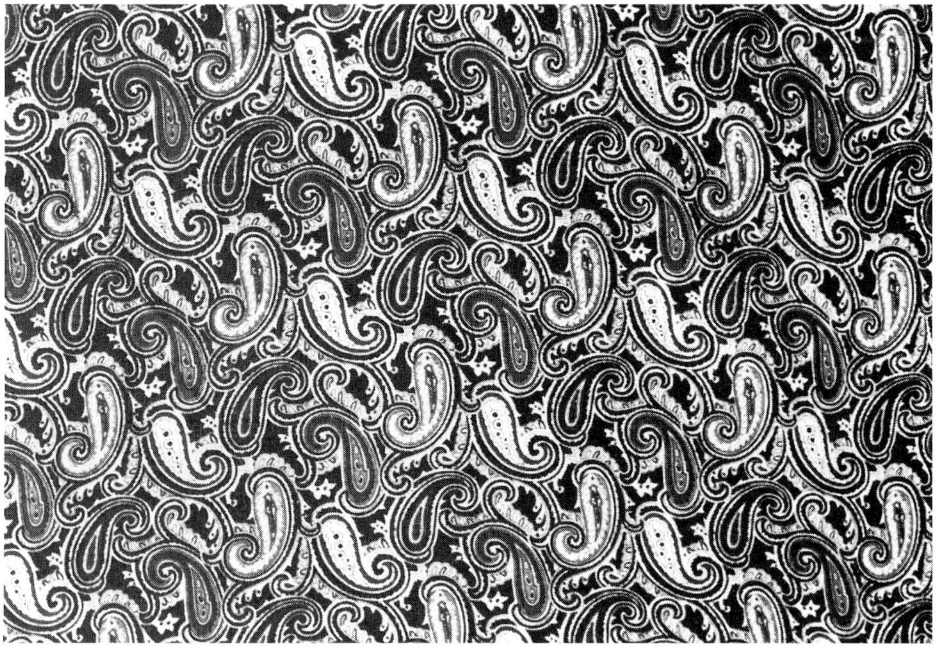

Figure 10–2

With fewer colors in the pattern, this fabric might cost only $4.25 per yard.

Figure 10–3

This fabric is printed with just one color over white, so its cost might go down to $3.50 per yard.

YARNS AND FABRICS

This has become one of the key areas of concentration for the fashion industry in the past 10 years. New fiber developments such as Tencel and microfiber, or new, more complex weaving or knitting techniques are becoming commonplace at all price levels. Consumers have many choices. Garment makers have to differentiate their products from the competition; fiber, yarn, and fabric are the most common differentiators. This is also the area in which retail buyers and other newcomers to product development, tend to have the weakest background. Eventually, you will need to learn a lot of technical information; but we'll begin here with a comprehensive introduction.

Fibers

These are the building blocks of yarns. They are either natural or manufactured. You're familiar with most of these:

Natural	**Manufactured**	
	Cellulosic (a natural fiber that's been heavily treated)	Petroleum-based
Cotton	Acetate	Polyester
Wool	Rayon	Nylon
Silk	Tencel	Acrylic
Linen		

These are either spun together or extruded (pulled) into yarns. Yarns are measured by their thickness. It's far too complicated to explain in detail, as different types of yarns use different measuring systems. But in general, the higher the number, the thinner (finer) the yarn. For example, the yarns in a blouse could be "40's" or "50's"; the yarns in heavy denim jeans would be "7's."

Each type of yarn has its own positive and negative characteristics. Natural fibers have a certain status, but they can wrinkle easily (linen) or can be fragile and difficult to wash (silk). The manufactured fibers have come a long way since the stigma of double-knit polyester in the 1970s (they never wrinkled!). Blends of manufactured and natural fibers are very common, as they can impart some of the good qualities of each. These fibers are also blended overseas to qualify them as *chief-weight natural fibers* (thus getting the lower natural-fiber duties) versus *chief-weight synthetic fibers* (getting higher duties).

Woven Fabric Construction

Following are several more advanced points that very few people know when they enter the industry. On their first trip to the Orient, their eyes pop from the technicality. But from then on, they're using this terminology daily.

A common blended broadcloth woven fabric (in a woman's blouse or a man's dress shirt) is quoted in construction terms as follows:

$$\frac{110 \times 70}{45 \times 45}$$

This means:

110 threads per inch in the warp (vertical direction)
70 threads per inch in the weft (horizontal direction)
"45" is the size of each thread in the warp
"45" is the size of each thread in the weft

This very accurately explains which thread and what density of threads are used in both directions of the woven cloth. It provides an exact *fingerprint* of the fabric.

Believe us, it can get complicated! Here, for fun, is the distinction between the oxford cloth used by one American designer in his status dress shirt and the oxford cloth used by another famous designer in his:

Designer A	**Designer B**
96 x 96 / 40 ǁ x 20/2	92 x 48 / 40 ǁ x 25/2

You need not remember this, but ǁ = parallel: two yarns are run next to each other as if they were one yarn, but not twisted together beforehand, and /2 = two ply: two yarns twisted together first, then woven as one.

Knitted Cloth Construction

Knitted cloth is measured by *gauge* (a measurement of the machinery that is used to knit it) and *weight* (how heavy is the cloth). The yarn size is usually quoted as well. In sweaters, for example, 3 GG (gauge) is a very heavy sweater knit (as in a fisherman's sweater). 12 GG (gauge) is a fine sweater-shirt type of knit (as in a fine merino wool turtleneck). In knitted fabric the higher the gauge, the finer and lighter the fabric (18 GG, 20 GG, 32 GG, etc.). Fabric weights used to be expressed in many different terms, but thankfully, most of the world is settling on grams per square meter. (Yes, we realize this is getting a bit overwhelming.)

FABRIC DYING

Three main dying techniques are used in the garment business.

Yarn Dying (Figure 10-4)

The yarns are dyed first, then either knitted or woven into a fabric. An example is a striped T-shirt, where one color yarn is knitted until the width of that stripe is achieved, then the machine picks up the second color yarn and knits that, and so on. In woven fabrics, the colored yarns are set up on the loom (in the warp) and then colored yarns are woven across them (in the weft, or fill). When alternating colors are used in both directions, the result is a plaid fabric.

Piece Dying (Figure 10-5)

The yarns are woven or knitted into fabric in their natural state (called *greige*). Then the already completed fabrics are bathed in dyes to color them. This is

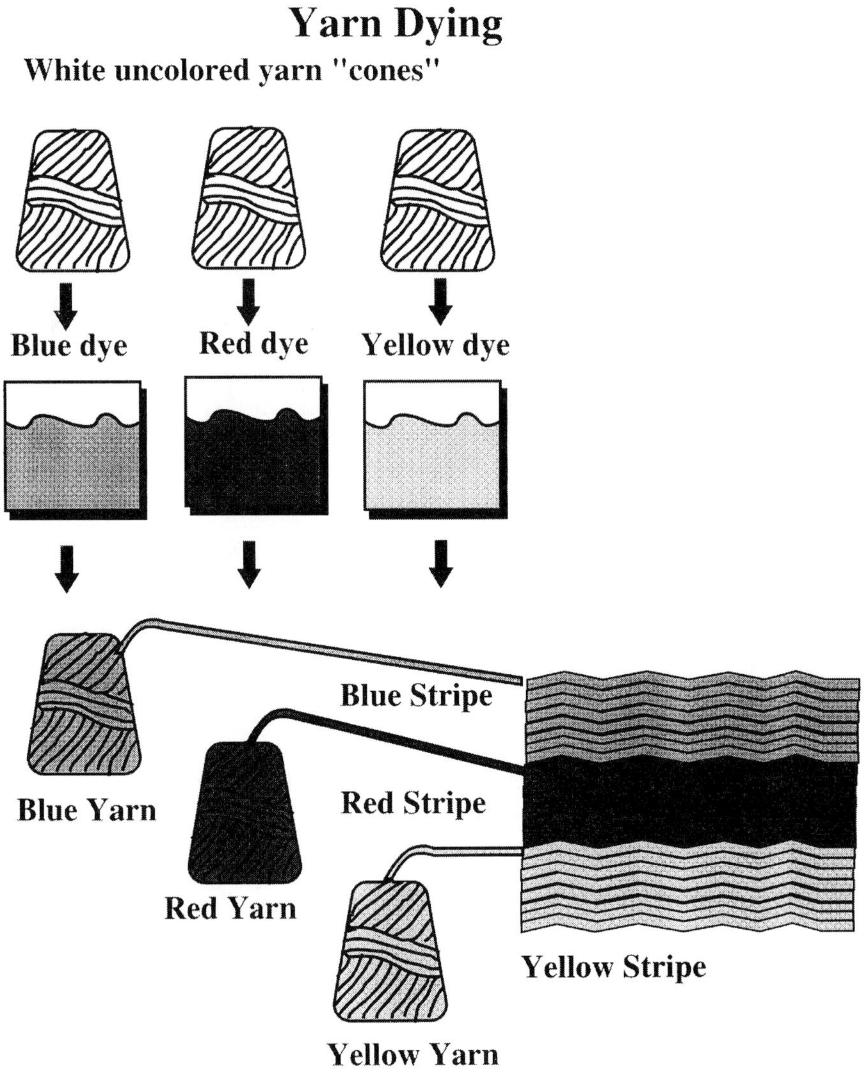

Figure 10–4

Yarn dying process. Artwork by Michael Carnegie.

the most common type of dying and is usually the most economical. This would be used for a solid-color T-shirt or a solid-color dress, for example.

Garment Dying (Figure 10-6)

This is a more uncommon technique and it has its pros and cons. Garments are actually sewn or knitted together out of the undyed fabric or yarn. Then, as full garments, they are dyed together in a big vat. This technique allows color selection to be made very late in the process (very close to selling time). But it generally works only on very casually constructed items, such as T-shirts, casual pants and shorts, and casual sweaters. The color effect is sometimes a bit uneven, the garments tend to look a little "funky," and they are more likely to fade in sunlight.

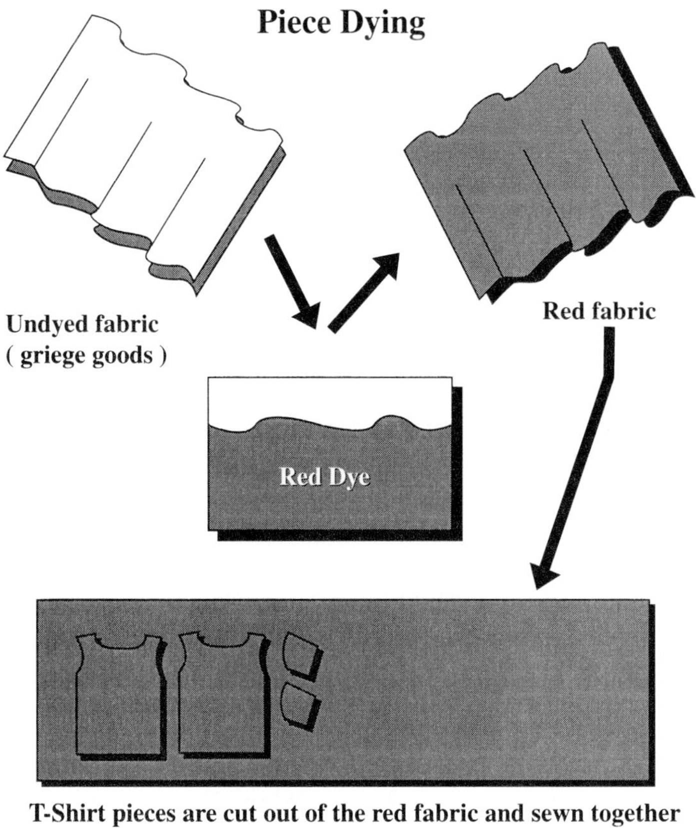

Figure 10–5

Piece dying process. Artwork by Michael Carnegie.

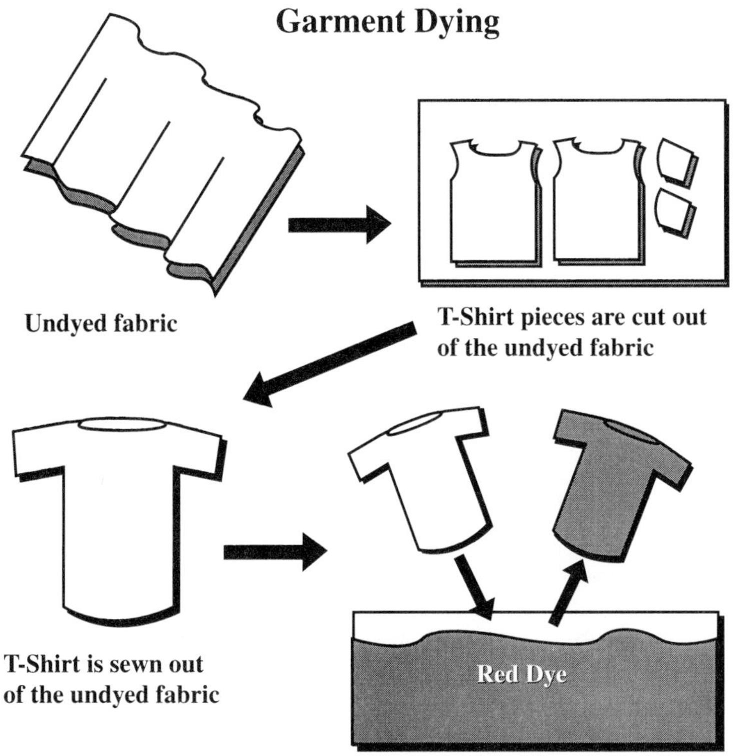

Figure 10–6

Garment dying process. Artwork by Michael Carnegie.

PRINTING TECHNIQUES

Prints come and go in fashion but they're never gone for long. They can transform a very ordinary piece of white fabric into a masterpiece (especially if you're talking about white silk and the printing is being done in Como, Italy). The two main printing techniques are screen printing and roller printing.

Screen Printing (Figure 10-7)

Screen printing is very similar to what you might have done in art class, only on a larger scale. Thick dye is "squeegeed" through a partially porous, partially solid screen, in a pattern onto the fabric below. Each different screen adds (only) one color to the garment until the total number of colors in the print is reached. ("three-color print" = 3 screens; "12-color print" = 12 screens). It can be done by hand or by automation (rotary screen). It's quick and not too expensive, but the design can't be too intricate.

Roller Printing (Figure 10-8)

The roller printing technique uses large metal rollers with designs engraved on them, one roller per color in the print. Fabric is run under these rollers very quickly and the pattern is applied continuously. The rollers are quite expensive to make up, so most printers will not offer this service if you are

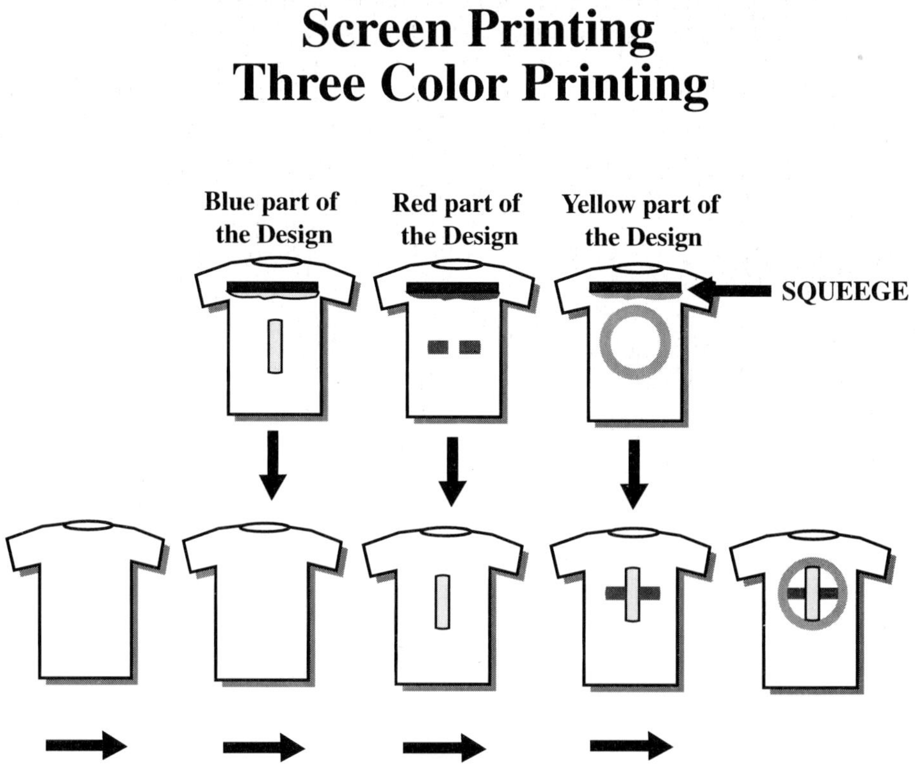

Figure 10-7

Screen printing process. Artwork by Michael Carnegie.

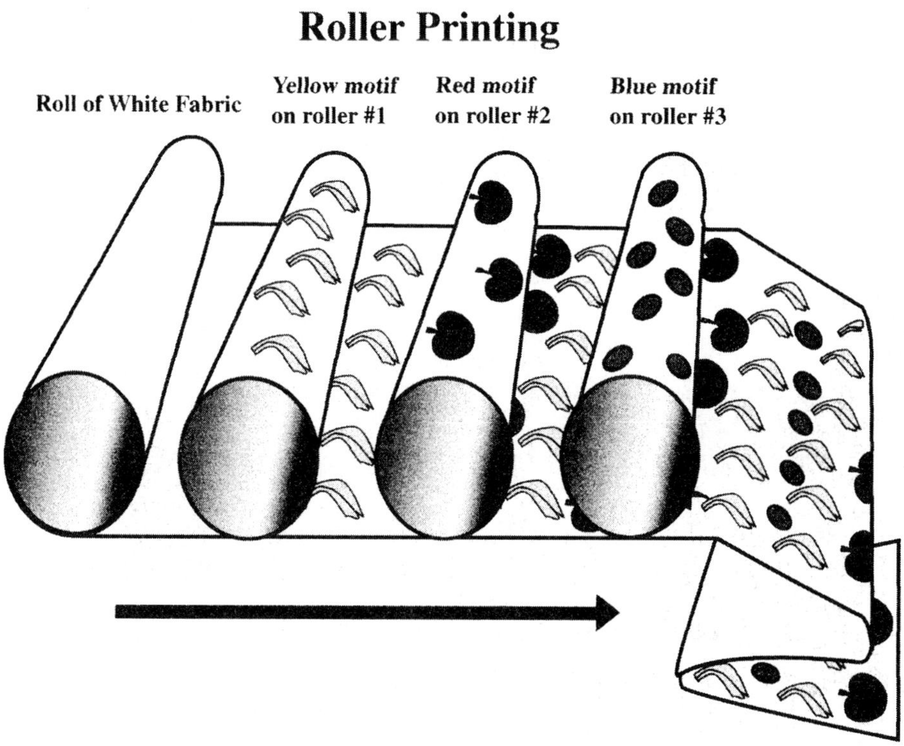

Figure 10–8

Roller printing process. Artwork by Michael Carnegie.

printing less than 5000 yards. Once set, however, this technique is very rapid, very accurate (fine detail), and can keep printing for large quantities without deterioration of the print quality.

In both cases, the cost gets more expensive the more colors there are in the print. Two to six colors is common—above that, and it gets both expensive and difficult to source. To check to see how the print is going to come out in production, printers will often prepare a preliminary hand screen version for the buyer to OK. This is called a *strike off.*

There is one other distinction that you need to know because it can cause some real complications, as you will see.

Direct Printing (Figure 10-9)

Direct printing is the standard method of printing dark designs on top of white- or light-colored fabric.

Dye and Discharge (Figure 10-10)

Dye and discharge is a much more expensive technique which starts with a dark solid-color fabric. Then, to have lighter-colored designs show up on top, the dark color needs to be *discharged* out (removed) in places. Then the lighter-colored design can be printed onto those places that are now white again. Picture yellow polka dots on navy.

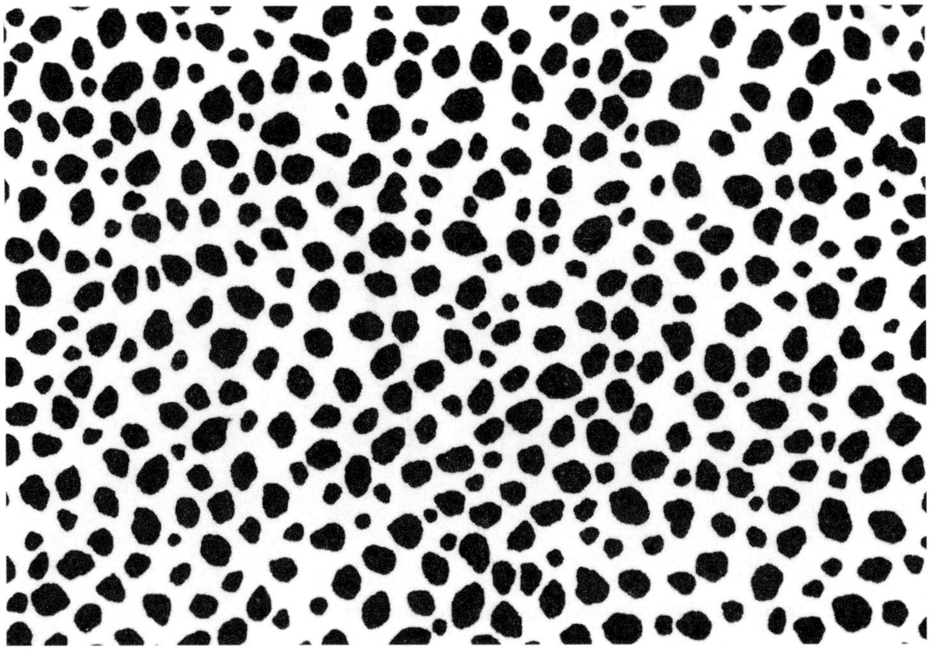

Figure 10–9

Direct print.

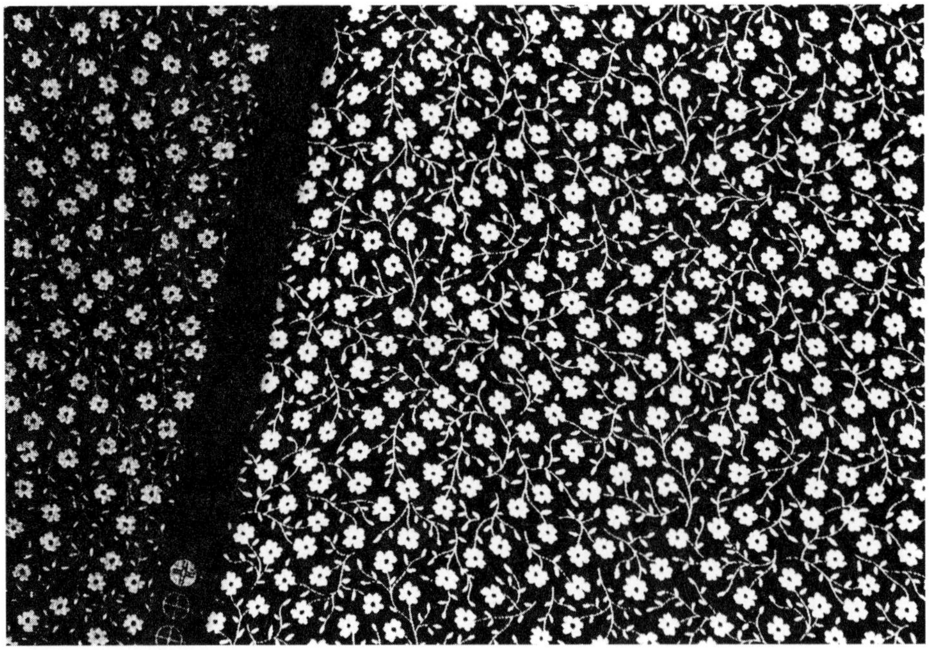

Figure 10–10

Dye and discharge print, turned back on itself. Note that the back side of the fabric shows that the discharging is not as strong on the back. Also, the edge of the fabric shows the original solid dark color.

THE INSIDE SCOOP

S. Y. Kim

A native of Korea, S.Y. graduated from Seoul National University with a major in fabrics and textiles. She then worked with several U.S. importers in their Korean offices. In 1982, S.Y. joined AMC–Seoul, where she rose through the ranks to divisional manager. After two years in New York, she moved to the AMC–Minneapolis office to service the Dayton/Hudson/Marshall Field's men's account as global sourcer. She is now at Sears.

On being brave enough to admit you don't know:

On his first trip to Korea, a product manager (PM) from New York negotiated a printed shirt program with our key Korean vendor. A 50–50 averaged price was struck for the two different kinds of printing—50% should be direct prints and 50% should be discharge prints. The product manager actually didn't know the difference between the two prints but was afraid to appear ignorant, so he didn't ask.

When the PM booked the program with the buyers in New York, he sent the patterns back to Korea. The vendor complained bitterly that of the 10 patterns, nine had to be done by the expensive discharge process. Only one was a regular (direct) print. The price quoted was based on five and five. The problem was that the product manager couldn't tell which patterns needed which process.

The faxes flew back and forth, and tempers flared. The vendor and the office thought the PM was trying to cheat. The PM thought the vendor was just trying to raise the price after the orders were in. Finally, I figured out that the product manager probably had not understood the distinction between the two prints. We carefully explained and gave him options to change color combinations to solve the problem.

The product manager faxed back the next day and said, "I feel like my eyes have finally opened." So I think rather than looking "smart" now and "not so smart" later, it's always better to admit you don't know something, and ask!

Now that you know how important these distinctions can be, here is one last printing distinction.

One-Way Print (Figures 10-11 and 10-12)

In one-way printing the pattern on the fabric has a definite top and bottom. All the motifs in the print point in one direction. It is more expensive to cut a one-way print because all the motifs must "point up" the same way on each piece of the garment.

Two-Way Print (Figures 10-13 and 10-14)

Many prints have motifs that point both up *and* down, so the fabric can be cut in either direction. This allows for a more efficient layout of the marker because the pattern pieces can go in either direction, thus saving money.

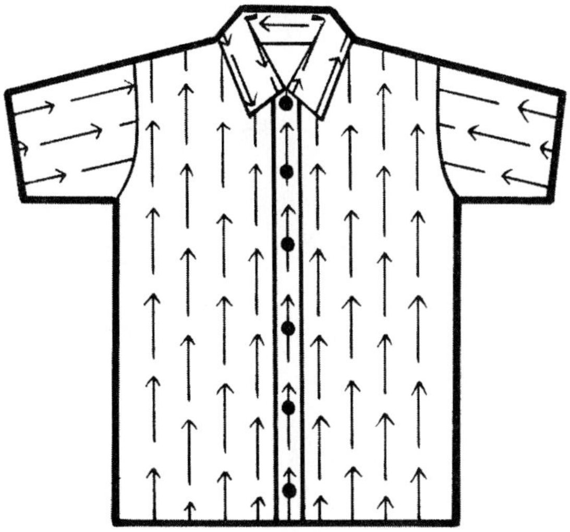

Figure 10–11
One-way print: Each fabric panel must be cut in the same direction. Artwork by Mary Lisa Caramico.

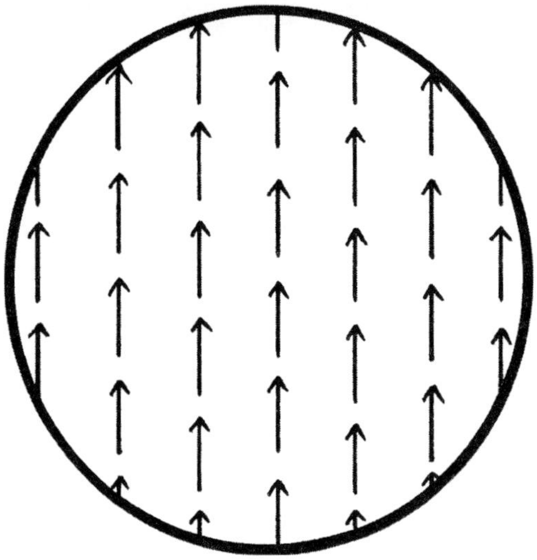

Figure 10–12
One-way print fabric. If you turn this fabric upside down, the arrows will all be pointing down. You can't have one side of the front of a shirt pointing up and the other side pointing down. Artwork by Mary Lisa Caramico.

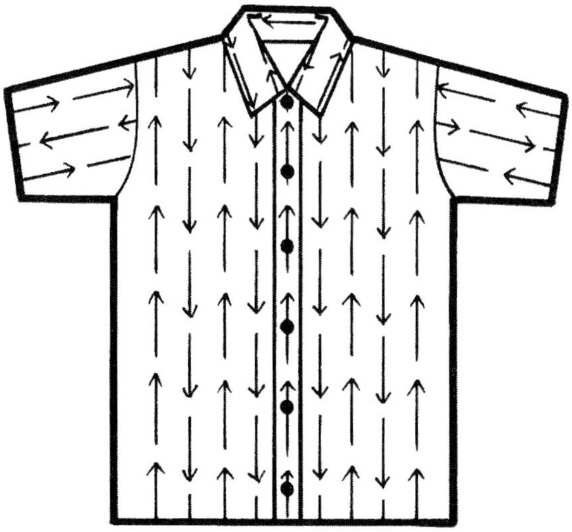

Figure 10–13
Two-way print: Each fabric panel can be cut in either direction. Artwork by Mary Lisa Caramico.

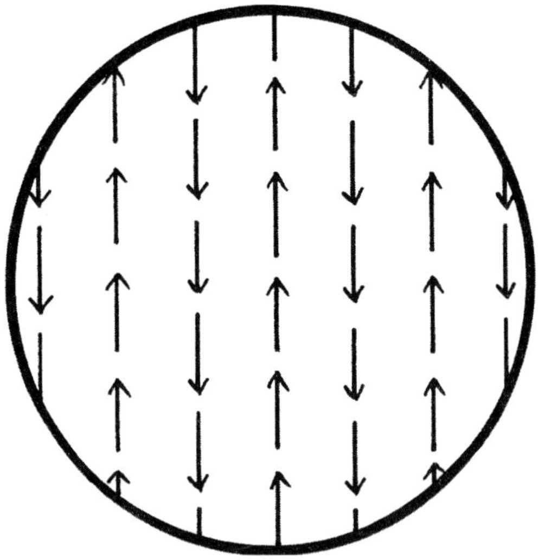

Figure 10–14
Two-way print fabric: If you turn this fabric upside down, it will look just the same. So it can be cut in either direction. Artwork by Mary Lisa Caramico.

SIZE SPECIFICATIONS/PATTERNS

A garment manufacturer cannot give an accurate price quote without knowing exactly how much fabric will be used for a garment. It is in the designer/merchandiser's best interest to be able to provide very exact measurements to the

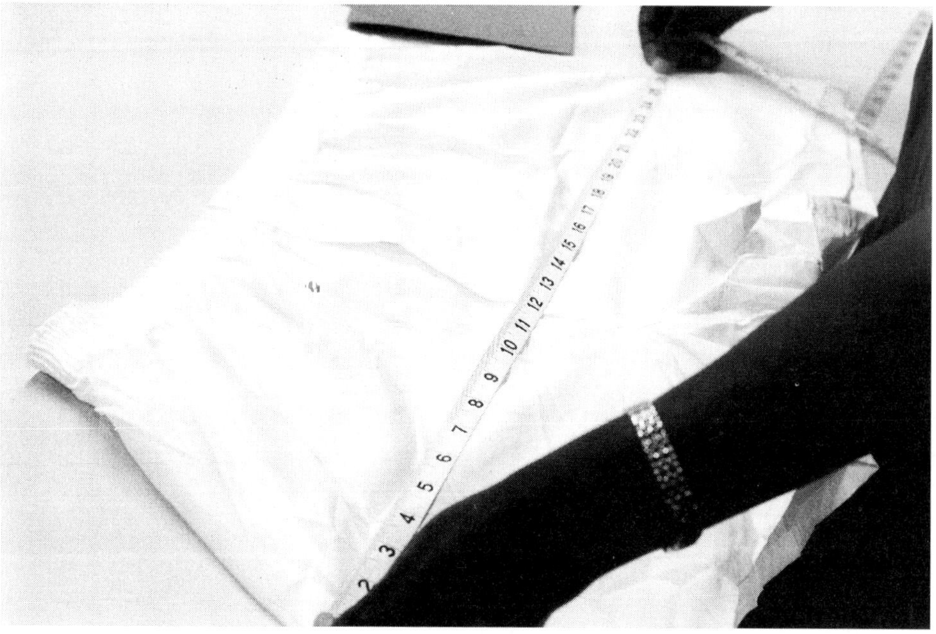

Taking a hip measurement on a boxer short. *Courtesy of the Harwood Companies, Inc.*

manufacturer in order to get the most accurate quote. If you remember, on the cost sheet there were actually two notations about marker yardage: one estimated and one actual. By having an accurate measurement from the start, designers are able to make more reliable business decisions as to whether or not a garment will be made.

How do you do this? It is done in one of two ways:

- Providing size specifications (specs) on standardized forms that show the measurements of each dimension of the garment
- Providing a **contract cutter** with a copy of your **marker** with the pattern pieces already drawn out for all sizes to be cut

Contract cutter
A subcontractor who cuts the pieces of fabric (only).

Marker
The paper pattern that is placed on top of the stacked fabrics, the pattern lines on the paper providing the cutting lines.

In either case, the manufacturer also needs to know the total number of sizes required, and the measurements of the sizes.

Let's take a look at the information a designer would work with. For example; four sizes might be required on a T-shirt: small, medium, large, and extralarge. The manufacturer also needs to know the **grade** or measurement increment between each of the sizes. An example of this would be:

Grade
Difference in measurement between sizes.

Size:	Small	Medium	Large	Extralarge
Chest measurement:	18 in.	19 in.	20 in.	21 in.

Note: This is the half-circumference chest measurement. (Figures 10-15, 10-16, 10-17 and 10-18 are technical work drawings of each size). Either half-circumference or full circumference can be used.

The above would be considered a 1-inch grade, because there is a 1-inch difference between each size. Grades vary by customer type and by brand, and they do not necessarily have to be even between all the sizes!

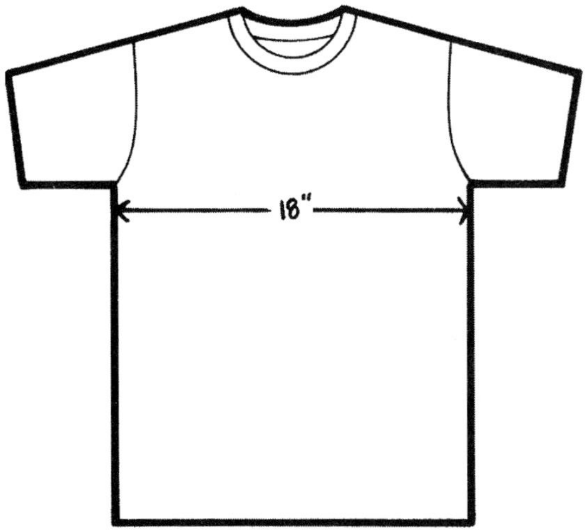

Figure 10–15
Half-circumference chest measurement, size small. Artwork by Mary Lisa Caramico.

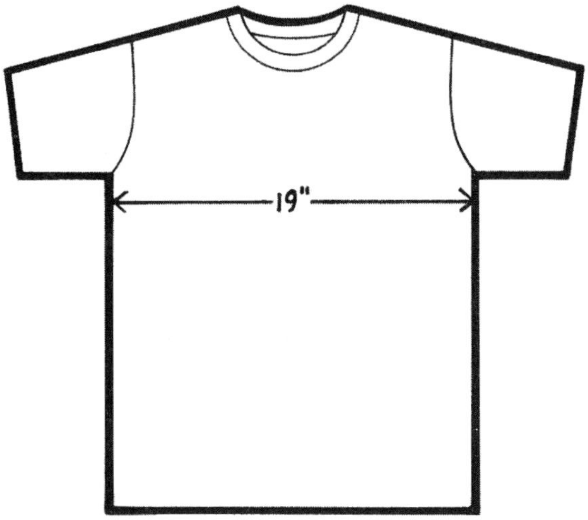

Figure 10–16
Half-circumference chest measurement, size medium. Artwork by Mary Lisa Caramico.

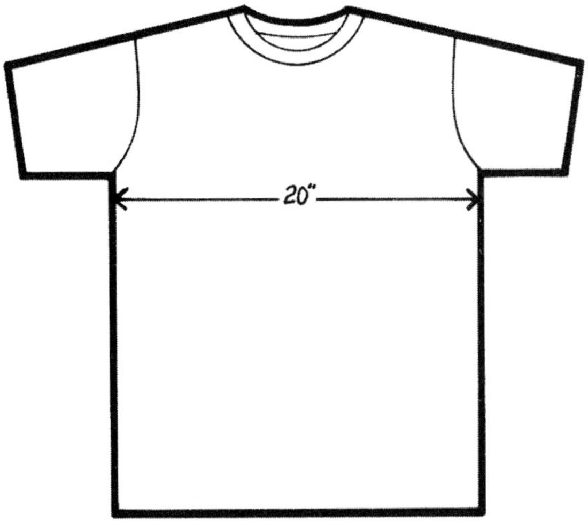

Figure 10–17
Half-circumference chest measurement, size large. Artwork by Mary Lisa Caramico.

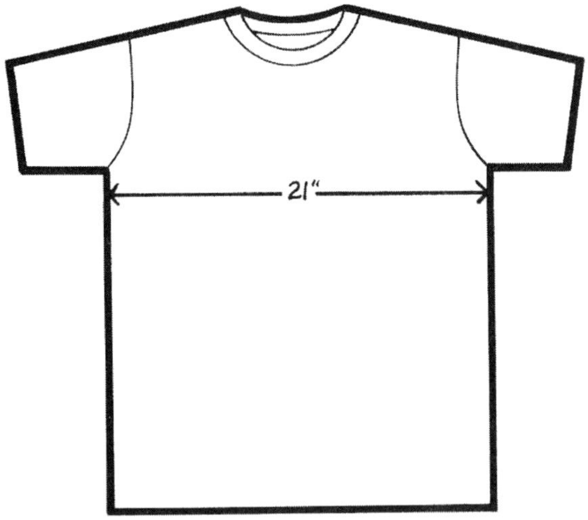

Figure 10–18
Half-circumference chest measurement, size extralarge. Artwork by Mary Lisa Caramico.

The manufacturer also needs to know the size scale or the number of pieces of each size that will be ordered. (Remember: the bigger the size, the more fabric it takes.) Size scales are often (but not always) expressed as the breakdown within one dozen: Here are some typical size scales:

	Small	Medium	Large	Extralarge	
	1	3	5	3	= 12 pieces
or	0	3	6	3	= 12 pieces
or	1	5	4	2	= 12 pieces

Now you know the number of sizes, approximate measurements, and how many sizes will be cut per dozen. Each of the factors above has a significant impact on the amount of fabric needed, called fabric *consumption*. This, in turn, has a significant impact on the price. By the way, which size scale above do you think will cost most?

IN GREATER DEPTH

SPEC SHEETS

To compile the information correctly to determine the accurate yardage, critical measurements are needed for each size. A design team works this out on a spec sheet. A spec (specification) sheet is a technical rendering of a garment, with the measurements and tolerance levels identified for each step. Often, companies have technical designers and/or patternmakers to make up the size specs or patterns. More and more, this is done on computers. But keep in mind that essentially every garment requires a new set of specs because there will probably be something unique on that garment that is different from a generic body.

In smaller companies, the designer, merchandiser, or product manager might be required to develop the specs themselves. This takes considerable training and/or experience. But it doesn't matter if the sheets are computer driven or calculated manually; everyone in the design industry must be able to read and use one.

Let's take a look at this spec sheet from Alan Stuart Menswear (Figure 10-19) and review what it means.

- *Style.* This is the numerical code that is used to identify each style.
- *Season.* Most wholesalers keep track of their styles first by season, then by style number. Silhouettes and styling can be similar, with slight design modifications from season to season. It is important to keep the information accurate and current.
- *Codes.* If you will take a look at the sketch on the right-hand side of the spec sheet, you will notice that there are the same letter codes as in the code column. These codes are important because they match up the measurements with the instructions (as to exactly how the measurements must be taken). For example, code K represents the chest measurement. On the sketch you will see that the line running horizontally across the shirt is identified as K.
- *Method of Measurement.* (Listed on the Alan Stuart spec sheet under "Top Specifications—Men.) Now it is time to match the measurement method to the codes and the drawing. In this case, for code K, it is noted

(Continued on next page)

PRODUCTION SPEC ☐

PRE-PRODUCTION SPEC ☐

Alan Stuart INC.

STYLE

SEASON

GARMENT SPECIFICATIONS - MEN

MEASUREMENTS : PLEASE MEASURE ACCORDING TO INDICATED GUIDELINES IF MEASUREMENT ARE IN CENTIMETERS OR INCHES. CIRCUMFERENCE MEASUREMENTS ARE GIVEN ON THE HALF.

CODE	TOP SPECIFICATIONS-MEN	TOLERANCE	SIZES					
K	"CHEST" MEASURED 1" BELOW ARMHOLE FROM SEAM TO SEAM	+/- 1/2"						
J	"SLEEVE LENGTH" MEASURED 2" FROM CENTER BACK NECK TO BOTTOM OF SLEEVE	+/- 1/2"						
P	"SLEEVE AT OPENING" MEASURED FROM FOLD TO FOLD	+/- 1/4"						
P2	"SLEEVE WIDTH" MEASURED 1" DOWN FROM UNDERARM SEAM FROM FOLD TO FOLD	+/- 1/4"						
I	"NECK OPENING" MEASURED FROM SEAM TO SEAM	+/- 1/4"						
L	"SHOULDER WIDTH" MEASURED FROM SEAM TO SEAM	+/- 1/2"						
M	"BOTTOM WIDTH" MEASURED FROM INSIDE TO INSIDE	+/- 1/2"						
N	"BODY LENGTH" MEASURED FROM CENTER BACK NECK TO BOTTOM	+/- 1/2"						

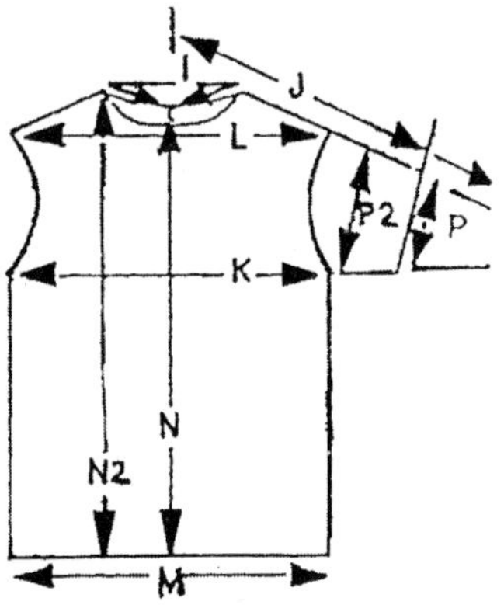

Figure 10–19

Garment spec sheet. Courtesy of Lezlie Johnny and Alan Stuart, Inc.

that the chest measurement is measured 1 inch below the armhole from seam to seam. You cannot assume that everyone is measuring the same way. There is no single standard in the industry. If you told someone to measure the width of the chest, where would they lay the tape? Would they place it at the armhole, 1 inch below, 2 inches below? It's done different ways by different companies, so the method of measurement must be stated clearly on the spec sheet to guarantee that everyone involved in the process will measure the same way on this garment. It is also important, as you can see on this spec sheet, to identify if you are measuring in centimeters or inches, and to note if a circumference measurement is given "on the half." That would mean that if a chest measurement shows 20 inches, that would only be the front half—the circumference would be 40 inches.

- *Tolerance.* Garment sewing is not like stamping out metal. No two garments are every exactly alike. The tolerance measurement is given here to indicate how much of a measurement deviation (plus or minus) will still be acceptable.
- *Sizes.* Each size to be cut has its own measurements. You learned in Chapter 7 that a well-balanced product must have a good fit. That good fit starts here, with each successively larger size getting larger in all proportions. Different garments might be cut in different ranges of sizes (Small, medium, large is one range. Small, medium, large, extralarge,

extra extra-large, is a different range, for example.) Only the sizes that will be used for this particular garment will be listed across the top. Then the exact measurements for each code (under each size) will be filled in.

- *Sketch.* This is the technical sketch of the garment being produced. With manufacturing taking place all over the world, it is always good to have a visual reference to support the statistics! If someone is reading this information overseas, the numbers and sketch alone would provide substantial information. (Please note that this particular Alan Stuart spec sheet does NOT show a sketch of the exact garment. You will see technical work sketches in this chapter's exercises.)

PRODUCTION SPEC ☑
PRE-PRODUCTION SPEC ☐

Alan Stuart INC.

STYLE T2930
SEASON Holiday/Spring 97

GARMENT SPECIFICATIONS - MEN

MEASUREMENTS : PLEASE MEASURE ACCORDING TO INDICATED GUIDELINES IF MEASUREMENT ARE IN CENTIMETERS OR INCHES. CIRCUMFERENCE MEASUREMENTS ARE GIVEN ON THE HALF.

CODE	TOP SPECIFICATIONS-MEN	TOLERANCE	SIZES S	M	L	XL	1X	2X
K	"CHEST" MEASURED 1" BELOW ARMHOLE FROM SEAM TO SEAM	+/- 1/2"	20 5/8	22 5/8	24 5/8	26 5/8	27 5/8	27 5/8
J	"SLEEVE LENGTH" MEASURED 2" FROM CENTER BACK NECK TO BOTTOM OF SLEEVE	+/- 1/2"	18 3/8	19 3/8	20 3/8	21 3/8	21 7/8	22 7/8
P	"SLEEVE AT OPENING" MEASURED FROM FOLD TO FOLD	+/- 1/4"	6 3/4	7 1/8	7 5/8	8 1/8	8 1/8	9 5/8
P2	"SLEEVE WIDTH" MEASURED 1" DOWN FROM UNDERARM SEAM FROM FOLD TO FOLD	+/- 1/4"	7 3/8	7 3/4	8 1/8	8 1/2	8 1/2	8 7/8
I	"NECK OPENING" MEASURED FROM SEAM TO SEAM	+/- 1/4"	15 1/2	16 1/2	17 1/2	18 1/2	18 1/2	19 1/2
L	"SHOULDER WIDTH" MEASURED FROM SEAM TO SEAM	+/- 1/2"	18	19	20	21	22	23
M	"BOTTOM WIDTH" MEASURED FROM INSIDE TO INSIDE	+/- 1/2"	11 7/8	12 7/8	13 7/8	15 3/8	15 3/8	17 7/8
N	"BODY LENGTH" MEASURED FROM CENTER BACK NECK TO BOTTOM	+/- 1/2"	25 5/8	26 5/8	27	28	28 1/2	29
N2	"FRONT LENGTH" MEASURED FROM HIGH SHOULDER TO BOTTOM	+/- 1/2"	26	27	27 1/2	28 1/2	29	29 1/2

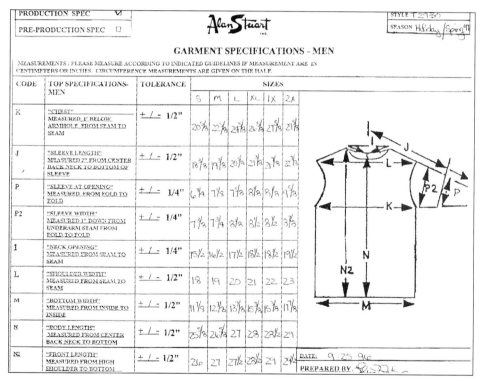

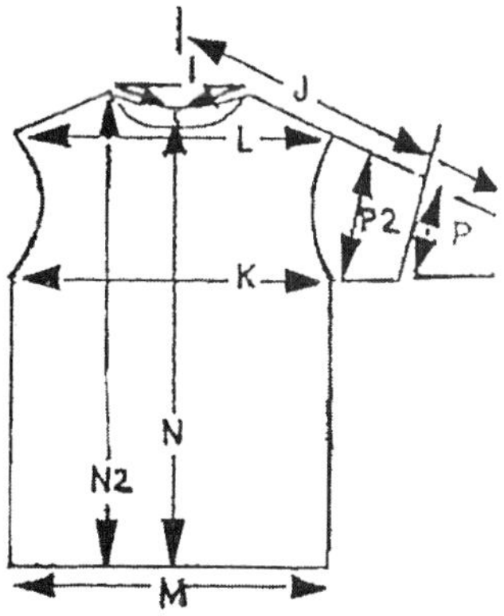

DATE: 9.25.96
PREPARED BY: [illegible]

Figure 10–20

Filled-in garment spec sheet. Courtesy of Lezlie Johnny and Alan Stuart, Inc.

Now let's take a look at an Alan Stuart spec sheet filled out (Figure 10-20).

The designer has coded this style T2930.

It is for the Holiday/Spring 97 season.

In the small size, the measurements are :

(Continued on next page)

Chest =	20 ⅝ in.	with a ½-in. tolerance
Sleeve Length =	18 ⅜ in.	with a ½-in. tolerance
Sleeve at Opening =	6 ¾ in.	with a ¼-in. tolerance
Sleeve Width =	7 ⅜ in.	with a ¼-in. tolerance
Neck Opening =	15 ½ in.	with a ¼-in. tolerance
Shoulder Width =	18 in.	with a ½-in. tolerance
Bottom Width =	11 ⅞ in.	with a ½-in. tolerance
Body Length =	25 ⅝ in.	with a ½-in. tolerance
Front Length =	26 in.	with a ½-in. tolerance

Then, looking at the size medium specs, you can see how these measurements increase as the size of the garment increases. Once the specs and then the patterns are set, they form the basis for the garment production. The written specs ensure the consistency of styling and fit from the sample to the production, and within production, from garment to garment. They are also used during production for the quality control department to make sure that everything is coming out correctly.

FIRST SAMPLES

After all this work, who knows what this line even looks like? So far, we just have lots of paper! *First samples* are made up of each item and evaluated for look, fit, construction, and value. Often, major adjustments to the line get made at this time. Whole segments might be dropped out, others added. Samples are usually made up in the manufacturer's or wholesaler's sample room, or perhaps by an outside sample-making service. But keep in mind that every style that is dropped now means that the time and money already spent on that style has been wasted. Often, the exact zippers, buttons, and/or other trims might not yet be available. The color of the fabric is usually whatever is immediately available. It takes a fair amount of imagination and experience to picture a great product in this sorry state—these samples usually look pretty rough.

To check to see if the proposed size specs or patterns are correct, this sample will be tried on either a mannequin (Figure 10-21) or on a live *fit model*, someone who is the perfect sample size in the perfect proportions for a particular kind of fit. A fit model that's right for a missy line, for example, will not be right for a junior line. And yes, even if you are a 3X, you might be just right as a big-sized fit model, as long as everything is in the proportions specified. Reviewing the garments on either the **mannequin** or fit model, the technical designer will then adjust the size specs to provide the best possible fit.

Mannequin
A wood-and-cloth form constructed exactly to the body measurements of a company's ideal customer.

Now we have a line of sample garments that have passed all the challenges to this point. It's finally time to start up the production line.

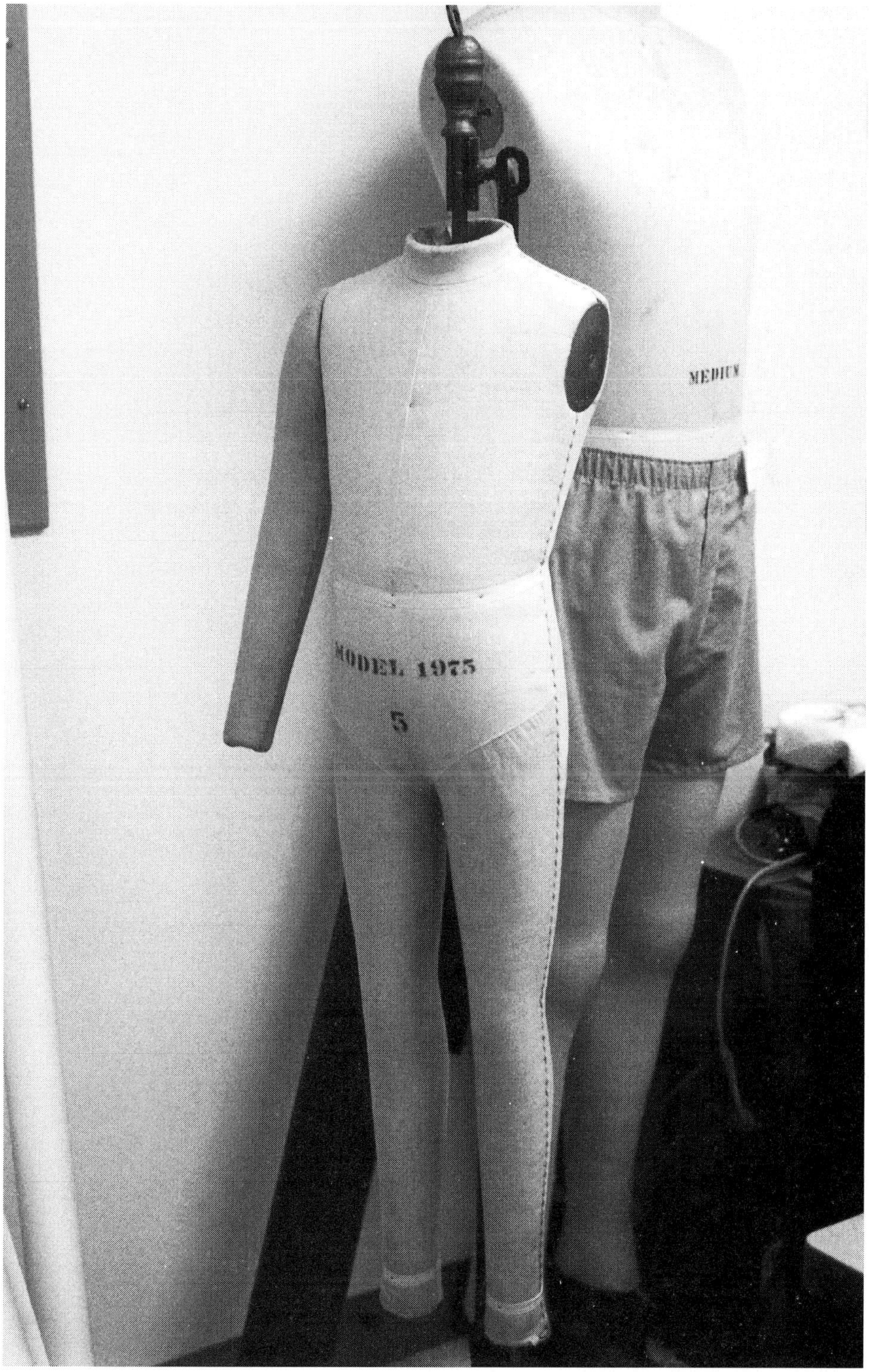

Figure 10–21

Mannequins for boys' and men's. Courtesy of the Harwood Companies, Inc.

SO YOU WANT TO WORK IN THE FASHION BUSINESS?
Here's How to Begin. . . Chapter 10

In Chapter 9 you worked with cost sheets, and now in Chapter 10 you have been introduced to spec sheets. We're sure that you can understand why these forms need to be so accurate: One wrong number and you could lose a lot of profit! If everyone measured things in his or her "own way," the design industry would be in a mess. So what we want to show you is not only how to measure, but also, how to fill in a spec sheet correctly. We're going to walk you through this step by step, so that you'll get a clear picture.

Before you start, you're going to get the retail industry involved, in addition to using your negotiating skills. Since you all understand the importance of networking, two or three students need to volunteer to go to a local Gap or Old Navy store and ask for some project help. What you want to do is ask to borrow a S, M, and L basic women's T-shirt, and a S, M, L, and XL men's T-shirt. It might take a little time in the store because they will have to prepare *a goods sign-out sheet.* This is a form used to check merchandise out of a store without selling it (for example, when placing merchandise in fashion shows).

Because paperwork can get tedious, it might be wise to call and make the arrangements with the store manager ahead of time. Keep in mind that if these garments can't be returned in exactly the same condition, the store will require full payment. (This means leaving the tags on, too.) If all else fails, perhaps the school could pay to purchase the seven samples.

With the women's basic T-shirts in hand, let's get to work.

First: Draw a Technical Work Sketch and Identify the Key Measuring Points

Draw a technical sketch of the T-shirt and, using codes, identify each of the two front measurements you will be making (look ahead at Figures 10-22 and 10-24). Put both coded arrows on the same figure.

Code	Measurement
A	Chest
B	Sweep

Now, draw the back side of the T-shirt (refer to Figures 10-25 and 10-27) and draw in the coded arrows for the two back measurements. Again, both back coded arrows should go on the same drawing.

Code	Measurement
C	Center back length
D	Sleeve length

Second: Measure the Garments to Identify the Spec Measurements

- Working with just the women's size small T-shirt, measure the width of the chest from 1" below the armhole. (Yes, this is the standard place where chest measurements are taken) (Figures 10-22, 10-23).

- Measure the bottom of the T-shirt from side seam to side seam across the bottom. This is called the "sweep" (Figure 10-24). Often, the sweep and chest measurements will be the same, but not always. Can you think of a top where they would not be?
- Place your tape measure at the center of the back at the bottom of the neck trim, and measure the length of the back (Figures 10-25, 10-26).

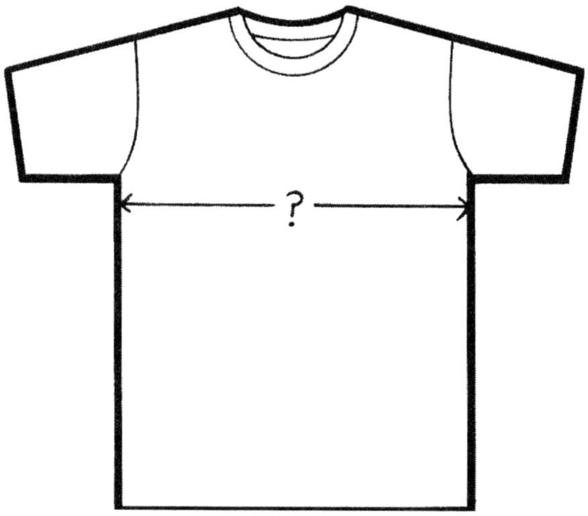

Figure 10–22

Chest measurement. Artwork by Mary Lisa Caramico.

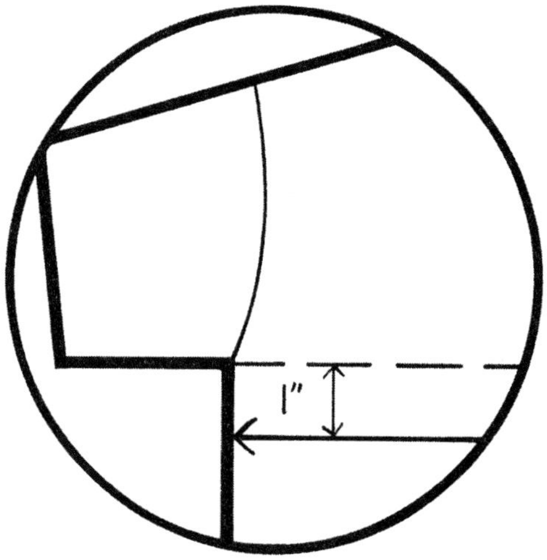

Figure 10–23

Chest measurement point, close up. Artwork by Mary Lisa Caramico.

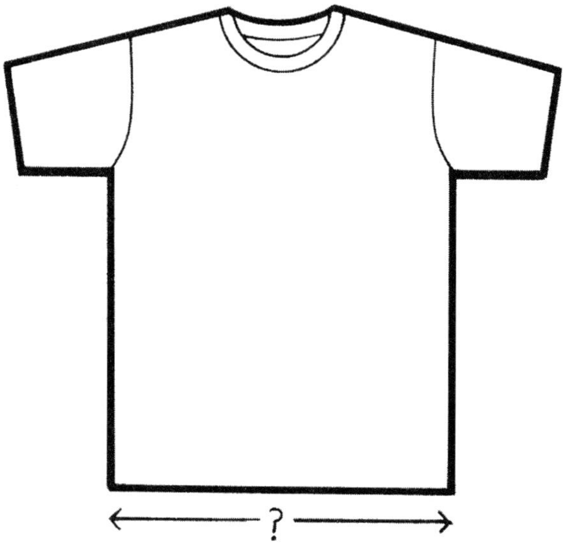

Figure 10–24

Sweep measurement. Artwork by Mary Lisa Caramico.

- Measure the sleeve length from the center of the back neck (the same point on the back that you used for the center back length measurement above), to the bottom of the sleeve (Figures 10-27, 10-28). Include any ribbed trim at the cuff of the sleeve

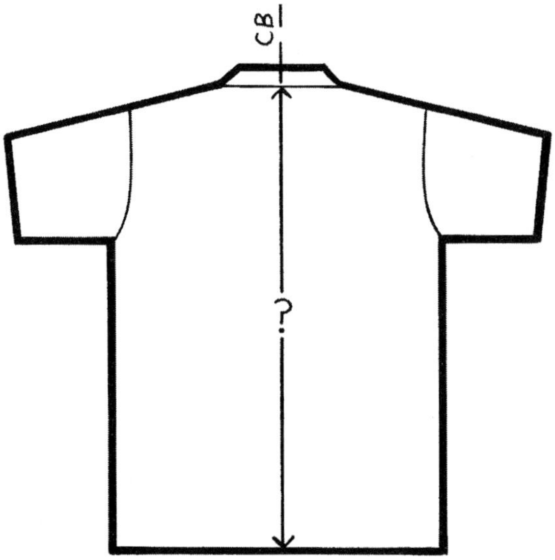

Figure 10–25
Center back length measurement. Artwork by Mary Lisa Caramico.

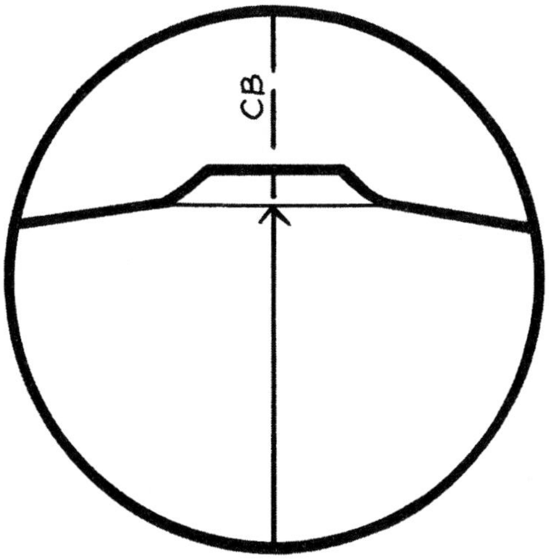

Figure 10–26
Center back length measurement point, close up. Artwork by Mary Lisa Caramico.

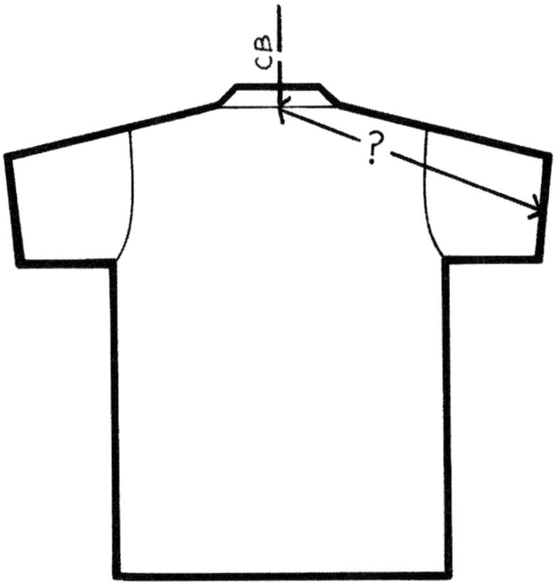

Figure 10–27
Sleeve length measurement. Artwork by Mary Lisa Caramico.

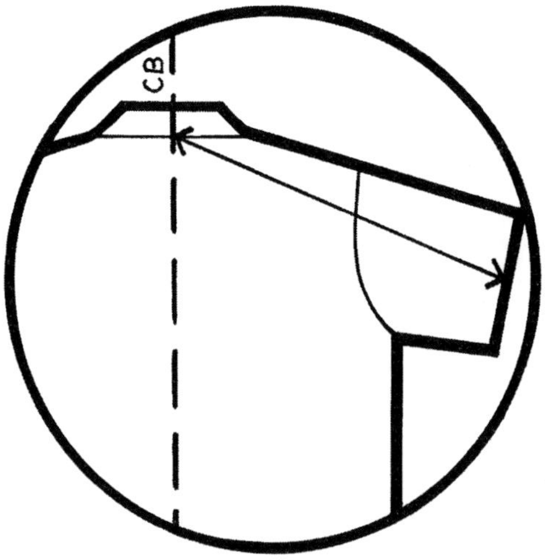

Figure 10–28
Sleeve length measurement point, close up. Artwork by Mary Lisa Caramico.

Put your measurements on this chart:

Code	Measurement	Size Small
A	Chest	_______ inches
B	Sweep	_______ inches
C	Center back length	_______ inches
D	Sleeve length	_______ inches

Obviously, there are many other points of measurement that would be taken for actual product development. Chest, sweep, body length, and sleeve length are usually the most important for tops.

Third: Complete the Spec Measurements for Sizes Medium and Large

Once you have finished with the size small, measure the medium and large women's T-shirts, following the same steps outlined above. Fill in the measurements for those sizes.

Code	Measurement	Small	Medium	Large	
A	Chest	_____	_____	_____	inches
B	Sweep	_____	_____	_____	inches
C	Center back length	_____	_____	_____	inches
D	Sleeve length	_____	_____	_____	inches

Are both your sketches (front and back) clearly identified with the codes? Are the measurements noted for each size on the chart? Now, exchange spec sheets with another student, and see if his or her spec sheet looks like yours.

- How many had identical measurements?
- Were all measurements taken at the right place(s)?
- Can you figure out what the grade is from size to size? Remember, grade is the difference between the sizes. For example, what is the difference in the chest measurement between size S and size M; between size M and size L, and so on?

Fourth: Repeat Steps One, Two, and Three Using the Men's T-Shirt in Four Sizes

For these exercises, divide the class into four groups of students. Each group should measure and spec one of each of the four Men's sizes. Then, by writing each group's findings on a large size spec sheet on the board, the class can "discover" what the grade is between the garments.

Code	Measurement	Small	Medium	Large	X Large	
A	Chest	_____	_____	_____	_____	inches
B	Sweep	_____	_____	_____	_____	inches
C	Center back length	_____	_____	_____	_____	inches
D	Sleeve length	_____	_____	_____	_____	inches

One note: We have told you that sewing garments is an imperfect science. We think you are going to discover this by looking at the grades. The group might come up with slightly irregular (but accurate) measurements. That is because each garment is not sewn exactly to spec, it is sewn within a specified tolerance or deviation from the spec. As a group, you might have to do a little creative "rounding up or down" to figure out what the intended grade is between sizes. (Actually, in the industry, you never rely on the measurements of just one retail sample to determine a competitor's spec. It's usually best to measure four to six garments of each size and then round off using all the measurements.) Note also that there might be a different grade between sizes, meaning between size S to size M, the grade could be 4 inches, from size M to size L, it could be 4 inches, but from size L to size XL, it might be only 2 inches.

CHAPTER 11

Production: Go, Team, Go!

IN THE FACTORY

The actual production of garments is a little like a football game. The quarterback (the production manager) leads a team of people, each with different skills, whose job is to complete production within the allotted time. There is no overtime; the retailer can legitimately cancel an order if it isn't delivered on time. This means that the whole team loses. Each team member makes a critical contribution:

Felix Garcia and Lawrence Behar discussing production issues on the Ike Behar factory floor. Courtesy of Ike Behar.

Production Manager

Generally, production managers are either gray or bald! Ultimate responsibility rests on his or her shoulders. If everything runs smoothly, he or she is just doing the job. If anything goes wrong, it is always the production manager's fault! The manager tries to schedule just the right flow of work through the factory. If there is too much, mistakes will be made in the rush. If there is too little, time (money) will be wasted. Some of the trained employees might even leave to find work elsewhere if they don't have steady work. The production manager must have seasoned managerial skills—all the rest of the functions outlined below fall under his or her jurisdiction. This responsibility can be pictured as an umbrella over everything and everyone in this chapter.

Quality Control (QC)

Making sure that every garment produced is of the appropriate and agreed-upon size specs and quality level is a bigger challenge than you might realize! There are numerous components and operations required for even the simplest garments. With so much pressure on keeping prices low, everyone in the process is trying to use the least expensive but still acceptable materials, put together in the shortest possible time. It's a very fine line between acceptable and unacceptable quality. Of course, in high-quality lines, only the best materials are used. But even there, quality control personnel need to stay alert.

THE INSIDE SCOOP

CLEO RYAN

Cleo is the vice president of worldwide quality assurance for the Donna Karan Company. Prior to that she had spent many years in quality control and management, including 14 months running AMC's Hong Kong/China office.

On the repercussions of quality:

While quality control is expected to have some immediate visible impact on product or service, the real return on investment may take several years. As QC policies and procedures are implemented consistently over time, the QC pendulum picks up momentum, having an ever-increasing positive impact on supplier and customer perception. Concurrently, the initial organizational "pains" suffered in setting a quality approach are usually "cured" with employee education and the time it takes for the process to become a routine way of business.

Conversely, inconsistent implementation of a quality control philosophy, or override of quality standards in favor of other short-term financial goals, can produce a slow, sometimes subtle erosion in quality of product and service. Unfortunately, by the time this erosion has the company's attention, the negative momentum of the pendulum may have swung so far already as to have caused irreparable damage to the organization's reputation for quality. The short-term goals for which quality was sacrificed are often a faint memory. Recapturing credibility with the customer becomes at best, an arduous task; at worst, a lost cause.

Most manufacturers and wholesalers entrust this responsibility only to very experienced, technically trained pros. Don't expect a startup job here! Chances are that a quality control (QC) professional will have an engineering degree plus significant production-line experience. They would be entrusted to:

- Evaluate yarn and fabric mills for suitability.
- Evaluate garment production plants to see if the required quality level can be achieved. They can also tell (after just a few minutes) how efficiently the plant is working.
- Know the capabilities of spinning, knitting, dying, cutting, and sewing machinery.
- After all this preliminary investigatory work, QC will typically inspect piece goods before they are cut (Figure 11-1) and monitor the garment production to be sure that all measurements and other requirements are being met. Most importers require that their own QC person or agent issue a *certificate of inspection* before the goods can be shipped.
- Tests for **shrinkage**, **seam strength**, **colorfastness**, and other points of performance will also be conducted by QC.

Shrinkage
Change in length and width after washing and drying.

Findings Buyer

The findings buyer is responsible to order findings (zippers, thread, linings) (Figure 11-2) and trimmings (buttons, appliqués, etc.). If a zipper ordered by the findings buyers is too short or if a button is late, the entire production has to be held. Problems or delays with findings are the most frequent reason for delivery delays. So it might not seem that ordering buttons is a big job until you grind the entire production line to a halt.

Seam Strength
Seams are tested by attempting to pull them apart. Minimum standards of strength are set.

Colorfastness
The ability of dyes to remain on the intended fabric (usually during washing) and not to run onto other fabrics.

Figure 11-1
Piecegoods waiting for inspection. Courtesy of Alan Stuart, Inc.

Figure 11-2

Even the correct thread color is critical. Courtesy of Alan Stuart, Inc.

Patternmaker

A patternmaker works closely with the designer and is sometimes called *assistant designer*. This person takes the designer's original sample pattern and modifies it so that the garment will be practical and easy to sew. The pattern will be drawn in the standard sample size (Figure 11-3). The itemized listing of all the pattern pieces and components for each style is called the *cutter's must* (Figure

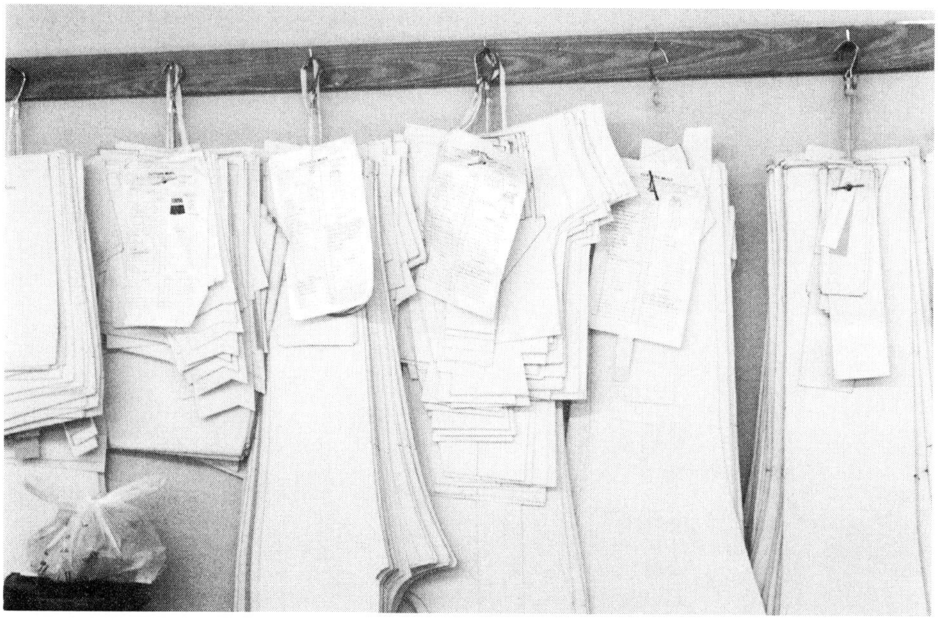

Figure 11-3

Pattern pieces. Courtesy of Alan Stuart, Inc.

11-4). This is used to make sure that every fabric, lace, button, or zipper that is needed to make the garment will be anticipated and accounted for.

Grader

The grader takes the pattern generated by the patternmaker and makes the patterns for the other sizes. Each pattern piece must be made larger or smaller (graded) for the rest of the sizes that are being made (small, large, extralarge, for example, if the patternmaker made the first pattern in size medium) (Figure 11-5).

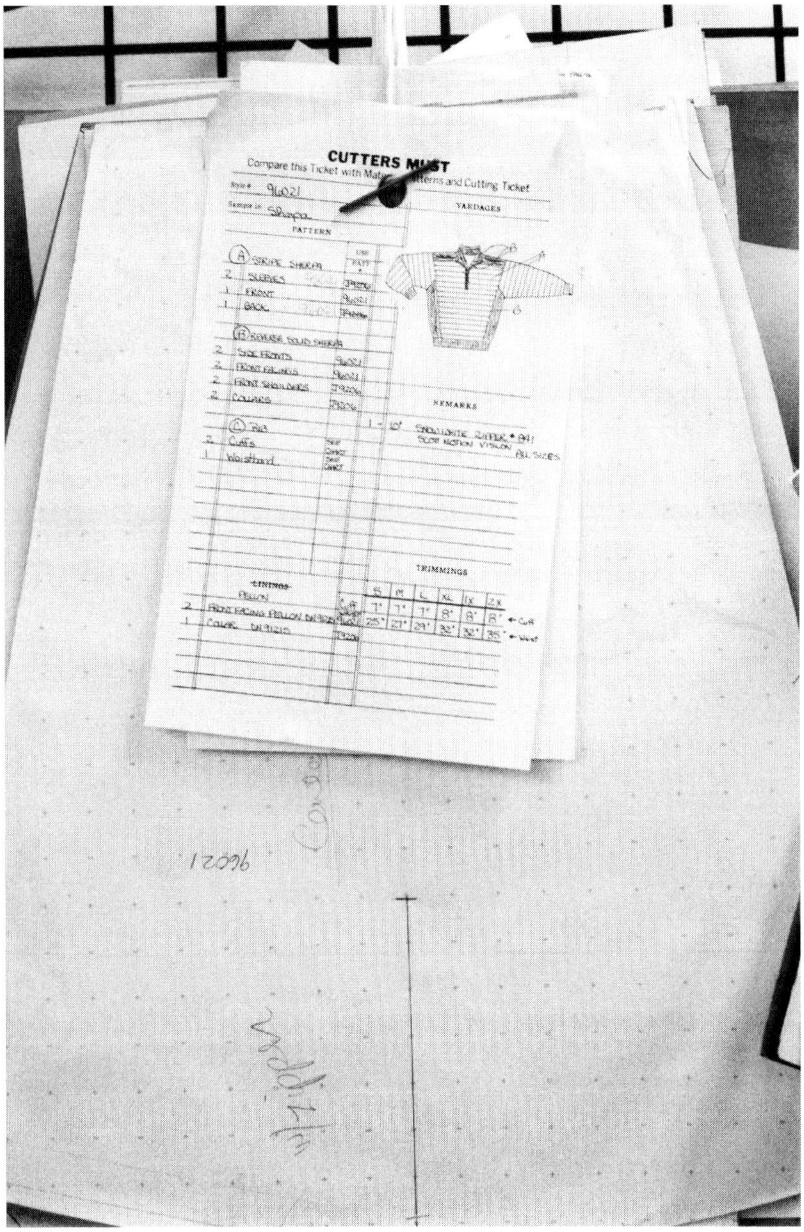

Figure 11-4

The "cutter's must" lists every component that the garment requires. Courtesy of Alan Stuart, Inc.

Marker Maker (Figure 11-6)

This team member arranges all the pattern pieces on a paper of the same width as the fabric. He or she will arrange and rearrange the pieces until they fit together tightly, wasting the least possible fabric. To give you an idea of how tricky this is, an experienced marker maker might lay out only one or two styles per day. If the pieces don't fit together as tightly as possible, profit will

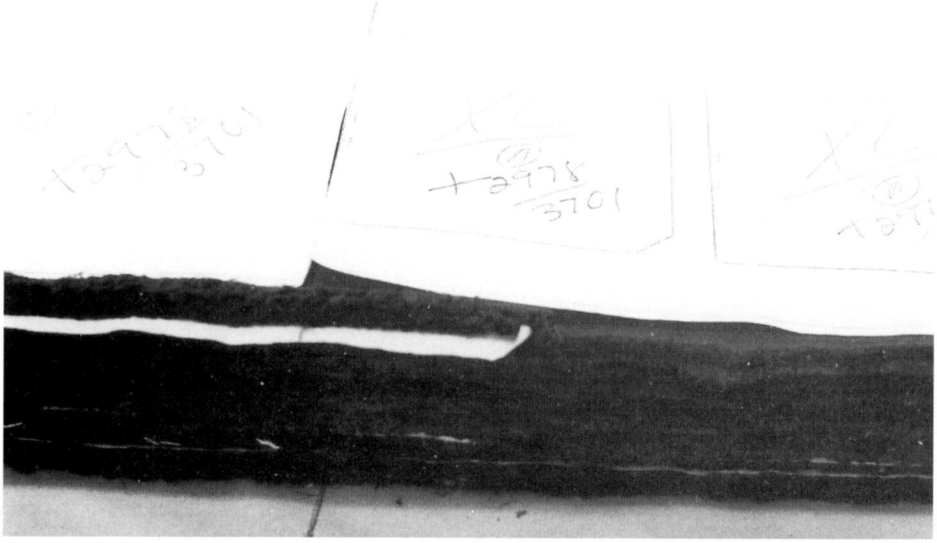

Figure 11-5

Components for different-sized garments are cut together. At this corner of the marker, you can see two XL pattern pieces. Courtesy of Alan Stuart, Inc.

Figure 11-6

The marker maker carefully arranges pattern pieces to use the least possible fabric. Courtesy of Alan Stuart, Inc.

THE INSIDE SCOOP

WENDELL WATKINS

Wendell is the vice president of manufacturing for Harwood Companies, Inc. Harwood produces private-label boxer shorts (2.5 million dozen a year) for customers such as L.L. Bean, Hanes/Michael Jordan, J. Crew, Polo, and J.C. Penney.

On the importance of marking correctly:

Fabric is the most important thing. It represents so much of the cost of the garment. It can be 40 to 60% of the total cost, depending on where you produce. If you throw even 10% of that fabric away, that's a lot of money! You can make or break yourself by saving fabric.

be lost. The pattern pieces are then traced in place on the paper, which becomes the marker. (In Chapter 14 you will see how many of these operations have now been automated on computers.)

Spreader (Figure 11-7)

The spreader rolls out layer upon layer of fabric on the cutting table. If the fabric is patterned (requiring matching at the garment seams), each piece must be lined up very carefully on top of the last one. Also, the spreader

Figure 11-7
Fabric spreader. Courtesy of Ike Behar

THE INSIDE SCOOP

S. Miller Harris

Miller joined Eagle Shirtmakers in 1946, almost 80 years after it was founded by his great-grandfather, and headed it for most of the ensuing 37 years. After a brief retirement he was called back by Smart Shirts Ltd. (Hong Kong) to head up their stateside office. His mission: to build an organization focused on design and merchandising in order to make an offshore contractor user friendly. His final assignment was the launch of Kellwood's (Smart's parent company) first men's branded venture, the Nautica dress shirt collection.

On squeezing out those pennies:

By the middle 50s at Eagle we were designing all our own patterned shirtings. We soon realized that since these fabrics were being woven to our specifications, we could engineer the design for maximum yield. It was also our custom to select the most aesthetically pleasing centerline for each pattern—the line on which the front buttons and buttonholes are sewn—so that every shirt of that pattern, no matter what size, had the identical repeat. If the repeat of the stripe was close to 1½ inches (the width of the top center), there was danger that the stripe on the placket edge would overlap the same stripe on the shirt and that since the placket was constructed with a folder, there was a chance that the placket edge would look wavy.

We devised a clear plastic template which we laid on top of the painting or handwoven sample of the proposed pattern. It had one stripe for the centerline flanked by two others to indicate the width of the placket. We could see immediately if the pattern as it then existed met our parameters. If it did not, we would adjust the repeat—either wider or narrower—a fraction of an inch on each side.

We then instructed the mill to weave every pattern with that center stripe precisely ⅞ inch (a figure developed by our cutting room staff for maximum yield) from one selvedge [this is the edge of the fabric]. The results: perfectly matched fronts and plackets; no wavy edges to the plackets; every shirt identical; and—most important to our controller—no wastage on the floor!

Fabric Shading
Slight irregularities in color from one part of a bolt to another or from one bolt to another.

watches closely for **fabric shading** within or between bolts of fabric. Finally, the paper marker is laid on top of these layered fabrics (Figure 11-8).

Cutter

The cutter uses a cutting "knife" (Figure 11-9), which is like a hand-held electric jigsaw, to cut out the pattern pieces from the whole layered stack of fabric at one time (Figure 11-10). The paper marker provides the cutting lines. If a mistake has been made earlier by the patternmaker or grader, it's almost impossible to reverse the error once the fabric has been cut.

Bundler (Figure 11-11)

The bundler ties together the various cutout pattern pieces. Then the production ticket is attached (for organization). Trims, findings, and care and main labels are bagged with the bundled pieces that will receive them.

Figure 11-8
A paper marker is laid on top of the stacked fabrics. Courtesy of Ike Behar.

Figure 11-9
A cutting knife is used to cut multiple layers of fabric. Courtesy of the Harwood Companies, Inc.

Figure 11-10

After cutting, there is a stack of identical pattern pieces. Courtesy of Ike Behar.

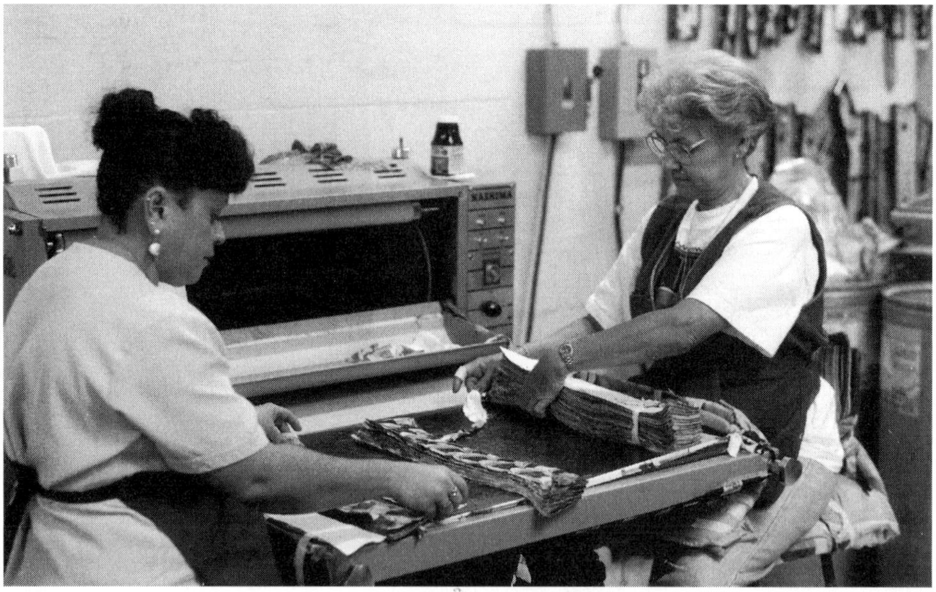

Figure 11-11

The cutout pieces are bundled together. Courtesy of Alan Stuart, Inc.

Operator (Figure 11-12)

The operator is the person who actually sews. Each person along a sewing line generally does one operation (buttonholes, closing seams, or attaching the collar, for example). Afterward, they pass that bundle on to the next operator, who does the next sewing step. Even for simple garments, a sewing line is often 15 to 20 people long, some using very specialized machines (Figure 11-13).

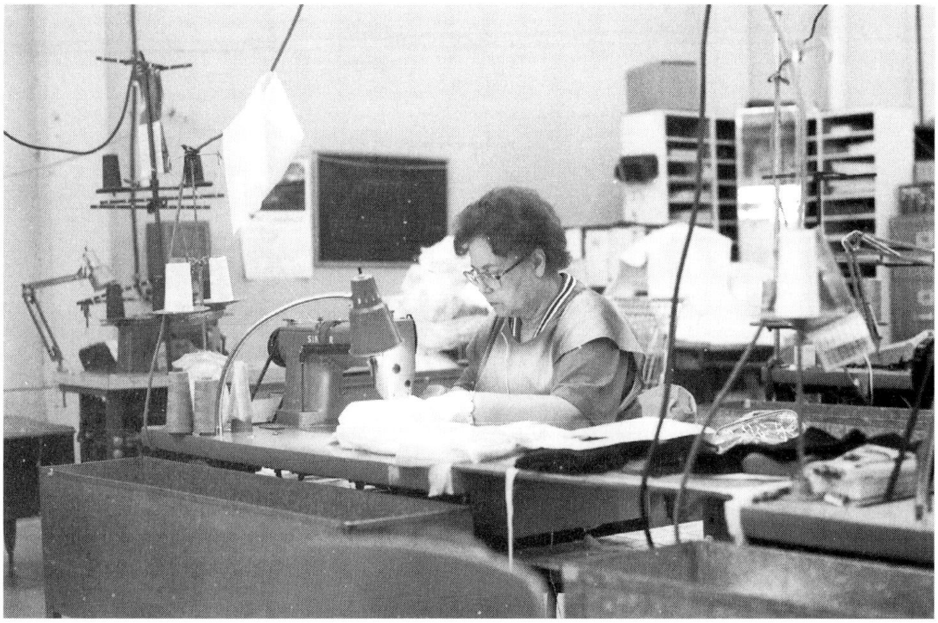

Figure 11-12

The operator sews the pieces together. Courtesy of Alan Stuart, Inc.

Figure 11-13

Specialized multineedle chain stitch machine. Courtesy of the Harwood Companies, Inc.

(*Note*: A new concept has also emerged, called *production pods* or *modules*. Fewer people do more operations each. As in the auto industry, this is being tried to counteract the carelessness that can come from assembly-line production.)

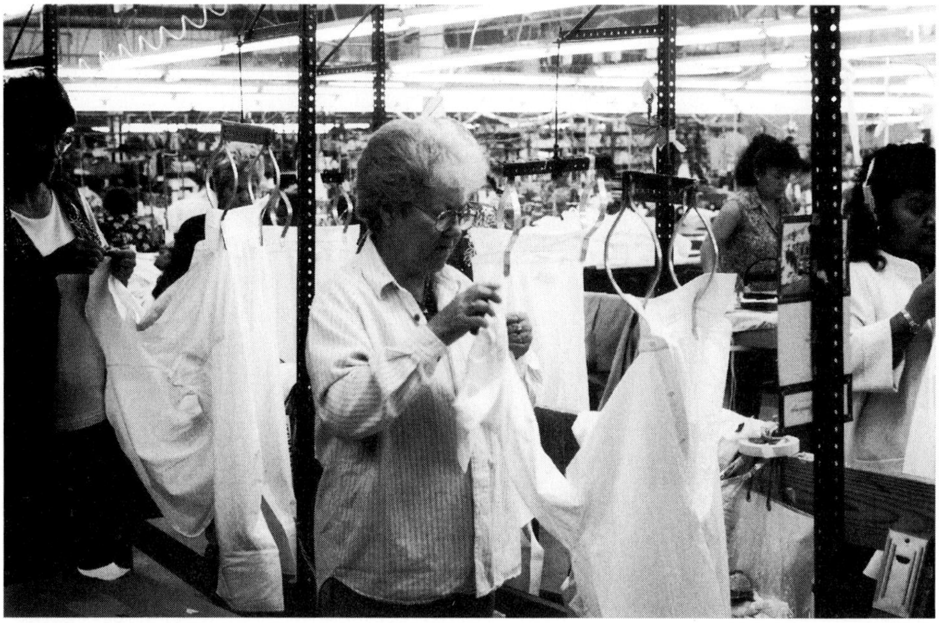

Figure 11-14

Each shirt is meticulously inspected at the Ike Behar plant in Miami. Courtesy of Ike Behar.

Operators have a difficult job. They have to sew at lightning speed with total accuracy. Half an inch off will be out of tolerance, and this garment becomes a reject. Just as they have gotten used to sewing one tricky style, that one is done and the next, different (tricky) style is now coming down the line.

Final QC (Figure 11-14)

Final QC people check for errors and decide if a garment is OK or if it must be sent back to the line for repairs or be discarded. Every garment that reaches this point but cannot be shipped represents a big loss (think how much time and material has already been invested). QC might also snip off loose threads and attach paper tags.

Finishers (Figure 11-15)

Finishers are the final pressers who make the garment presentable for sale. Folding is sometimes partially mechanized (Figures 11-16 and 11-17).

Packing/Shipping

Packers and shippers put the garments in bags (Figure 11-18) or in boxes or on hangers. They must pull and pack accurately because the packing slip and invoice (the bill to the customer) must match exactly (Figure 11-19). If there is a discrepancy, bills don't get paid. The department also arranges the transportation of garments from the factory.

Delivery

After solving dozens of little problems along the way, our precious shipment is ready to be delivered. In some cases, this could be as simple as carting it across

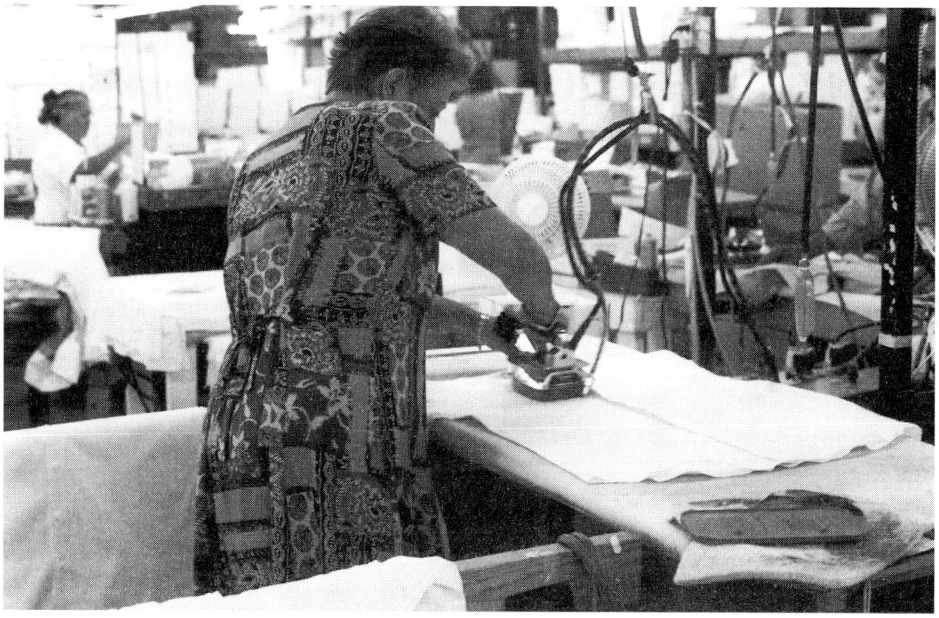

Figure 11-15
Final pressing. Courtesy of Ike Behar.

the street to the wholesaler's warehouse—or more likely, shipping it halfway around the world from the contractor's sewing plant in Bangkok to the wholesaler's warehouse in Bayonne. Sea freight delivery from some of the more remote locations (Pakistan, Mauritius, Zimbabwe) can take as long as 60 days until it has reached the port, cleared **Customs**, and been delivered to the warehouse.

> ***Customs***
> The U.S. government agency that monitors imports and collects duty (tax) on them.

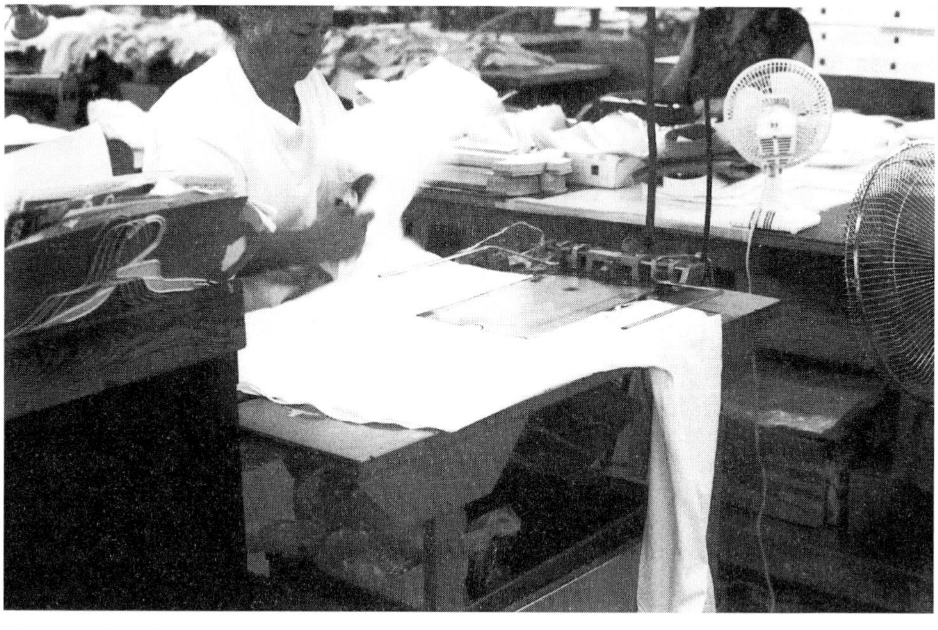

Figure 11-16
A folding machine...Courtesy of Ike Behar.

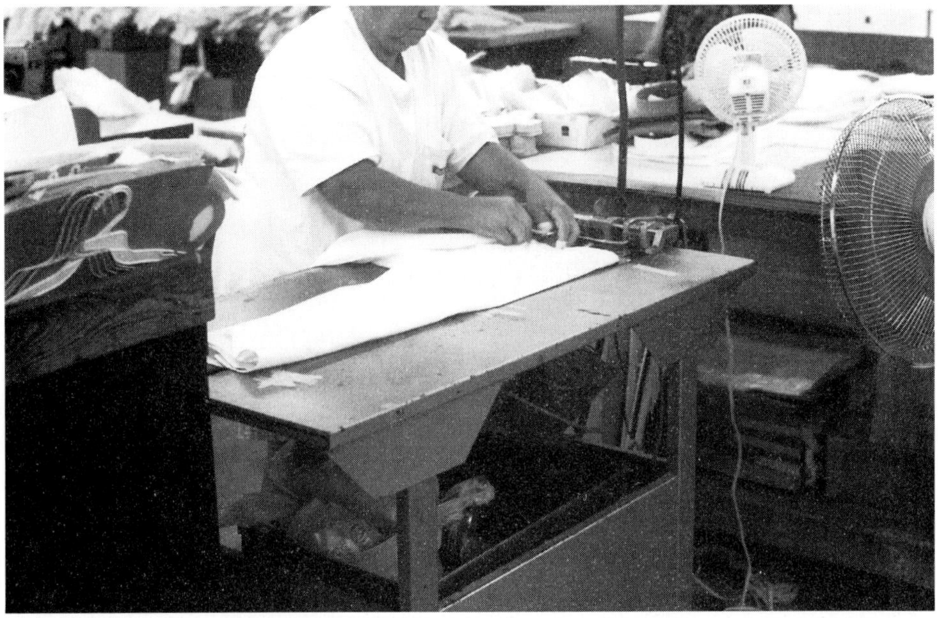

Figure 11-17

...ensures a crisp, consistent fold. Courtesy of Ike Behar.

Figure 11-18

Each shirt is carefully pinned and bagged. Courtesy of Ike Behar.

Cartons and Freight

Glamorous it's not, but important it is, that your merchandise get from factory to selling floor in good condition. Most garments shipped from overseas are folded, put into poly bags, then (usually) 12 to 48 pieces will be packed into a sturdy cardboard carton for shipping (Figure 11-20). Alternatively, some garments will have hangers already inserted and then laid flat in a carton. This saves time when they are received—the stores' receiving rooms don't have to put each garment on a hanger. It's already done (by someone earning less!)

Figure 11-19
Pulling and packing the correct assortment per order. Courtesy of Ike Behar.

Figure 11-20
Shipping folded garments in boxes. Courtesy of Alan Stuart, Inc.

There are even shipments on hangers hung on a rod in a wardrobe-type carton. This allows each garment to hang for the entire journey. Both of these alternatives cost more in packaging, and in the case of the wardrobe hanging boxes, a lot more in freight cost. But if the garments are very expensive and if shipped hanging they won't wrinkle, it might be worth the cost because they won't have to be repressed (expensive, again!) when they reach the United States (Figure 11-21).

Most cartons that are shipped by sea get packed into huge steel boxes (containers) that are 20 or 40 feet long. One container can hold as much as 20,000 adult turtlenecks, or 44,000 kids' turtlenecks. That's a lot! So imagine when you get this fax: "Your container of turtlenecks suffered water damage crossing the Pacific. Will have to unpack in Long Beach to see extent of damage. Thanks and best regards!"

If a store or importer orders enough to fill an entire container (FCL = full container load), it can travel intact all the way to the warehouse without being unpacked or repacked. This saves a considerable amount of money.

Knowing that almost anything could happen to delay production or shipping, most wholesalers give themselves a 30-day cushion from the planned arrival time in the warehouse to the required ship date to the stores. This cushion is doubly important if different components of a collection are being made by different contractors and/or in different countries. Even with the best planning it is impossible to have all the shipments arrive at precisely the same time. With the 30-day cushion, they can stagger in, and still all get shipped back out together as a package to the retail stores. Also during this time, a spot QC inspection might be conducted in the wholesaler's warehouse to make sure that there are no problems with the completed merchandise (Figure 11-22).

Figure 11-21

Shipping garments on hangers (called "g.o.h." in the trade). Courtesy of Alan Stuart, Inc.

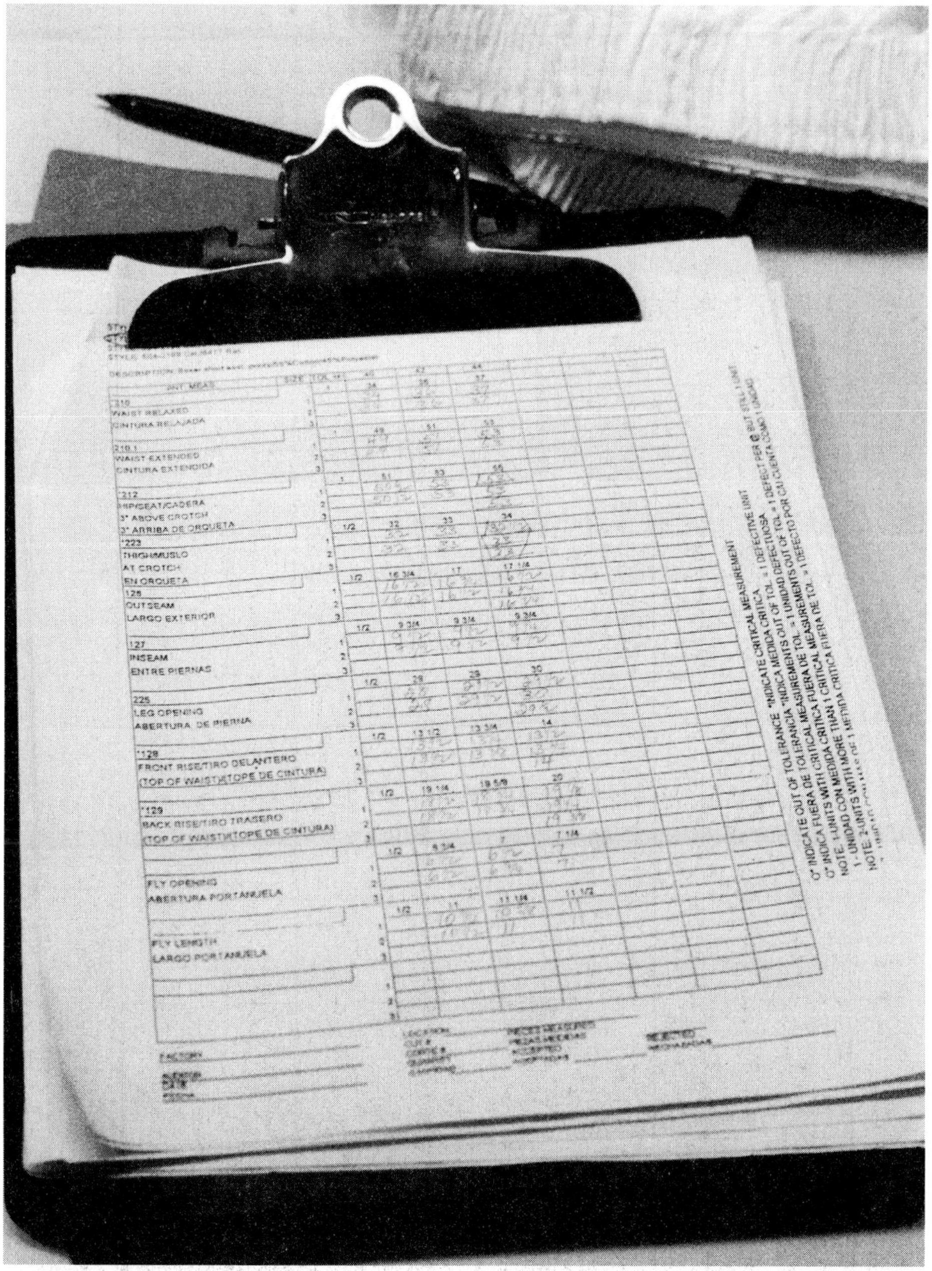

Figure 11-22

Spot quality control log: checking a selected number of garments to make sure they measure "to spec." Courtesy of the Harwood Companies, Inc.

More and more, retail stores are requiring smaller but more frequent deliveries of merchandise. In the past, they might have "loaded up" with a whole season's inventory at the start of the season. Today, stores want to receive some new merchandise every month: This is better for their **cash flow**, and it gives their customers something new and exciting to see every time they come into the store.

> ***Cash Flow***
> One measure of corporate wealth, based on that company's ability to access its funds.

ONE'S EASY; NOW TRY 1000 DOZEN!

It's at this point that we like to take our students to see a real garment factory in operation. Standing in the middle of a building bigger than a football field, with the steady bustle of hundreds of workers, one student always says, "Yikes, how do you get from sewing one garment to this!" She's right: Sewing one garment and sewing 1000 dozen nearly identical and perfect garments are two totally different things. The "football team" usually means hundreds of people, not just a few dozen. And these team members depend on each other for their livelihood.

When you are a student in school, either your parents are supporting you or you are working outside the classroom to put yourself through school. But let's say that you have graduated and have now become the designer of a good-sized manufacturer. You walk the factory floor on your first day and see the hard-working and dedicated sewing operators, packers, pressers, and cutters busily filling a large order. It's at this moment that you realize that your obligation to do a good job is not just to yourself, to your boss, or even to your customer. It is also to all these people who don't make a lot of money, but what they make often supports entire families. They count on you to design a successful line so that they can keep their jobs. Their job is in your hands!

Ouch! What responsibility! But that's what teamwork is all about. You have to count on them to cut, sew, and press the garments correctly so that your efforts will be successful, too. When dealing in large-scale manufacturing, everyone has to understand clearly what he or she needs to do, and then needs to do it well. If not, the result is not an F on a report card—it is a financial disaster for many.

SO YOU WANT TO WORK IN THE FASHION BUSINESS? Here's How to Begin. . . Chapter 11

The cost sheets have been prepared, the spec sheets are complete, and now it is important to get that information communicated correctly to the production team. You've probably already surmised that the production teams are usually not next door to the designer studio. They could be miles away, or even in another country. Clear and professional communication skills are the foundation of success in any field. This becomes doubly important if you are working with people long distance (in the mills, in the factories, etc.) It becomes triply important when some of those people are overseas, where English is not their first language!

There are a few "tricks" to specific and clear communication in the garment world!

First: Gather All the Information Before You Start

Have everything related to this issue in front of you. It gets too easy to skip a few specifics (such as style number or spec measurement) if the information is not in front of you, but in a file someplace. Skipped specifics lead to misunderstandings every time!

Second: Assume Almost Nothing!

Don't assume that the reader "knows what you mean." Your job is to provide specific and crystal-clear details. Remember, you do not know to whom this message might be passed. Your primary recipient might "get" what you are saying, but how about the production manager or shipping clerk whom you've never met? Avoid slang: "This fabric looks cheesy!" will not be understood.

Third: Ask Your Questions

Be certain to include any questions that you need answered. People often don't reply if they are not asked to respond to specific questions. To make them very specific, number each question and ask that each question be answered by number.

Fourth: Establish a Time Line

If time is an important part of your correspondence, set up checkpoint dates, which will help you know what is going to happen when. When you promise something, always specify when you will deliver it. When you request something, specify when you need it.

Fifth: Always Sound Reasonable!

Strong emotions expressed in writing, such as faxes and E-mails, somehow end up sounding very emotional and severe. Keep your tone reasonable—firm if necessary, but not negative or accusatory.

First, let's give you some examples of unclear and clear phrases that were intended to say the same thing. . . Then afterward, let's see if you can "clear up" some fuzzy phrases.

Unclear Phrase	***Clear Phrase***
T-shirt style.	T-shirt, style 123.
Scheduled for February delivery.	Scheduled for February 28 delivery.
The shorts are too long.	Shorts, style 456: Inseam measurement of sample is 5 inches. Our spec calls for 3 inches.
Will shipment be on time?	Please advise: 1. Vessel name 2. Vessel number 3. Exact sailing date
Blouse collar looks funny.	Blouse collar point spec (code F) calls for 2 inches. Sample has been made to our spec; collar point measures 2 inches. However, now that we see the sample, the 2-inch collar looks too short. Please change collar point spec (code F) to 3 inches, remake sample with new collar, and resend. Please advise when you will be able to resend.
Have sent skirt sample to you, please advise your price.	Have sent skirt sample to you. Based on the specs of the sample itself, please advise your price. Please also advise the exact fabric construction on which this price is based. Sorry for the rush, but I need this answer no later than June 25. Can you get me the information by then?
Have sent toddler short sample and the size specs to be used for this style. Please advise your price.	Have sent toddler short sample. Have sent the size specs to be used for this style. Plan to use a S–M–L size scale of 2–6–4. Please advise your price.
Your lab dip looks too dark.	Lap dip is not approved. It needs to be 10 percent brighter (chroma) and 20 percent lighter (value).
Rush this shipment, or I'll never do business with you again!	Garments must leave factory no later than November 2.
[No reply]	Sorry, I still do not have an answer. Will be able to give you complete explanation tomorrow.
Will send you orders in April.	Orders will be in your hands no later than April 10.

Will be visiting Hong Kong in September. See you then!	Will be working in Hong Kong September 15, 16, 17. In advance of our appointment, please cost out objectives 31, 32, and 37. Specs are attached. Please bring to the appointment a swatch of each fabric on which the prices are based.
Do you have a jazzier fabric for this style?	Need to upgrade this style with a better fabric. Would prefer a softer, brushed hand. Can only increase garment cost by $0.50, however. Please advise exact fabric (and fabric construction) you would propose.
Dress is too expensive.	Sorry, price is too high on ladies dress style 567. Need to come down at least $1.00 on first cost. Fabric cannot be changed! Can you suggest any other changes that might save $1.00?
We need this jacket to ship from Hong Kong no later than September 15. What do we have to do?	We need this jacket to ship from Hong Kong no later than September 15. To achieve that ship date, please advise the trigger dates when you will need the following decisions: 1. Date you must have exact quantity. 2. Date you must have exact fabric construction. 3. Date you must have exact colors and the quantity for each color. 4. Date you must have finalized styling.

Now it's your turn to try this. Let's see if you can be more specific than these phrases are. and when you're finished, why not compare several in the class and decide which are the most clearly communicated?

Unclear Phrase	***Clear Phrase***
Our blouse	______________________
When will it ship?	______________________
	______________________
Color is "off"	______________________
	______________________
Sleeves look too long	______________________
	______________________
Sweater price is too high	______________________
	______________________

Orders are coming soon

This fabric is sleazy!

Need goods by January 10, or else!

Where's my order?

I want this T-shirt in October. What's it going to cost me?

CHAPTER 12

Selling the Line: How Final Is the Sale?

SALESMAN SAMPLES

Once the kinks get worked out on the first samples, most wholesalers have a number of **salesman samples** made up. The exact **production fabric** is ordered (but in a smaller quantity of 15 to 200 yards, depending on the size of the sample line). This is so that garments and swatches can be assembled for selling purposes. Retail buyers are under tremendous pressure to perform. They have to see what they will be shipped. These samples really have to be exact representations (color, fabric, make, styling) of what will be shipped if the buyer places an order. To save money (samples can cost up to five times as much as the same garment will cost in production), wholesalers will often show just one color or pattern in full garment form and have the other colors or patterns represented on a **swatch card**. CAD printouts are also widely used to represent secondary colors or patterns.

With a full **sample line** completed, where does the wholesaler meet his or her customer, the retail store buyer?

Salesman Samples
Sets of samples for salespeople to use when showing the line to their retail accounts (buyers).

Production Fabric
Not a sample, this is from the actual fabric that will be used to make the entire run of this style.

Swatch Card
A card with small pieces of fabric attached to show alternative patterns or colors that are available.

Sample Line
A full collection of sample garments that will be shown to retail buyers.

FOUR OPPORTUNITIES FOR SELLING

New York Showrooms

The New York Garment District is the "capital" of U.S. fashion. Along 7th Avenue and Broadway in the 30s are thousands of **wholesalers' showrooms**. Retail store buyers from all over the country come to New York to visit these showrooms and **to shop** the wholesale lines. Some showrooms are owned by one manufacturer or designer. Others could be multiline showrooms where the salesperson represents several different lines.

> ***Wholesalers' Showrooms***
> The offices where wholesalers have their sample lines and where they show these lines to buyers.

> ***To Shop***
> To visit, to look.

There are specified *market weeks* during which the new season's lines are unveiled. Most buyers come in at these times to see the lines as they open. The women's ready-to-wear market generally has five such weeks during the year:

Market Week	***Season Being Shown***
Mid-January	Summer/transitional
End February	Fall 1
End April	Fall 2
Early August	Resort/holiday
Early November	Spring

Men's, kids, and accessories are similar, if a little less frequent.

What is an appointment to "shop a line" like? Let's say that you're the buyer of moderate missy sportswear for Huxtable's Department Store in Tampa, Florida. You've flown in on Sunday afternoon so that you could start promptly at 9:00 a.m. on Monday of market week. Your first appointment is at 1407 Broadway, with Mar-Lee Casuals, a small but up-and-coming missy separates line. Over coffee the saleswoman will ask you how your current group from Mar-Lee is selling in the store. What's been good? What hasn't? She'll also probably ask what other vendors or items in your department are selling well. How is business overall? Are you planning increases or decreases for the upcoming season?

Before getting into the individual styles on the new line, your saleswoman might point out that the showroom has been set up (*trimmed*) to capture the mood of the new line. Perhaps there are props and backdrops to evoke a rustic feeling, or maybe a sleek, sophisticated tone, depending on the look of that season's line. Mannequins might be dressed in the most striking combinations of styles from the line.

The saleswoman will start with a description of the designer's concept for this delivery, based on international fashion direction merged with the knowledge of what the Mar-Lee customer has purchased (or not purchased) in the past. Presentation boards can be used to illustrate the concept. With this done, she will proceed to show the line style by style. Cost prices are quoted on most, if not all styles.

Here's where we go back to the concept of knowing your customer. Our saleswoman has probably worked with you and maybe even with the Huxtable buyers before you. From that experience, she knows that specifically at Huxtable's, the best-performing parts of past lines have been, say, the brighter and less expensive styles. In addition, from her other Florida accounts, she knows that she should steer you away from all long-sleeved styles. With this knowledge, our saleswoman steers you toward certain styles and away from others. She might even opt to skip a portion of the line that she knows won't sell at Huxtable's. After all, she wants you to be successful with her line so that you will come back the next season! Also, she knows your time is limited.

After the overview, you might go back to double check that you have noted down all the important styles for your purchase. You could have the saleswoman hang up just your proposed selection from the line, for your final review. With these notes by style/cost, you can either write your orders on the spot or when you get back to the store. Chances are that you will want to see more of the competing lines this week before making the final decision.

Three Other Ways to Shop

Even though New York is the center of fashion in the United States, there are *regional market centers* across the country with their own marts full of showrooms. It is easier for some stores to use these (more accessible) market centers. Some of the larger ones are in Los Angeles, Dallas, Atlanta, Chicago, and Miami (Figure 12-1).

Next, there are temporary marts set up in the form of *seasonal trade shows*. Minishowrooms are created by thousands of wholesalers, giving retail buyers a very efficient way to see lots of lines (including new ones) in a short period of time. Again, styles represented as CADs rather than samples help make these presentations more portable. The industry that has done the best job of

THE INSIDE SCOOP

ZACHARY SOLOMON

Zach trained at Abraham and Straus and then followed the important back-and-forth merchandising line/stores line career path: assistant buyer, department manager, buyer, branch divisional, DMM, MM branch store. After that he was GMM of ready-to-wear at May Company–Los Angeles, president of The Emporium in San Francisco, vice-chairman of May Company–Los Angeles. At that point he switched from retail to wholesale, becoming president of Perry Ellis and then of Ellen Tracy. He has also been the president and CEO of Associated Merchandising Corporation in New York.

On selling:

1. *Don't Oversell.* If you push a buyer to overbuy, he or she will always come out with a bad season, and this always comes back to haunt you.
2. *Be honest and realistic.* A buyer has to have confidence in what you're saying. She can't have the feeling that you're just trying to get the order. Don't let her buy what you know she won't be able to sell. She needs to know that you are getting the best assortment for her.
3. *Tailor each buy to the customer who will be coming into that particular store.* Your taste level is not always the same as the customer's. In fact, different parts of the country have different taste levels. When I was at Ellen Tracy, we found that the customers who bought Ellen Tracy in Texas, Oklahoma, Arkansas, and Louisiana were very conservative. So every season I would fight to be sure that we included a couple of 25-inch skirts that would cover the knee. Short skirts were great in New York, Los Angeles, or Chicago—but not in the southwest!
4. *Know when the sale is complete.* Don't keep selling when the sale has been made. Know when to stop!

Figure 12-1

Miami International Merchandise Mart. Courtesy of the Miami International Merchandise Mart.

this is menswear, with their show, MAGIC, held twice a year in Las Vegas. The women's ready-to-wear end of the industry has also started to participate (MAGIC/WWD).

There are shows all over the country featuring specialized market segments:

International Kids Fashion	New York
Designer's Collective	New York
Super Show (sports)	Atlanta
Surf Expo	Orlando
Southern Apparel Exhibitors	Miami

and many more.

The final area of sales is one that has seen better times: *road salespeople*. Not too many years ago, most purchases (even by major department stores) were handled by a local salesperson. They traveled from store to store with the line in the trunk of their car. But as we have learned, with the nationalization of retail, there are already just a handful of megaretailers left. They tend to negotiate directly with the heads of the wholesale companies (this is called *corporate selling*) rather than with a local road salesperson. Those salespeople left tend to service the small independently owned specialty stores in small markets across the country.

AFTER SELLING, ADJUSTING THE INITIAL BUY

Like any other business, the more inventory you have invested in what your customers do want and the less you have of what they don't want, the more successful you will be. Unfortunately, however, the wholesaler has to commit to (most of) the line before any retail buyers come in and place their orders. Something in the line might "take off" and book in much greater quantities than expected. Conversely, an item could have been projected to be a big booker, only to fall on its face. (These styles are called "dogs.")

Here is where that scrambling comes in that Dianne Ige told us about! How can existing orders be adjusted so there will be just the right amount of inventory for each style? There are quite a few tricks; we discuss here some of the most common.

Swing

When the wholesaler makes advance commitments for fabrics and/or garment production space, the mill and/or cutter might be willing to take the order with a clause that at a specified future date, this quantity could be altered up or down by 10 or even 25%. This adjustment is referred to as the **swing** quantity. It acts as an easy cushion if demand turns out to be greater or less than anticipated.

> ***Swing***
> The ability to adjust or alter a specified amount.

Switch

If a yarn commitment is firm and can't be changed, sometimes it is possible to take that yarn and knit it or weave it into something slightly different. For

Flat Interlock
Interlock is a knitted fabric, a variation of rib knit, which is made on a special interlock machine.

Drop-Needle (Ribbed) Interlock
The same interlock fabric but with a ribbed pattern (which is achieved by skipping some needles during knitting).

Twill
Fabric woven is such a way that it produces small, raised diagonal lines on the cloth.

Denim
A twill fabric made with white and indigo-dyed yarns.

Canvas
A heavy plain-weave cotton-type fabric.

Jersey
Plain-stitch single-knit fabric: All stitches on the face are knit stitches; all on the reverse side are purl stitches.

Jobbed Out
Sold off; usually implies sold at a loss.

Bulk
Same as production fabric.

example, the same cotton yarn would be used to knit **flat interlock** as it would to knit **drop-needle (ribbed) interlock**. If the flat interlock styles in the line underbook and the drop-needles overbook, you can switch the same (committed) yarn from one knitting technique to the other. An even more obvious example would be a gingham check fabric, which is shown in the line as a jumper and as a dress. The jumper's great, the dress is a dog. So switch all the piece goods to jumpers. ("Kill the dress, cut the jumper!")

Mill Goods

Mill goods are basic, running fabrics that are readily available and used extensively. This would include woven fabrics such as **twill**, cotton **denim**, **canvas**, and knitted fabrics such as **jersey** or interlock. If you need to back out of a commitment on one of these, chances are that the mill will be able to sell it quite easily to another customer (and thus, might not hold you responsible). Novelty, specially woven or specially knitted fabrics, or even mill goods dyed in unusual colors, become much more difficult to back away from. These fabrics will probably have to be **jobbed out** at a loss, with the loss being absorbed by the wholesaler who made the (unfortunate) commitment. But if you say, OK—for safety's sake I think I'll stick to mill goods in basic colors for my first line. Well, just picture how boring and "unspecial" a line like that would look! You've got to take some risks to be successful!

Shared Fabrics

One trick that many designers use is to repeat a fabric several places in the line, so adjustments can be made like the gingham example above. They can also be used as trims: for example, using a shirt fabric as the lining in a jacket. If the jacket is a "dog," you can shift the lining fabric back to shirts.

Sample Looms

With some woven mills it is possible to place just a limited order of, say, 500 to 1000 yards of a pattern (a *sample loom*). A designer might put five patterns into work and have the fabric woven and this limited number of shirts made (250 to 500 shirts, approximately). Then, when the line is sold, it could be that only three of the patterns book well, so the designer would go back to the mill and place the **bulk** piece goods orders on just the three patterns. With all the preliminary set up and color matching already done, the mill can now produce more quickly the needed 5,000 or 10,000 yards, for example.

Staggered Trigger Dates

No, this is not a drunken brawl in a cowboy bar! As explained earlier, *trigger dates* are drop-dead due dates that are agreed upon by all partners. The point is to wait until the last possible moment to make the (irrevocable) decisions. Each decision is probably required at its own specific time. The later that each decision is made, the more booking or selling information you will have on which to base this decision.

REORDERS

When you're hot, you're hot! Sometimes, based on the strong initial orders received from buyers, or sometimes, based on very fast sales at retail (**check-outs**), a wholesaler might want to get more of a particular item. The trick is to produce it much more quickly than the original production, so that it can be made available as soon as possible. At times, available trims or fabrics might have to be substituted rather than waiting for customized materials all over again. There is a real art to making subtle substitutions that won't be noticed by either buyer or customer. It is common on reorders from overseas to pay the **surcharge** for **air freight** (over the regular, less-expensive **sea freight**) in order to gain 15 to as much as 45 days.

Checkouts
Merchandise that has sold quickly.

Surcharge
An extra charge.

Air Freight
Shipping merchandise via airplanes (expensive).

Sea Freight
Shipping merchandise via ships (less expensive).

Moving merchandise as quickly as possible in New York's garment district.

THE STUFF THAT DOESN'T SELL

This is not a perfect world! With every wholesale line release, there are going to be items that do not sell up to the level of already committed **inventory**. A good wholesaler minimizes this problem by taking the steps outlined in the preceding section, but it never works out exactly right. So what happens to the merchandise that you can't sell? The best thing is to try to recoup as much of the cost as possible, and there are several different routes to do this.

Inventory
Merchandise owned by a wholesaler or retailer at any given time.

Your Current Customers

The first choice is always to make a reduced-price (*off-price*) special offer to your current retail store accounts. This will allow them to run a special sale and encourage traffic in their stores. With this, the existing relationship

To Dump
To get rid of quickly and usually at a loss.

between wholesaler and retailer is actually enhanced. Conversely, this keeps the wholesaler from having **to dump** the goods in different stores, which might compete with the regular client stores. Keeping off-price goods in the regular client stores and not in off-pricers or other less desirable outlets is called *keeping your distribution clean.*

Outlets

The next most desirable place to sell off problems is a relatively newer phenomenon: the wholesaler's own clearance or off-price stores. Outlet malls filled with brand-name stores have become such a huge business that these stores cannot rely just on overruns and mistakes. These stores also buy and develop merchandise, especially for themselves. Still, they will often absorb the wholesaler's overages, even though they have become more independent and can no longer be forced to take something they feel they can't sell.

Off-Price Chains

Next are the national or regional off-price store chains, such as Marshall's/TJ Maxx, and Loehmann's. These very large organizations can absorb a lot of merchandise, but they will negotiate for sharply reduced prices on the wholesaler's overruns. To get this branded merchandise, however, most of these chains will agree not to use the brand names in advertisements. This is to help the wholesalers preserve their relationships with the stores that buy from them at full wholesale price.

Special Situation: Overages Overseas

Diverted
When merchandise gets sold or transferred to an unauthorized customer.

If merchandise is produced overseas and there is an overage, or even if there are seconds, sometimes the wholesaler/importer will buy this merchandise back from that overseas contractor. This is especially true for high-end status brands. They don't want this merchandise to be **diverted** and sold to unauthorized outlets. Some importers whose merchandise features highly recognized trademark logos or embroideries might insist that any merchandise that gets canceled (for example, if the manufacturer couldn't complete it on time) be destroyed! (We know of one importer who required videotapes of the burning of the garments!) Again, this is to protect their highly valuable and recognizable trademarks from ending up in the wrong places!

DIRTY LITTLE SECRETS

Vendor Matrix
A management-set listing of wholesalers from whom buyers must buy; an unapproved vendor is "off the matrix."

Here's what really goes on between wholesalers and retailers. As you have learned, there are fewer and fewer stores for wholesalers to sell to. The biggest chains of departments stores tend to have a **vendor matrix**, set by top management. This means that buyers are only allowed to buy from resources that have been preapproved by management. If you're not on the matrix, you might not even get a buyer to come in and look at your line!

The result of all this is a certain level of desperation on the wholesaler's part. They are desperate to get on the matrix, and they are desperate to stay on it. To ensure that their line will be profitable for the store, they might give that store some up-front guarantees:

- *Taking goods back.* There might be an agreement that if the store has merchandise left over at the end of the season, it can simply be returned to the wholesaler for a full refund.
- *Markdown money.* If the store has to take more markdowns than planned to clear the inventory, some wholesalers will reimburse them with a check to make up the difference.
- *Guaranteed gross margins.* This is similar to the above. The store and wholesaler agree at the start of the season what the store's percentage of profit would be on the line (*gross margin*). If at the end of the season, the gross margin falls below the agreed-upon figure, the wholesaler reimburses the difference.

The sad truth is that this game is an illusion. The only way that a wholesaler can afford to offer these guarantees is to inflate his original offering price. So the value of the merchandise is suspect from the beginning.

Our editorial on the subject of these dirty little secrets is this: An unhealthy trap has been created by this practice. Store buyers now often seek out the best deal, the best protection, rather than the best merchandise for their customer. The buyer comes out all right in the end as far as profitability is concerned, but there are more and more disappointed customers who don't find what they are looking for; and the overinflated initial prices just encourage shoppers to wait for the sales. It's a vicious circle. It's our opinion that this practice has been one of the major factors contributing to the accelerating demise of department store chains in the 1980s and 1990s.

This ends our production unit. We've made and sold our line. The process you have seen is the standard one. In Unit 3 you'll learn about some of the changes that are making this process easier on the one hand and more challenging on the other.

SO YOU WANT TO WORK IN THE FASHION BUSINESS?
Here's How to Begin. . . Chapter 12

FASHION TRENDS AND BRANDS PROJECT

It is now time to start putting all the information you have been researching in your journals together with what you have learned in this course. This project is designed for you to take a look at the garments being produced in the industry and compare their value, based on design, construction, and consumer acceptance. It is important to note that this project will reflect your opinion, based on your research, and there is no "right" answer as to what is the better product. Ultimately, your opinion will be a key factor projecting the success of a product or group line. A good fashion forecaster must always ask himself or herself, will the customer be willing to pay the price I am asking for this garment? Your research, knowing if your product is at the right place with the right value, will provide you with the foundation to make qualified decisions. Suggested research tools are identified in Chapter 6.

Part One: Identify the Balance of a Leading Designer

Identify an item or group line produced by a leading designer and discuss:

a. The philosophy of the products created by this designer
b. The consumer market being targeted
c. The store type (with examples) of where the product is sold
d. The characteristics of the product itself (the look, the price, the fit and durability, and if possible, where it was manufactured)

Part Two: Identify the Balance of a Leading Private-label Product

Identify an item or group line produced as a store's private label and discuss:

a. The philosophy of the products created and how these products relate to the store they are designed for (for example; the Arizona Jean Co. for Penney's: How does the product reflect the store image?)
b. The consumer market being targeted
c. The promotional approach and customer service presented in the private-label store
d. The characteristics of the product itself (the look, the price, the fit and durability, and, if possible, where it was manufactured)

Part Three: Identify the Balance of a Leading National Brand Product

Identify an item or group line produced as a national brand label and discuss:

a. The philosophy of the products created
b. The consumer market being targeted
c. The promotional approach and customer service presented in the store for these product labels.
d. The characteristics of the product itself (the look, the price, the fit and durability, and if possible, where it was manufactured)

Part Four: Compare and Contrast

a. Are each of these products meeting their consumers' needs?
b. Which product do you feel is more on track with the consumer market, and why?
c. Based on your research of the consumer, economic, fashion, and lifestyle trends, which product do you feel is the one most likely to generate the strongest sales? Why?
d. Based on your product knowledge, which product do you feel is the strongest value? Discuss why!

UNIT 3

Scale, Technology, Politics, and Geography: Where in the World Is All This Going?

In Unit 2 you learned the step-by-step process used to produce a garment. Surely this is enough to know, right? Well, no, not exactly. To make this work on a commercial scale and at appropriate pricing, you need just a few more skills.

In Unit 1 we learned that fashion is founded on an understanding of the customer, customer segmentation, and the spectrum of stores. In Unit 2 we saw what it takes to actually make a garment. Now, in Unit 3, we're going to look at the rest of the business tools that you will need to find success:

- What the calendar looks like when all seasons are figured in
- How technological innovations are making radical (good!) changes in the industry
- How government rules and regulations continue to have a big influence on what you can and can't make; and where you can and can't have things made
- Where you'll need to travel to produce affordable clothing
- Whether or not you can still have some garments made here in the United States.

Yes, there's lots more to this business than just design! Beautiful designs don't make you successful. Well-executed and well-priced garments that sell, do.

CHAPTER 13

Three Seasons at Once: Spinning Plates on Poles

As noted in Unit 2, we worked our way step by step through the product development process, from the first ideas right through to shipping and selling. In our example (fall season) we started with those first ideas in July (of the year before) and kept building for 13 months. At the end, we were finally ready to ship the completed merchandise to the stores. In graphic form, it would look like Figure 13-1.

Fall Line Development: The Timing and Action Calendar

July	*START HERE FOR FALL (F) First brainstorming, first ideas.
August	(F) Brainstorming continues.
September	(F) Dollars, SKUs, and deliveries broken down.
October	(F) Colors decided.
November	(F) Final line planner set; price and color information sent overseas.
December	(F) Manufacturers work on samples; price bids are submitted.
January	(F) Overseas trip; finalize vendors, prices, deliveries.
February	(F) Vendor orders piece goods and trims.
March	(F) Countersamples are sent from the manufacturer; patterns and specs are final.
April	(F) Piece goods and trims arrive; production begins. Line goes on sale.
May	(F) Production completed; shipped to warehouse.
June	(F) Goods arrive at warehouse.
July	(F) Merchandise is finally shipped to the stores.

Figure 13-1
Fall line development: The timing and action calendar.

Whew! It took a long time and a lot of thought and effort, but we did it—we shipped Fall! But don't stop to congratulate yourself yet! The next season, Holiday, doesn't start now. It started already! It actually overlaps with Fall! Holiday goes through exactly the same sequence, but it starts just a few months after Fall started (because you will ship Holiday to the stores just a few months later).

Thus, the first Holiday brainstorming starts in October (rather than in July for Fall). But then it plays out in the same sequence month by month. Also keep in mind that in October, when you are starting your first thoughts about next Holiday, you are actually also shipping the current year's Holiday line. So in the thirteenth month, the same season actually overlaps itself! Here is the same calendar again, but with the Holiday time and action sequence added to it (Figure 13-2).

Fall Line Development

Holiday Line Development

July	(F) First brainstorming, first ideas. *(H) Piece goods and trims arrive; production begins. Line goes on sale.*
August	(F) Brainstorming continues. *(H) Production completed; shipped to warehouse.*
September	(F) Dollars, SKUs, and deliveries broken down. *(H) Goods arrive at warehouse.*
October	(F) Colors decided. *(H) Merchandise finally shipped to stores. *START HERE FOR HOLIDAY (H) Brainstorming next Holiday.*
November	(F) Final line planner set; price and color information sent overseas. *(H) Brainstorming continues.*
December	(F) Manufacturers work on samples; price bids are submitted. *(H) Dollars, SKUs, and deliveries broken down.*
January	(F) Overseas trip; finalize vendors, prices, deliveries. *(H) Colors decided.*
February	(F) Vendor orders piece goods and trims. *(H) Final line planner set; price and color information sent overseas.*
March	(F) Countersamples are sent from the manufacturer; patterns and specs are final. *(H) Manufacturers work on samples; price bids are submitted.*
April	(F) Piece goods and trims arrive; production begins. Line goes on sale. *(H) Overseas trip; finalize vendors, prices, deliveries.*
May	(F) Production completed; shipped to warehouse. *(H) Vendor orders piece goods and trims.*

June	(F) Goods arrive at warehouse. *(H) Countersamples are sent from the manufacturer; patterns and specs are final.*
July	(F) Merchandise is finally shipped to the stores. *(H) See July above.*

Figure 13-2

Fall line development calendar with holiday line development slotted in.

Hey, this is getting complicated! But no, we are not done yet!! The Spring line is going to overlap both Fall and Holiday. And they keep overlapping all year (Figure 13-3).

Fall Line Development

Holiday Line Development

Spring Line Development

July	(F) First brainstorming, first ideas. *(H) Piece goods and trims arrive; production begins. Line goes on sale.* (S) Overseas trip; finalize vendors, prices, deliveries.
August	(F) Brainstorming continues. *(H) Production completed; shipped to warehouse.* (S) Vendor orders piece goods and trims.
September	(F) Dollars, SKUs, and deliveries broken down. *(H) Goods arrive at warehouse.* (S) Countersamples are sent from the manufacturer; patterns and specs are final.
October	(F) Colors decided. *(H) Merchandise is finally shipped to the stores. Brainstorming next Holiday.* (S) Piece goods and trims arrive; production begins. Line goes on sale.
November	(F) Final line planner set; price and color information sent overseas. *(H) Brainstorming continues.* (S) Production completed; shipped to warehouse.
December	(F) Manufacturers work on samples; price bids are submitted. *(H) Dollars, SKUs, and deliveries broken down.* (S) Goods arrive at warehouse.
January	(F) Overseas trip; finalize vendors, prices, deliveries. *(H) Colors decided.* (S) Merchandise is finally shipped to stores. *START HERE FOR SPRING (S) Brainstorming next Spring.
February	(F) Vendor orders piece goods and trims. *(H) Final line planner set; price and color information sent overseas.* (S) Brainstorming continues.

(Continued on next page)

March	(F) Countersamples are sent from the manufacturer; patterns and specs are final. *(H) Manufacturers work on samples; price bids are submitted.* *(S) Dollars, SKUs, and deliveries broken down.*
April	(F) Piece goods and trims arrive; production begins. Line goes on sale. *(H) Overseas trip; finalize vendors, prices, deliveries.* *(S) Colors decided.*
May	(F) Production completed; shipped to warehouse. *(H) Vendor orders piece goods and trims.* *(S) Final line planner set; price and color information sent overseas.*
June	(F) Goods arrive at warehouse. *(H) Countersamples are sent from the manufacturer; patterns and specs are final.* *(S) Manufacturers work on samples; price bids are submitted.*
July	(F) Merchandise is finally shipped to the stores. *(H) See July above.* *(S) See July above.*

Figure 13-3

Fall line development calendar with both holiday and spring line development slotted in.

Take, as an example, the month of December. In this month alone:

- For Fall, you will be evaluating the price bids as they come back from the manufacturers on the new styles.
- For Holiday, you will be taking your design ideas and breaking them down into a line, by style, by price, and so on.
- For Spring, you have this Spring's line arriving at the warehouse, ready to be shipped to the stores. And for next Spring (to follow the Holiday line above), you are just 30 days away from starting your first ideas on that!

You can't be serious! Yes, we are—and now you really know why they call it "work"! Every day you will find yourself addressing some issue on each of the three seasons. As you're planning a new season, you've got buyers in to buy the current line, and you've got a stack of faxes saying that the line under production has just run into some technical problem!

The best way to visualize what this job is like is to picture those old TV novelty acts where a man kept a whole row of dishes spinning on top of a row of poles. He would race back and forth to respin each plate just before it was about to drop to the ground (Figure 13-4). That's what your job will be like—running back and forth from season to season snatching each line from some unexpected disaster!

Oh, and just to make it even more vivid, keep in mind that many ready-to-wear companies have five lines a year, not three. Picture how many plates you'll have to keep spinning for that!

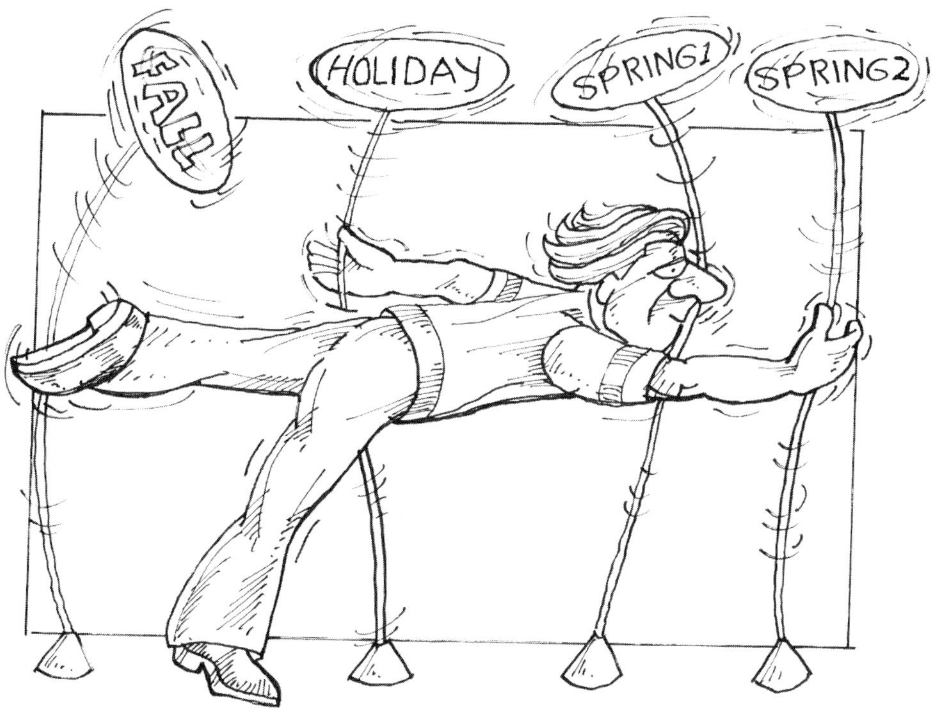

Figure 13-4

Artwork by Michael Carnegie.

SHORTENING LEAD TIMES

The battle cry of the 1990s. Great, let's just spin those plates even faster! In the calendar above it takes 13 months from idea to final sale. So you can imagine that finding a way to do all this in less time has become a hot topic!

Here's the ideal situation: On Thursday, a retailer sells one piece of a blue jumper size 10. On Friday the blue size 10 replacement jumper is shipped back into stock. If this were possible, it would be very hard for a buyer to guess wrong when he or she was ordering!

The opposite scenario is this: A complicated item in a complicated fabric is being custom-woven and custom-sewn for the store. A plaid jumper made from yarn-dyed cotton twill from China could take nine months or more from the time it is ordered by the buyer and the time it hits the selling floor. The further in advance you have to buy, the more likely customers might not want that item anymore by the time you finally get it!

So everyone in the process is looking for a way to order and receive merchandise in as short a time as possible. It's quite tricky, but there are several successful techniques:

- *Trigger dates.* Making each individual styling decision at the last possible moment to allow for more selling information to be factored into that specific decision. For example, 180 days in advance of shipment, commit to fabric construction; 150 days in advance of shipment, commit to fabric color; 120 days in advance of shipment, commit to garment styling, and so on.

- *Local production.* Cut out the shipping times. Using fabric from China to be shipped (30 days) to Sri Lanka, garments sewn and then shipped (60 more days) to the United States means that 90 days are spent just for transportation. Instead, you could use American fabric and American sewing and gain most of the 90 days back.
- *Quick response.* As we have already seen, this means speeding up the information flow between all parties so that nothing waits even one day.

When many of these techniques are put together and the process is clearly understood and agreed upon by all parties, the time frame can be shortened dramatically. We've even heard of start to finish in six weeks! This is called *speed sourcing,* but just leave it to the seasoned pros right now—it is really difficult. (The Limited is famous for being able to produce and ship merchandise out of the Orient in a matter of days! The advantage for them? To replenish inventories as soon as they discover what customers are starting to buy.)

CHAPTER 14

Apparel Goes On-Line

YOU'RE TELLING ME THAT "THING" AGAIN, AREN'T YOU?

You're telling me that I'm going to have to sit in front of a computer all day, right? Thank you very much, but I'm studying fashion, not accounting. I want to be a designer, not a computer geek.

Well, what can we say? Most designers have resisted the move to computer designing and sketching—that is, until they get the hang of it. It's kind of like the hassle you went through learning to drive a car. Once you mastered it,

Student Jonathan Grimes working with the Gerber system.

you couldn't imagine not driving. The systems makers have been sensitive to this problem and have redesigned many of them to be more "designer friendly." In fact, designers can now "draw" right on a computer screen with a cordless pen. They can select the look of water color, charcoal, or crayon. Patternmakers can work full-size on a board very much like their old paper pattern setup. More and more of these applications are compatible with MAC, PC, Windows, and UNIX.

There are other really significant reasons why these new systems can save lots of time, energy, and money. Once you get started with these tools, you will wonder how people ever did without. Because of this new technology, production can also be made more efficient. The main reasons for a wholesaler/manufacturer to invest in this (expensive) equipment are:

- Many tasks can be done much more quickly.
- Changes can be accommodated more easily, right up to the last minute, and everyone who is on-line will be aware of these changes.
- Much more uniform quality can be achieved, especially in an area such as cutting.
- Smaller, customized orders of many more styles can be handled more efficiently.
- Time is saved all along the design and production process, resulting in cost savings.
- One of the most remarkable advantages of all: Each step of the process can be done in a different location. Design could be in New York, patternmaking in Los Angeles, and cutting and sewing could be

THE INSIDE SCOOP

MICHAEL McKEITHAN

We met Michael, the CAD designer for Tommy Hilfiger, earlier.

On maximizing CAD:

It's not about just simply "working" the CAD machine. You can learn the functions in a week. No, it's what you bring to the machine, what else you know. You need an understanding of knitting, weaving, and printing techniques. If you don't know how cloth gets printed in a factory, you won't be able to get the most out of CAD. It's also a matter of trial and error. When I first started working with "repeats," some [repeats within certain] designs were not always apparent. It took a long time to figure it out, but then one day the lights went on and Boom! I was flying!

I love the challenge of CAD. It's like accomplishing the impossible: to take something really difficult and render it so it looks like an actual knitdown or hand-drawn art. And then to color it and make it look not just fashionable, but salable!

done in Mexico. All participants are linked electronically with the very latest information. Designs, patterns, and markers can be transmitted by modem or direct line between all locations.

Are We Convincing You?

It tends to get quite technical, but here is further proof of how much you are going to love your new computer helper. The two industry giants are Gerber and Lectra. Their capabilities are quite similar and here are some of the downright amazing things that their systems can do. In *design*:

- A huge library of prints, patterns, trims, buttons, and styles is stored in the computer. Do you need to see how your tunic sweater would look if it was done in a jacquard instead of a solid color? Push a button (Figure 14-1).
- Do you want to see how a patterned fabric will "drape" on a gathered skirt silhouette? The computer will make a three-dimensional image for you.
- Do you want to select different colors for your range of printed T-shirts? Some of these machines store 16 million individual colors to work with (Figure 14-2).
- Do you want to design a new fabric for your collection? You can simulate different weaves, knits, jacquards. You can **graph sweater** patterns automatically. You can print your newly created print right on a

Sweater Graph
To design a knitted item like a sweater, it is necessary to show the color and style of *each stitch*. This is usually drawn by a designer on graph paper, each box representing one stitch.

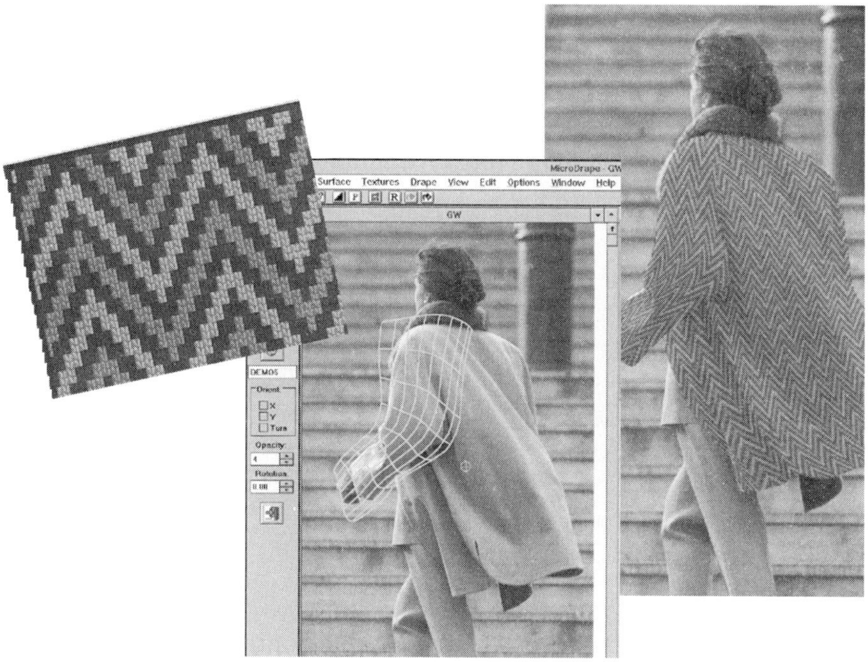

Figure 14-1

The jacquard pattern is "placed" on the solid sweater so that the designer can see what it will look like. Courtesy of Gerber Garment Technology.

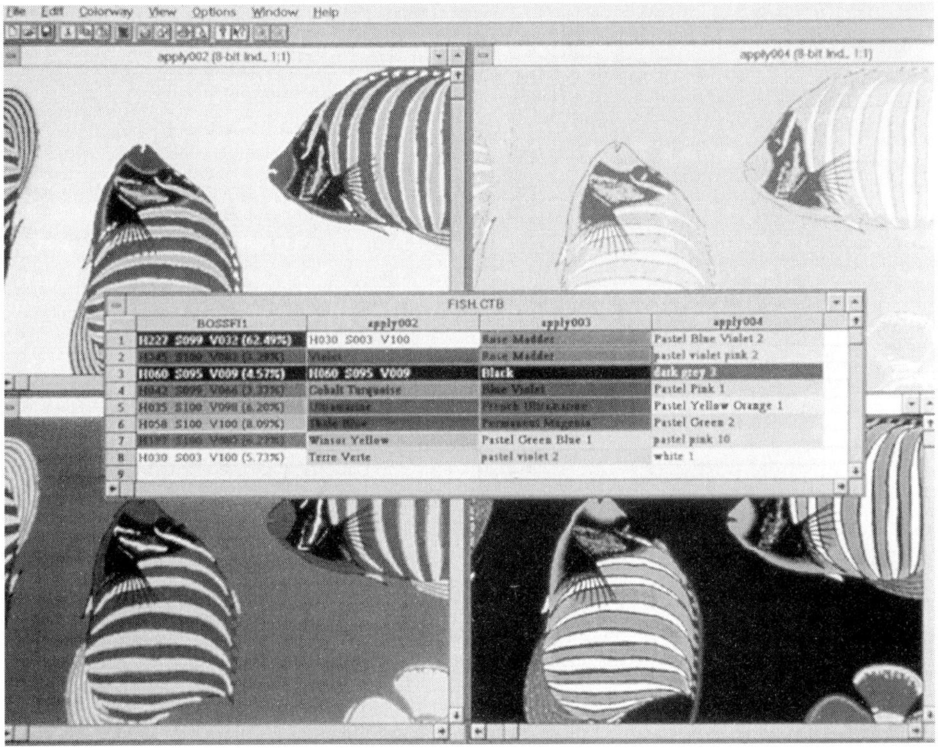

Figure 14-2

Four different color combinations of the same print. Courtesy of Gerber Garment Technology

sample fabric and then have a sample made up (Figure 14-3). You can also transmit your new print design directly to the fabric mill for bulk production.

- You can cost out each item with a built-in cost sheet calculator. You can do a "what if" check to see what a change in the design will do to the price. Change the buttons? Change the length? Change the fabric? The computer does the cost recalculations for you (Figure 14-4).
- You can take all your sketches and arrange them into work boards without resketching. You could also make final presentation boards and send them by modem to the sales force, who could preview them with key customers and send back their reaction! You could send out the completed collection on CD-ROM for customers to view in their own offices (Figures 14-5 and 14-6).

Are We Starting to Change Your Mind?

Without getting into too much detail, let us just tell you that this is only where it begins. The most important part of this computerization is that it links together many different stages in design and production. Next we'll look at just a few highlights of the current technology for the production end.

Figure 14-3

Scanning and printing fabrics. Courtesy of Gerber Garment Technology.

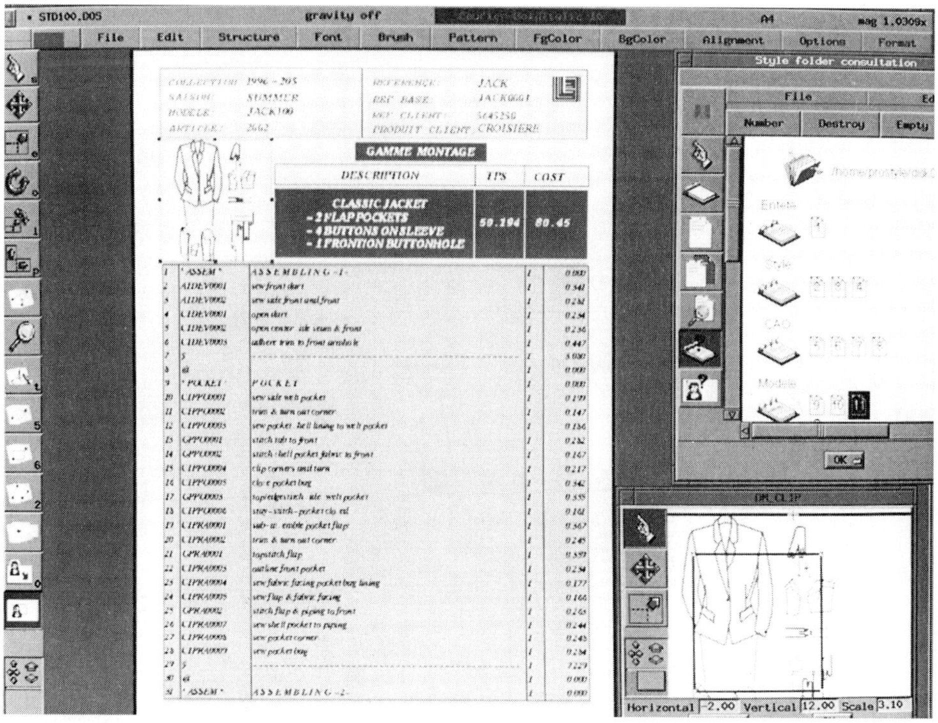

Figure 14-4

Cost sheet calculator. Courtesy of Lectra Systemes.

Figure 14-5

Work boards can be assembled automatically. Courtesy of Gerber Garment Technology.

Figure 14-6

Presentation boards showing alternative color combinations. Courtesy of Lectra Systemes.

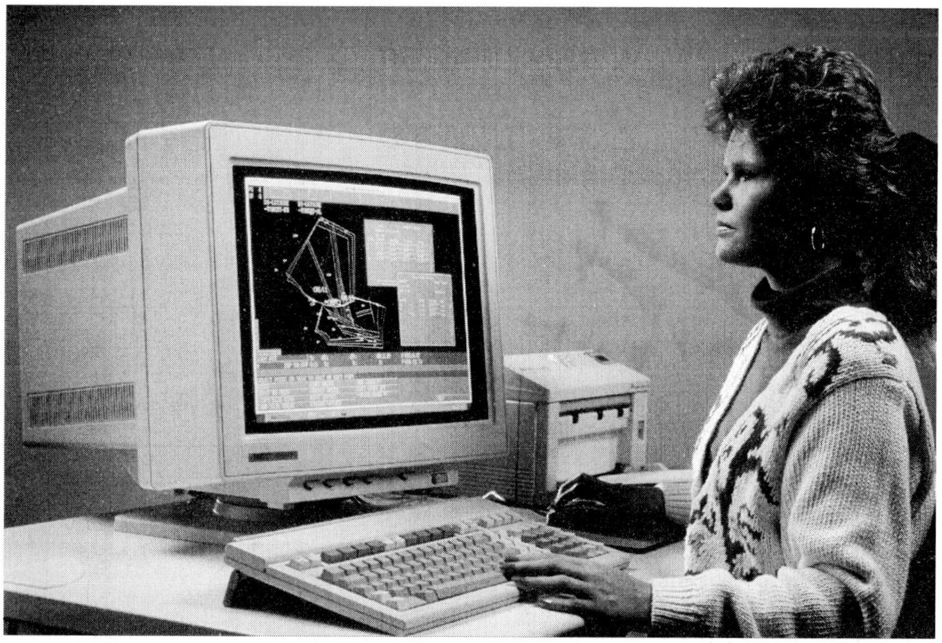

Figure 14-7

Patternmaking on screen. Courtesy of Gerber Garment Technology.

Patternmaking and Grading

Previously used patterns can form a quick basis for new patterns (Figure 14-7). These can easily be stored, retrieved, and tweaked on the screen. For experienced patternmakers who are only comfortable working fullsize, there is a system that can handle that. Some systems are able to call upon a database for the various body shapes of different population groups. Grading from size to size can be automatic, based on previously determined fit distinctions between sizes (Figure 14-8). Automatic adjustments can be made for seam allowances and even for shrinkage.

Marker Making

The marker maker can be programmed to find a way to allow only *x* percent of the fabric to be wasted, and it will work all night (by itself) until it finds the right layout of pattern pieces (Figure 14-9).

Spreading

This is when layers of fabric are laid out on the cutting table. Not only do these new automated machines do this to the exactly right length (they get the information on-line from the marker maker machine), but they can also handle the really difficult fabrics like stretch knits and **tubular knits** in such a way that they don't get stretched out during the process (Figure 14-10).

> ***Tubular Knits***
> Most knitted cloth is knitted on a circular machine that revolves, adding courses of stitches with each revolution. The fabric comes out like a giant tube—and is usually cut down one side to open it into a flat fabric.

Cutting

The fabric layers are held down with a vacuum system and then the already programmed cutter cuts them together (Figure 14-11). But how's this for amazing: The cutting knife knows when to resharpen itself, and on

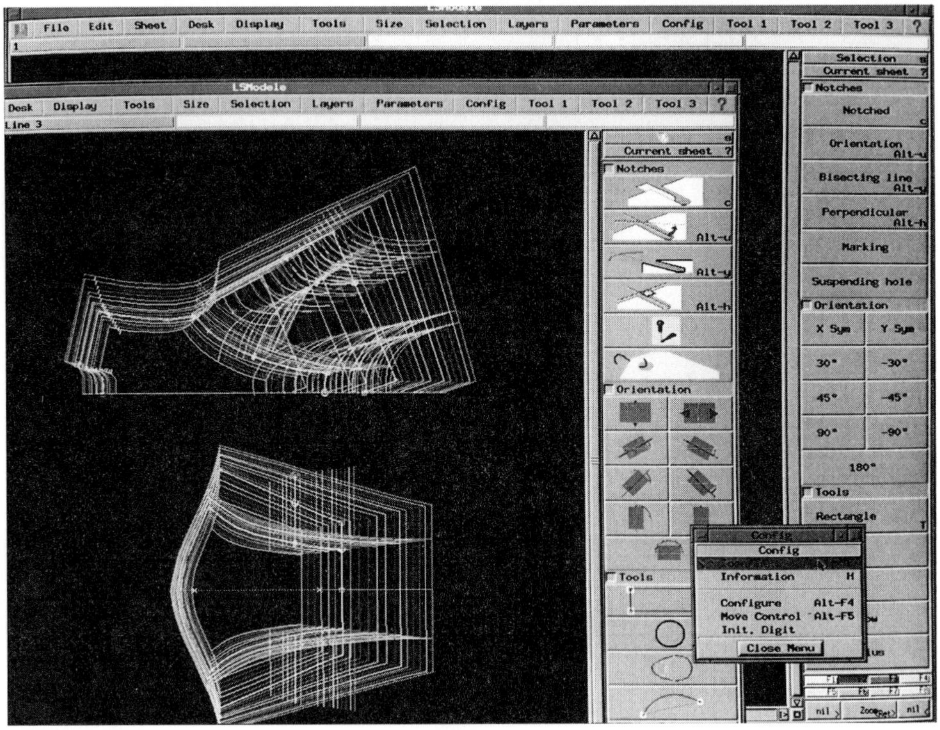

Figure 14-8

Grading on screen. Courtesy of Lectra Systemes.

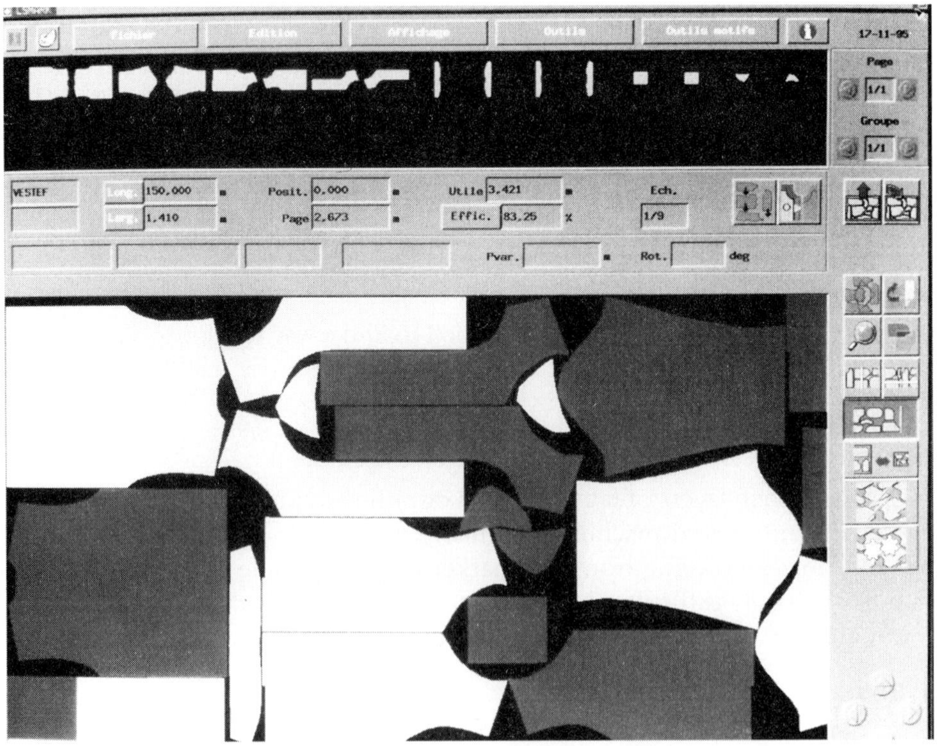

Figure 14-9

Marker making on screen. Courtesy of Lectra Systemes.

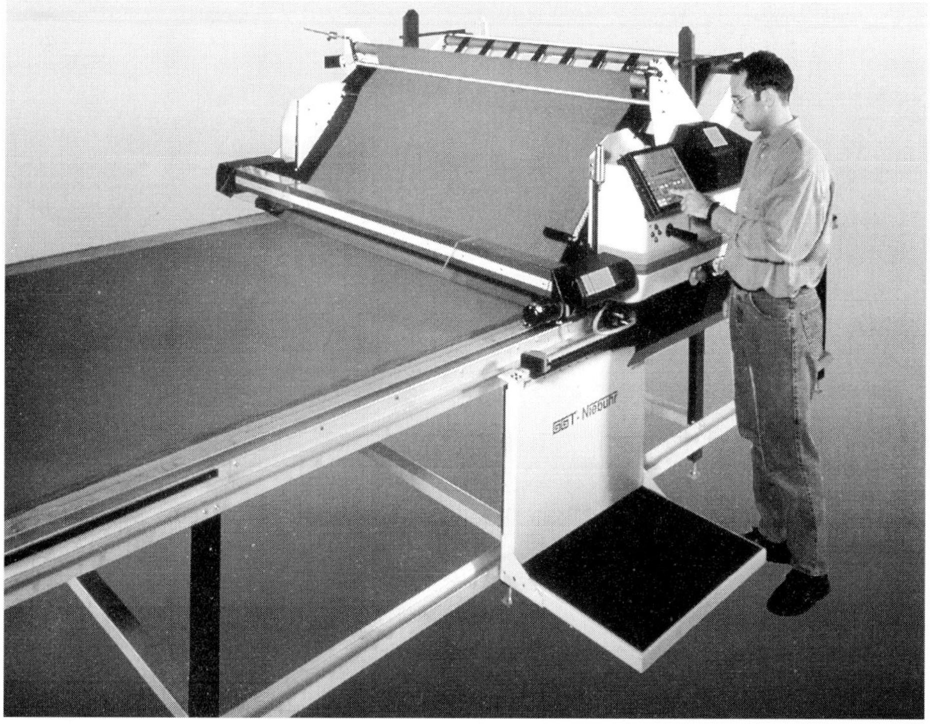

Figure 14-10

Computerized fabric spreading. Courtesy of Gerber Garment Technology.

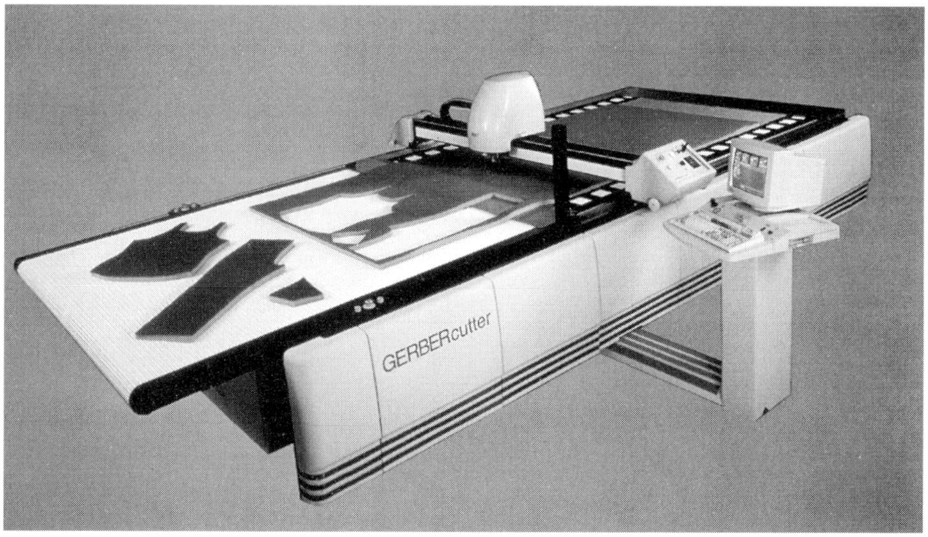

Figure 14-11

Cutting multiple fabric layers by computer. Courtesy of Gerber Garment Technology.

some specialized machines, it uses a camera to view a single layer of plaid-patterned fabric, sees the irregularities in that particular section of cloth, and adjusts the cut so that when the garment is sewn together, all the plaid pieces will match (Figure 14-12). These cutters can also be used on some plastics

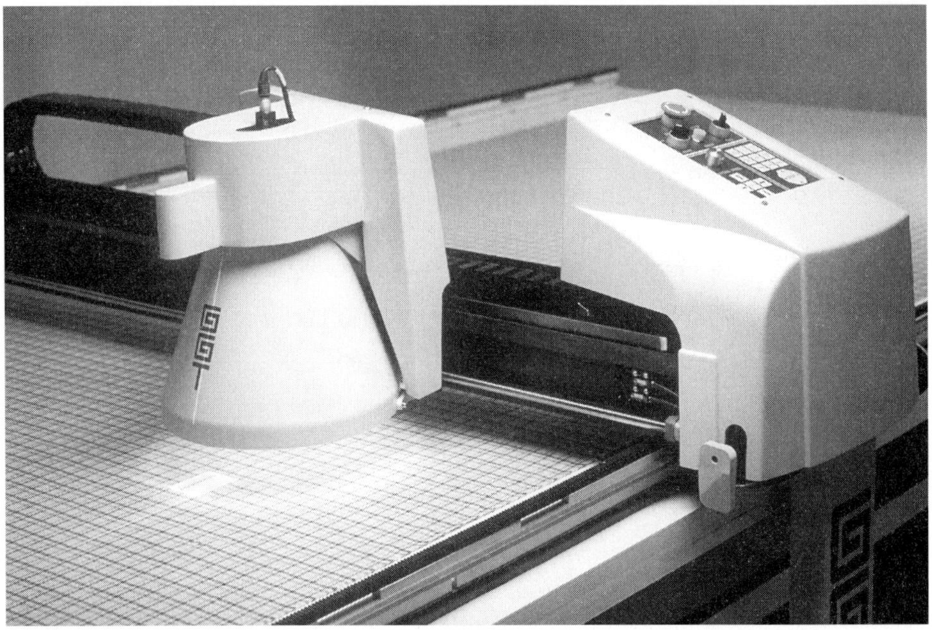

Figure 14-12

This machine "reads" the irregularities in the plaid fabric and adjusts the cut so that the pattern pieces will match. Courtesy of Gerber Garment Technology.

and leathers. Laser cutters can be used to seal all the cut edges. To keep all the cut pieces straight, there is an automatic marking machine that puts an adhesive ID stamp on each stack of pieces.

Sewing

Sewing is still the weakest link in the automation process. It is very difficult to handle the flimsy and floppy individual pieces of cloth in a machine. That is why even with all the automation listed above, imports from low-labor-cost markets continue to take more and more of the market. Yes, there are automatic pocket applicators and collar makers, but this is a drop in the bucket.

Factory Flow Systems

One of the few advances that has been made on the sewing floor is a system to move goods around the factory automatically. Hanging overhead, they move from operator to operator to finisher with greater ease (Figure 14-13). But if high-labor-cost markets such as the United States think that this will be enough to make them competitive, be forewarned: We have seen this technology in places as unlikely as Singapore and Egypt.

Linkage and Tracking

Actually, linkage and tracking is the biggest breakthrough of all. Everyone along the way is working with the same information since it is all on-line. Updates or changes are communicated to everyone instantly. The head office can check in on a collection to see where it is in the entire design and production cycle. (Does this mean that no one will ever be late again? We doubt it.) These systems continue to be made easier and easier to get into. Now they

Figure 14-13

Garment moving system. Courtesy of Gerber Garment Technology.

are PC, MAC, and in some cases E-mail compatible. Along the way, designers or pattern makers or cutters can "attach" comments for someone down the line. One of our favorite features is that a pattern maker in Los Angeles can attach a visual video explanation in Spanish for the production manager in Mexico!

IF THAT'S WHERE WE ARE, CAN THERE BE MORE IN THE FUTURE?

Many things once deemed impossible are commonplace now. The sewing part of the process is the weak link at present. But you can be sure that some clever person will figure that out. Is that you? The trend among the biggies, Gerber and Lectra, seems to be more and more interconnectivity, more compatibility with standard systems such as Windows and MAC, and more comfortable user-friendliness. With all of these improvements, it will probably be actually easier for you to get on-line when your time comes...

ANY OTHER HIGH-TECH IN THE WINGS?

Technical improvements seem to arise on a daily basis. Let's just say that the Internet is starting to open up with images and fabrics that designers can download for use in their designing. FIT in New York is putting its huge textile collection on CD-ROM for use by designers. The links between manufacturers and retailers for quicker and more accurate replenishment will certainly continue to grow. The New York buying office, Doneger, is planning to offer its members up-to-date market information and digital photographs of trend items over the Internet [*Women's Wear Daily*, January 22, 1997] Levi's custom-fit jeans program for women is booming! Your body measurements are punched into a computer at one of the 30 Original Levi's Stores, and two weeks later, a custom-fitting pair has been produced just for you! Started in 1994, this service now accounts for 25% of women's jeans sales at these stores! [*New York Times*, April 6, 1997]

You have managed it through the technology part. Now how about a trip to faraway lands?

CHAPTER 15

The Politics of Apparel Importing: Rewards and Punishments

FIRST COMPUTERS; NOW POLITICS?

Sounds boring. Do I really need to know this? Well, how about this: If you are importing something from overseas and willfully break the rules of importation, you can go to jail! Now, do you think it's worth checking out? We'll make it as brief as possible.

BACKGROUND

Textiles and apparel making are important to the United States, as they are to almost every other country. Unlike a product such as airplanes, which are made in only a few countries, apparel is made almost everywhere. There are lots of dollars and jobs at stake. In fact, it is estimated that 23.6 million people work in textile and garment factories worldwide [International Labor Office, October 28, 1996 release]. To show how important this industry is to some countries, consider that garments represented 66% of Bangladesh's total exports in 1995, amounting to $2.5 billion [*Daily News Record*, Dec. 16, 1996, "Bangladesh's Textile Sourcing Goes Local"].

Because of a long history of strong lobbies, the textile and apparel industries are among the most protected in the United States. U.S. makers want to limit the amount of imports, and they want to tax them so that they will be less competitive in price. Now, in fairness to all, let's quickly point out that other countries do exactly the same. Europe and Canada have very similar setups, and some Third World countries have been so restrictive on all imports that their people can only buy locally made goods.

So, with all this hassle, why go overseas to have garments made? There are still a couple of compelling reasons:

- Labor costs can be so much less in some countries that even with all the duties, their products are still cheaper.

Full-Fashioned
A method of shaping a knitted fabric during the knitting process.

Hand Work
Artisanship done by one person on one garment at a time: for example, hand embroidery.

- Some machinery is much more available overseas (for example, **full-fashioned** knitwear machinery). Also, **hand work** is prohibitive if done in a developed country, but it is still affordable in the Philippines, India, and China, among others.
- Perhaps because so much is not automated overseas, it has been easier to produce smaller quantities and more variations. Also, we have found a more flexible attitude overseas, more of a willingness to try something new.

U.S. RULES AND REGULATIONS

The basis for all this, is that the United States wants to limit the amount of imports and put a tax (duty) on them to make them less competitive. But we also reward some countries and penalize others, so it gets a bit messy. We'll now review briefly what you need to know.

THE INSIDE SCOOP

JULIA HUGHES

Julie is the vice president of trade and government relations for the USA ITA (U.S. Association of Importers of Textiles and Apparel), based in Washington, DC. She is a veteran of the government scene, having covered it for years at AMC.

On moving from protectionism to globalization:

When I started in Washington in the early 1980s, my job was pretty much "What's under quota and how much is left?" We were just reacting to a system that had been in place for over a decade. The mid-80s brought a "sea change." The domestic industry was pushing hard to limit imports, via legislation like the Jenkins bill. Lee Abraham, chairman of the AMC, had the vision to see that we needed a concerted counter-effort among retailers, overseas producers, and private label importers.

Up to this point, "our side" had never worked with Congress. One Senator told us, "Where have you been? I have stacks of letters from unions and the domestic garment industry—where are your letters?" We lobbied, we initiated letter-writing campaigns. When we finally defeated the Jenkins bill, it was suddenly a whole different ball game.

At a reception at the U.S. Embassy in Geneva during the GATT talks, the domestic industry representatives wouldn't talk to us or even shake our hands! They had never had to deal with someone who had another view! Now, we're substantively involved in all negotiations. We provided a lot of information for the NAFTA and Uruguay Round Talks, for example.

But I think the point is not "us versus them." We're a global industry that's linked. The same domestic manufacturers are now going offshore via NAFTA or 807, or they are trying to export U.S. goods. For the first time, they're running into protectionism in those other countries.

If we all work together globally, we can have the best opportunities. For example, the United States produces lots of cotton. What if there were some incentive given for anyone in the global industry to use U.S. cotton? Politics has kept us apart, but—exports, imports—they're really all becoming the same!

Duty

Also called a *tariff*, duty is the tax that the U.S. government applies to imported articles. It is collected by the Customs Service and goes to the U.S. government. Duties are very slowly decreasing for apparel products; most items still fall between 16 and 26% ***ad valorem***. This means that if an importer paid his Hong Kong contractor $10.00 in Hong Kong for a cotton sweater, the duty on this item when it arrives in the United States would be 16.5% of the **first cost** ($10.00), or $1.65 (16.5% is the current duty rate for cotton sweaters). This is one more cost that must be figured into the selling price.

> ***Ad Valorem***
> In proportion to the value; duties levied on imports according to their invoiced value.

> ***First Cost***
> The actual cost paid to an overseas manufacturer before additional charges such as freight and duty.

Quota

Quota is a limit on a particular category of apparel that will be allowed to enter the United States from another country. Most of these agreements were worked out country by country, so the amounts vary widely. The United States (as of 1995) "had quota agreements with 42 countries, covering 40% of total U.S. textile imports and 50% of U.S. apparel imports" [U.S. International Trade Commission, Industry Trade and Technology Review, October 1996]. Recently, there was an agreement reached by the World Trade Organization (WTO), which will eliminate quotas by the year 2005. However, most of the changes won't be seen until the last year. Countries with much more capacity than quota, such as Bangladesh and Pakistan, will end up benefiting most dramatically. But in the meantime, apparel quotas are being loosened up very slowly.

At times, when there is too much demand for a particular category (say, women's wool sweaters, or men's cotton outerwear, etc.), quota becomes "hot." In some countries it is legal for manufacturers who own quota (because they have shipped this category in the previous year) to sell the quota to another manufacturer who needs it to ship his orders. This price is purely what the market will bear, but we've seen it go as high as $4.00 to $5.00 per piece on superhot categories in Hong Kong. This cost is put into the cost of the garment, which means that eventually, the customer ends up paying for it. (By the way, a $5.00 per piece quota charge in Hong Kong would mean that the customer has to pay a $20.00 difference at retail, with absolutely no difference in the garment to show for it!)

When a quota category is filled from a particular country, all remaining shipments are **embargoed**. This is not a happy situation. It means that your precious jackets are sitting in a warehouse in Long Beach, you are paying the warehouse charge, the contractor has already gotten your money for the jackets, and now Customs is telling you that even though today is September 15, you can't touch those jackets until January 1 of the next year when the new quota year opens. ("But they're jackets! What do I do with jackets in the spring?")

> ***Embargoed***
> If shipments of a particular imported category exceed the allowable limit set by the U.S. government, Customs has the right to stop all remaining shipments at the port and to refuse entry until the new quota period opens up again.

Country of Origin

Because of the quota allocations by country, manufacturers and importers have gotten very creative in trying to find a way to have a garment come from one country (with lots of quota) even if it might be partially made somewhere else (where quota is tight). Fraudulent disregard for these laws gets you into that "jail" problem we mentioned. But the rules themselves have gotten so complicated that it is often hard to pinpoint the official country of origin. In very general terms, in most cases the country where the garment is assembled is deemed to be the country of origin.

Most Favored Nation
A status conferred by the U.S. government on most nations, calling for standard duties; the few countries that do not have this status, such as Vietnam, receive significantly higher duties.

Most Favored Nation

Almost all countries charge each other their standard duty rates whether or not there is a full agreement on all political points. But there are some instances where this is not the case. Unlike other **most favored nations**, China has to be recertified by the United States every year. It's always a nail-biter, because if it is not renewed, the duties (and thus costs) go way up. There are also some countries that do not have MFN status at all, so their products are penalized with much higher duties. This includes Afghanistan and Vietnam. Still other countries have total trade embargoes imposed by the United States. No trade is allowed, for example, with North Korea or Cuba.

Special Programs

Here is where we get into some of the "rewards." There are special agreements with some of our neighbors and closest political allies to give them a trade boost. Some of these include:

- *Israel Free Trade Agreement.* The United States and Israel signed the first free trade agreement in 1985. Duties were phased out over a 10-year period, and quota is open.
- *807 (now called 9802).* The fabric must be of U.S. origin, and part of the manufacturing (often the cutting) has to be done in the United States to qualify, but assembly then can be done in the Caribbean or Central America. Duty is paid only on the value added in the other country, and there are special quota considerations as well.
- *NAFTA.* This is the North American Free Trade Agreement. In 1992, the leaders of the United States, Mexico, and Canada signed this agreement, which will eventually allow most merchandise to cross their boundaries without duties or quotas.

Ironically, since NAFTA was introduced to help Mexico, the Caribbean suppliers who had benefited previously under 807/9802 are now paying the price. "In the last two years, more than 150 apparel plants closed in the Caribbean and 123,000 jobs have been lost. Since NAFTA took effect in 1994, Mexican textile exports have grown at a rate three times those of the Caribbean as a whole. In 1996, the Caribbean Textile and Apparel Institute estimates Jamaica's garment exports fell by 7%, with 7000 jobs eliminated. The creation of new jobs in this nation of 2.3 million people has stopped altogether and overall unemployment has risen to 16% from 9.5%" [*New York Times*, January 30, 1997, "Blows from NAFTA Batter the Caribbean Economy"]. In the month of May 1997 for the first time in history, more apparel came from Mexico and the Caribbean than from the Far East [*Daily News Record*, August 18, 1997, "U.S. Textile Leaders Praise NAFTA," Brenda Lloyd].

Marking

> **Marking**
> The labeling requirements on garments.

All garments that come into the United States must have the following permanently attached:

- Fiber content of the garment
- Country of origin
- Legal identification (a trademarked brand, a store name, a registration number)
- Care labeling

These requirements, in some cases made by the FTC (Federal Trade Commission) are mostly to help consumers know how to care for what they have bought and how to trace the maker in case of a problem.

In 1997 a new system of international care symbols (pictograms) will also be allowed to specify washing and care instructions. For example, a triangle means bleach, a square means dry, and so on. In 1999, garments will only be required to carry these symbols. This will move the United States one step closer to the symbols used in much of the rest of the world. Look for the new symbols on detergent boxes.

CAN WE GO NOW??

OK, so now you've done all your homework on the legal requirements involved in importing. (By the way, you can just imagine the paperwork that comes along with all this!) So now, let's finally get on that plane and go!

CHAPTER 16

The Geography of Tomorrow's Manufacturing, or "I Have to Change Planes in Kuala Lumpur?"

BAD KARMA!

> To get to Madras, India, we flew overnight from New York to Frankfurt. After a long and drowsy layover, we changed planes for yet another overnight flight to Bombay. From Bombay it was a couple more hours to Madras, which is situated in India's steamy south. We collapsed in the hotel only to find that we couldn't even get a beer to unwind: Madras is a "dry" state in India.
>
> The next morning, after getting about two hours sleep, we set off on a 90-minute ride through blazingly colorful streets. The car crawled because the roads were impassable with carts and animals plus men and women dressed in brilliant colors and plaids (this is Madras, after all).
>
> So, after creeping through, we finally arrived at the office of the very famous Mr. Iyer. He is well known in the industry for his stunning and original woven cloth. We were asked to wait in the hallway next to a pungent, smoking religious shrine for almost 30 minutes.
>
> Finally, we were escorted into Mr. Iyer's office, expecting to be greeted as the big buyers we are. Instead, we found him glowering from behind a huge desk. Suddenly, we felt like kids called into the principal's office.
>
> After a long, dramatic pause, Mr. Iyer finally broke the silence: "Your company is the most disreputable company I have ever met. I refuse to do any further business with you, so you might as well just go back to New York right now!"

Yikes! This actually happened. It turned out (when we calmly, politely, but firmly pressed the issue further with Mr. Iyer) that someone else had "knocked off" patterns that he had designed exclusively for us last season. Mr. Iyer thought we had knocked him off. After a couple of hours, we were all friends again; there were no hard feelings, and business continued.

There are a couple of international sourcing lessons to be learned by this experience:

1. *Don't panic.* Stay calm, reason things out, don't shout. People overseas are usually embarrassed by strong emotions.
2. *Anything can happen!* Who knew after flying for 2½ days that the whole point of the trip would be in jeopardy? Be ready to scramble at all times!
3. *All business is personal.* Doing business between any two people from any two countries requires that these two people find a way to establish a level of rapport and trust, sometimes despite major cultural differences.

WHERE IN THE WORLD?

The majority of garment manufacturing, especially in your young careers, will be done in **developing countries**. Garment making is still quite labor intensive, which means that cheap labor is the only way to stay competitive. Wholesalers have to keep shifting contractors and countries to keep costs low. As wages in a given country increase, garment manufacturing tends to get replaced with more sophisticated, higher-tech industries such as fabric weaving and electronics assembly.

Developing Countries
These are the economically less-developed nations, such as Pakistan, Indonesia, and Sri Lanka.

Korea is a good example of a country that has gone through all the manufacturing stages within 25 years or so. In the late 1960s, believe it or not, one of the biggest Korean exports was human hair! Wigs were in fashion then, and the only skill a hair-grower needed was "combing." From wigs came clothing exports in the early 1970s. Korean workers were low paid but disciplined and highly trainable. The industry boomed, the country benefited, wages went up. The newer workers came in with more education and higher expectations, so they no longer wanted to work in hot, cramped sewing lines. The electronics giants started luring these workers away with higher pay in air-conditioned factories. (American garment wholesalers joke that as soon as the hotels get nice in a country, this is a signal that it is time to move on to a poorer country with funky hotels. With envy, they say that the electronics guys don't arrive until the nice hotels are built!)

By the 1980s, Korean factories were making cars and ships. Those companies that had developed expertise in garment production over the years had to find a creative solution to stay in business. Their own workers were just too expensive. Along came the invention of triangle shipments.

Triangle Shipments

Triangle shipment is a term used to describe an increasingly common multi-country procedure. For example:

The manufacturer's company headquarters is in:	Korea
An American wholesaler flies to: to put together a flannel shirt program at the sharpest possible price.	Korea
The fabric is best and cheapest if it is woven in:	Korea
But it is too expensive to sew the shirts there, so the manufacturer ships the fabric to their own factory in: where the garments are assembled by Nicaraguan workers under Korean supervision.	Nicaragua
The completed garments are shipped to: directly from Nicaragua.	the United States

The term *triangle* is used to signify that there are three different locations for fabric, construction, and customer. (Previously, fabric and construction were almost always done in the same country as the manufacturer's headquarters.) Most of the original Far East garment countries (Korea, Taiwan, Hong Kong) are holding on to fabric production, but all of them have had to move to triangle arrangements to find low-cost garment assembly. "At present, more than 60% of world clothing exports are manufactured in developing countries" [International Labor Office, October 28, 1996 release].

In the mid-1990s, some of the more important garment assembly countries included Indonesia, Pakistan, India, China, Egypt, Caribbean countries, and Central American countries. Where will this go when you are sourcing? Probably China, India, Central America, Vietnam (depending on the politics of the situation), and Africa (Figure 16-1).

There are even some very artificial situations caused by quota (which we learned about in Chapter 15). Some countries actually have a significant amount of quota, but their own labor force is too small or too expensive for garment making. As a result, some garment companies set up factories in those countries and import the workers just as they would import the fabric! In Saipan (a U.S. territory) there are dormitories full of Chinese workers. In the United Arab Emirates, workers might be from Pakistan; in Malaysia, they might be from Sri Lanka. These workers live in what we would consider pretty spartan conditions for two or three years, separated from their families. But at the end, they return with much more money than they could have earned at home.

If all this sounds complicated, just look at what "triangle" shipments are now turning into.

The manufacturer's headquarters is in:	Singapore
The fabric is woven and dyed in:	China
Special fabric finishing is applied in:	Hong Kong
The fabric is sent to:	southern Malaysia
where the individual pattern pieces are cut and sent to:	northern Malaysia
where they are embroidered by Sri Lankan workers, then trucked back to:	southern Malaysia

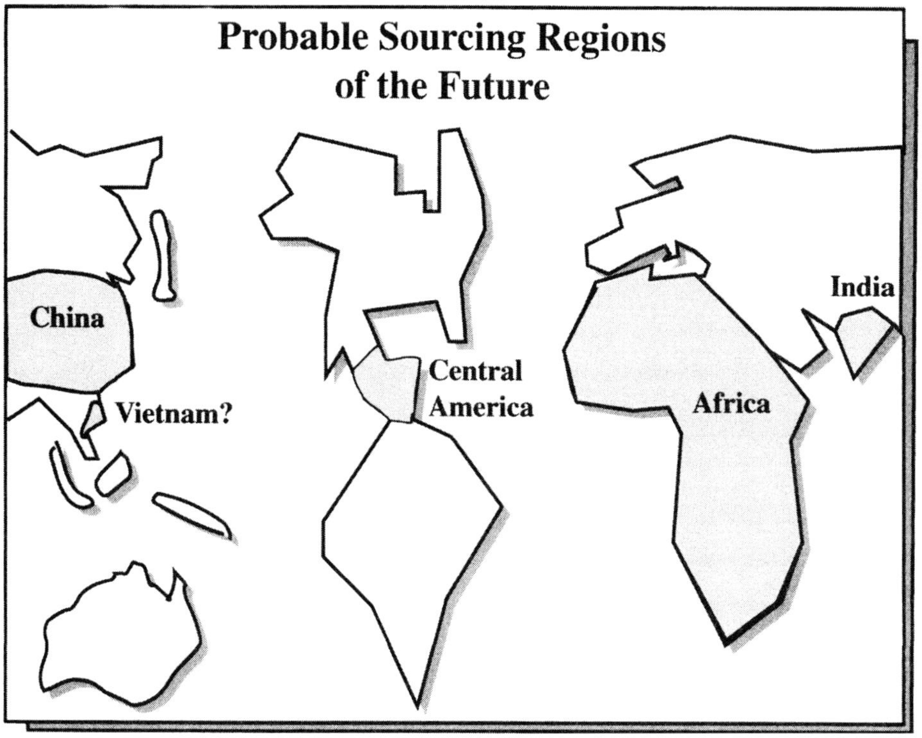

Figure 16-1

Artwork by Michael Carnegie.

where the pieces are assembled into garments, but then are trucked to:	a different town in Malaysia
where they are garment-washed and then trucked back to:	southern Malaysia
where the washed garments are pressed and packed in the original factory and then finally shipped to:	Taiwan
where they go from the smaller ship (feeder vessel) to the larger ship (mother vessel) for shipment to:	the United States

This is more than a triangle. This is called "asking for trouble." It might come as a shock to you, but most of your clothes are better traveled than you are!

HOW DOES THIS COMPLICATED BUSINESS GET MANAGED?

Most American and European wholesalers and retailers work overseas via agents or with their own offices. As you can imagine, there are so many details to be attended to that quite a few people are required on-site in each producing country. *Agents* are independent operators who provide these services

THE INSIDE SCOOP

SARA BAVLY

Sara is the senior merchandise representative in AMC's Tel Aviv, Israel, office.

Doing business in Israel is a little different from other countries. It is a very small and friendly market. If a manufacturer is quoting a price, he might say that another Israeli manufacturer might be able to quote you a better price!

The textile business in Israel is mostly made up of generations of the same families. The first generation all know each other and the second generation probably all went to technical school together. These manufacturers prefer to tell a buyer up front if he anticipates that there might be technical difficulties knitting or dying their requested style. But to do business with these manufacturers, buyers need to arrive fully prepared with designs, specs, colors, price targets.

for a fee (usually some percentage of the cost of the shipments). Two of the largest independent agents in the Orient are Li and Fung, and Connors. Other U.S. companies are so large that they have their own network of offices (May Company, Macy/Federated). Or they band together and share offices (Dayton-Hudson Corp., Eaton's, Bloomingdale's, Saks at AMC, the Associated Merchandising Corporation).

Most of the jobs in these overseas offices are filled with people from that country. By the way, this would be an exceptional opportunity for foreign students who have studied in the United States and then returned home. They would be viewed as highly desirable employees because of their exposure to the American wholesale and retail scene, their newly acquired technical skills, and their native language facility. From time to time, there are also opportunities for skilled and experienced Americans in some of these offices.

LABOR CONDITIONS AND UNDERAGE WORKERS OVERSEAS

Labor overseas is a highly complex subject, and we don't pretend to be legal or moral experts. Let us just state up-front that we feel no one should be forced to work, no one should have to work in unsafe or unhealthy conditions, and no child should ever be exploited as a source of cheap labor. Having said all that, this is still not a black-and-white issue. There have clearly been abuses—Chinese forced labor in prisons, for example, or young children in factories in places like Bangladesh. Most American wholesalers and retailers have been trying hard to make sure that their merchandise does not end up in such shops. Not in anyone's defense, but sometimes it is very hard to know where your garments are actually getting made. Contractors often subcontract out to cheaper, less sophisticated operations. Like the layers of an onion, this can actually go down several levels, with no knowledge on the part of the buyer. We've seen garment components flying back and forth in taxis (going where?).

"Manufacturers, contractors, and organized labor contend that the swell of **sweatshops** here and abroad is directly linked to intense price pressures from retailers as well as consumers and that weak apparel sales in recent years have exacerbated the problem" [*Women's Wear Daily*, June 11, 1996, "Fashion's Blame Game," Arthur Friedman]. The issue of legal working age is also complex. The United Nations charter states that the legal working age in a country should be no younger than 14. In some countries it is expected that 14-year-olds will work. The alternatives might be even less desirable.

> **Sweatshops**
> Factories where labor law(s) are being violated, such as minimum wage, underage workers, and unsafe conditions.

Still, abuses continue to occur and this has been appropriately raised as an issue of concern. President Clinton's 1997 task force on this subject was able to reach some guidelines to be applied to overseas suppliers to the United States but there is still a long way to go, especially considering the profound differences from country to country.

A FEW TIPS ON SOURCING OVERSEAS

As with anything else, skills develop in this arena through (good and bad) experience. Doing business overseas is very different from doing business in the United States. As our friend S. Y. Kim (AMC account executive) of Seoul, Korea, explains, "There is only one America. Don't expect other countries to be America also. Please respect that they have their own values."

America has been quite isolated through history, as well as linguistically spoiled. (Relax: Even though we shouldn't be so lucky, there probably is no place left on earth where we can't get by with English.) When we Americans set out in the international business world, we're often not really prepared to deal on someone else's terms and turf.

Next we'll look at some basic pointers to guide you on your international way.

Careful, Clear Communications

Always speak clearly, slowly, don't mumble. Don't talk baby talk! (You would not believe how many Americans start doing this when they get to the Orient! How embarrassing!) Words don't always mean the same things overseas. For example, did you know that "I'll try" is the polite way of saying "no" in much of the Orient? They don't want to insult you with "no," but then you go merrily along assuming that they are still working on it, which they aren't.

Setting Everyone Up To Succeed

Some wholesalers, designers, or sourcers get on the plane to fly overseas, ready to do battle with everyone! If they are tough on agents and contractors, their thinking goes, they will come out the winner. But this goes back to our section on negotiating. Everyone has to make his or her profit. You just need to make sure that no one's profit is overinflated and that everyone will earn their profit. Some travelers feel that they should "dare" the contractors to do the almost impossible. It's really much healthier to try to make things as

THE INSIDE SCOOP

GUNSAN CETIN

Gunsan is the managing director of GAP's Istanbul, Turkey, office. She is a mechanical engineer with training in textile machinery, patternmaking, and designing. In her seven years as the head of AMC–Istanbul, she increased the business 40-fold.

On doing business in another culture:

To be able to succeed in business in Turkey, you will need a close and professional relationship with the manufacturer. If your approach is strictly business, you can't be successful. Also, if a manufacturer knows you don't know what you're talking about, for example, if you don't know what goes into the cost of a garment, he won't respect you.

If you do need a favor, the best approach is to ask for the manufacturer's help rather than to demand that something be done. A Turkish manufacturer might break a business relationship if his or her ego has not been taken care of properly.

Having said all this, if you do use the right approach with Turkish manufacturers, there is nothing that can't be done!

"possible" as you can. Talk all the details through with the contractor, anticipate problems, and avoid them now, when it's easy. Don't load your partner up with so many "challenges" that it will be a miracle if he or she succeeds. You might be forgetting that this also means that it will take a miracle for you to get your goods the way you want them when you want them. You can't succeed if he or she doesn't succeed!

Oy, the Problems!

When you're working all over the world, it's not a case of "there might be problems." There will be problems! Lots of them, most of them totally unexpected. Our friend, Hope Cohen, vice president, Polo, Ralph Lauren tells about an earlier trip to Uruguay to design sweaters: "We were sitting in the vendor's showroom in downtown Montevideo when suddenly the lights went out. Time was tight, so we moved over to the window, lit some candles, and proceeded to pick colors for the sweater jacquards in semi-darkness. It must have worked, because we had our most successful season ever! So what's the moral of the story? Always pick your colors in the dark?!"

This E-mail came in to our friend May Cygan (AMC associate product manager): "Your shipment mistakenly put into refrigerated container rather than regular garment container. Garments now frozen. Will advise status once they thaw out" (Figure 16-2). The key is keeping your cool at all times, and looking for solutions, not people to blame. Now that you're in the big leagues, when the teacher passes out the construction paper and popsicle sticks, she might surprise you with a blindfold. You still have to find some way to make that airplane!

Figure 16-2

Artwork by Michael Carnegie.

Sticking With a Good Partner

Another very common mistake that newcomers make is to move their program from one contractor to another, or even from one country to another, for a small savings in cost. Going back to our football metaphor, that would be like tossing out your most experienced team members near the end of the season and bringing in a bunch of rookies who have never played together before. The old plays that everyone on the team understood before suddenly run into new misunderstandings. Yes, there are times when it's right to make a change. But most importers make the mistake of changing partners too often rather than not often enough.

There are many more pointers for this end of the business. But for now, let's just tell you about one entry-level position that could start you off in this international direction.

Import Production Assistant Follow-up

After production orders have been placed with the manufacturers, and wholesale orders have started to come in from store buyers, the follow-up begins. You've gotten a glimpse of how complex all this is. This becomes the responsibility of the production assistant, a possible entry-level position for someone starting in the wholesale industry. Coming in with the following abilities is a must:

- Good oral and written communication skills
- Meticulous attention to detail
- Ability to keep the "big picture" in mind even while immersed in hundreds of details

Some of the duties of the production assistant include:

- Confirming exact quantities, styles, colors, and deliveries to the various manufacturers
- Proactively watching the calendar to make sure that all trigger date deadlines are anticipated and met
- Ensuring that all fabrics and trims have arrived on time
- Maintaining the merchandiser's cost sheets (usually on Lotus or Excel) as price changes or competitive bids come in
- Tracking the production of the salesman samples and swatches so that everything is ready for the line opening
- Following up on color approvals (**lab dips**), fit comments, and trim details
- Monitoring ex-factory deliveries closely so that shipments will be on time

> ***Lab Dips***
> A small piece of fabric or yarn that has been dyed as a trial to see if the color will be acceptable to the buyer.

It Is an Adventure!

So this gives you a bit of the "flavor" of international product sourcing. As you have seen, it always seems to come with "experiences," good and not-so-good. With all these adventures, it's easy to forget that there are still lots of garments made right here at home.

In Chapter 17 we find out how that is going.

CHAPTER 17

Manufacturing in the United States: Is There a Future?

TOUGH GLOBAL COMPETITION

Is there a future in manufacturing apparel in the United States? Yes and no. It's getting harder and harder to be priced competitively if your labor costs are in the United States. However, there are new ways of doing business and there are niches of business that can still work here. According to the U.S. Department of Labor, Bureau of Labor Statistics [Labstat Series Report, August 1995], the annual average employment in the United States for textile mill products decreased from 691,000 in 1990 to 666,500 in 1995. Employment in apparel and other textile products decreased from 1,036,200 to 930,400 in the same period. Even with these decreases, "the textile industry accounts for nearly 10% of all manufacturing jobs and represents the second largest employer among non-durable industries" [Global Trade Talk, July–October 1996, Vol. 6, Nos. 5–6, U.S. Department of Treasury].

Just these few statistics make it clear that while the textile and apparel industries are still important in the United States, they are not having an easy time of it; and the fall-off continues. According to *Women's Wear Daily* [January 13, 1997, "61,000 Jobs Lost in 1996 in Apparel," Joanna Ramey], "the U.S. apparel industry in 1996 lost more jobs than any other private-sector business, 61,000 to be exact. In the last two years alone, 16% of the apparel work force has disappeared. The reality of lower labor costs in Third World countries, and demands by retailers for low wholesale prices, remain driving factors behind apparel companies either shuttering or moving production jobs off-shore."

As we have seen earlier, this industry continues to be dependent on a high amount of manual labor in its garments. So all countries with high-paid workers are experiencing similar declines, especially in apparel production. Don't think that this is just happening here: Japan, Korea, Taiwan, and Hong Kong have also been going through the same scenario.

Empty racks and "going out of business" sales in New York's garment district.

In dollars and cents, it becomes quite clear why manufacturers and importers have sought out other countries to produce clothing. Following are average hourly apparel worker wages in selected countries:

Italy	$14.00
Canada	9.88
United States	9.56
France	7.81
United Kingdom	7.38
Hong Kong	4.55
Costa Rica	2.38
Dominican Republic	1.62
Eastern Europe	1.11
Mexico	1.08
Colombia	1.05
Thailand	1.02
Philippines	0.94
Nicaragua	0.76
Haiti	0.49
Indonesia	0.34
Sri Lanka	0.31
India	0.26
Vietnam	0.26
Pakistan	0.21

China	0.20 to 0.68
Bangladesh	0.10 to 0.16

[*Women's Wear Daily*, December 31, 1996, "Labor Costs: Where and How Much?" *Source*: Werner International]

With such a huge difference, importers can add duties and freight to their overseas (first) costs and still come out at a lower price than if they had made it here. This has ballooned the annual textile import volume into the United States to a staggering $44 billion [Global Trade Talk, July–October 1996, Vol. 6, Nos. 5–6, U.S. Department of Treasury].

FIGHTING BACK

Well, domestic textile mills and apparel manufactures weren't about to just let this happen. The stakes are high, especially in certain states. Following are the states with the largest number of textile workers:

North Carolina	206,000
Georgia	108,000
South Carolina	91,100

And those states with the largest number of apparel workers:

California	138,600
New York	100,100
North Carolina	72,400

[Global Trade Talk, July–October 1996, Vol. 6, Nos. 5–6, U.S. Department of Treasury]

There has been a huge push to remain competitive, including steps such as:

- *Modernizing equipment.* We've already learned about Gerber and Lectra. There are similar advances in textile technology.
- *Quick response.* By electronically linking together all players (fiber and fabric producers, garment makers, and retailers), U.S. suppliers can offer quicker replenishment of best-selling merchandise.
- *Combination operations.* Most U.S. garment makers originally did all of the production steps with their own employees. This is called *in-house labor*. This has been followed in recent years by a number of innovations.

  Subcontractors. Manufacturers send partially completed items to subcontractors who can add the next operation more efficiently and thus less expensively because they specialize in certain operations (pleating, embroidering, or simply sewing.

  Cottage labor. People who can do certain work in their own homes, such as hand-knitting sweaters, can reduce cost substantially.

  Offshore and other combinations. Many manufacturers in the United States are now doing part of their production overseas. The 9802 (807) laws encouraged U.S. makers to do their cutting in-house but then to send the pieces overseas (usually the Caribbean) for lower-cost sewing assembly. NAFTA is going to accelerate the trend to go offshore in the next 10 years. Ironically, while the 9802, super 807, and NAFTA rules are all encouraging the use of U.S.-made fabrics, they are also speeding up the movement of apparel-making jobs to other countries.

Joint ventures. At times manufacturers will share in the ownership of a subcontractor (either here or overseas) in order to tighten the relationship and reliability.

SWEATSHOPS

The squeeze on prices has also produced some abuses within the United States. There have been some highly publicized cases of "sweatshop" labor in the United States. Recent immigrants with few skills (business, language, or legal) fall prey to contractors who take advantage of their naiveté and force them to work unusually long hours, sometimes in unhealthy surroundings, for insufficient pay.

"The Labor Department estimates that about half of the 23,000 contract shops in the country are sweatshops—places where inspectors uncover illegal practices, including violations of wage and hour laws, employment of illegal aliens and unsafe working conditions" [*Women's Wear Daily*, January 7, 1997, "Shaking the Sweatshop Stigma"]. As a result, the Labor Department initiated a "No Sweat" campaign in 1996 [Garment Enforcement Report, April–June 1996, Wage and Hour Division, U.S. Department of Labor] to try to end such abuses. By singling out known abusers, by encouraging known compliers, and by trying a "No Sweat" hangtag campaign (Figure 17-1), the Department of

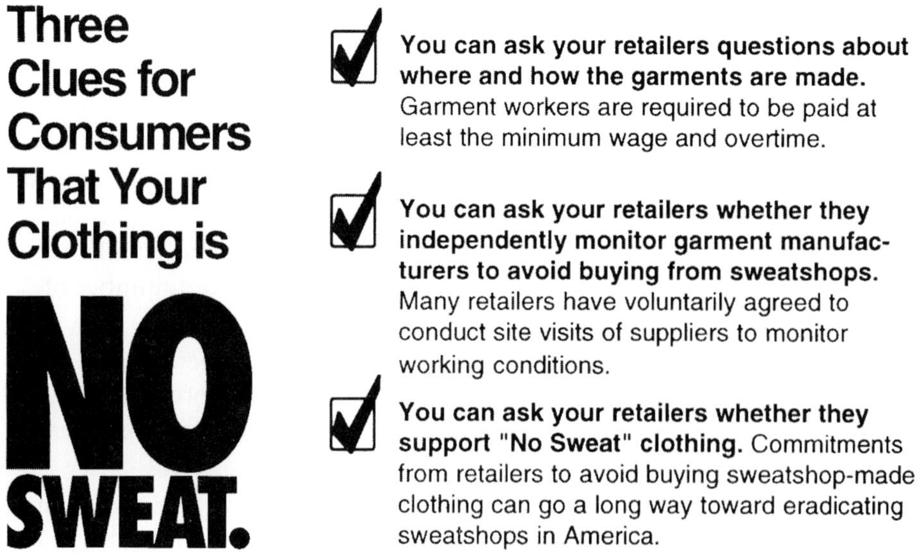
Three Clues for Consumers That Your Clothing is
NO SWEAT.
You can ask your retailers questions about where and how the garments are made. Garment workers are required to be paid at least the minimum wage and overtime.
You can ask your retailers whether they independently monitor garment manufacturers to avoid buying from sweatshops. Many retailers have voluntarily agreed to conduct site visits of suppliers to monitor working conditions.
You can ask your retailers whether they support "No Sweat" clothing. Commitments from retailers to avoid buying sweatshop-made clothing can go a long way toward eradicating sweatshops in America.

Figure 17-1

Consumer information provided by the "No Sweat" campaign. Courtesy of the U.S. Department of Labor.

Figure 17-2
UNITE union members. Photo by Cara Metz/UNITE.

Labor hopes to change this situation. Former Secretary of Labor Robert Reich said: "We hope that the administration's emphasis on encouraging manufacturers not to do business with known unscrupulous contractors and to monitor formally their contractors for compliance with minimum wage and overtime laws can buy long lasting positive changes in the working conditions for this country's workers" [*Women's Wear Daily*, January 7, 1997, "Shaking the Sweatshop Stigma"].

Also quite recently, the two apparel unions, ILGWU and ACTWU, merged to form a combined union, UNITE (Figure 17-2). "The union label certifies that the garment came from the hands of U.S. workers who belong to UNITE, the Union of Needletrades, Industrial and Textile Employees. These workers are guaranteed at least minimum wage, health-care benefits and worker's compensation for on-the-job injuries" [*Glamour*, April 1996, "Sweatshops: Fashion's Dirty Little Secret"].

OPPORTUNITIES OTHER THAN SEWING

Even if the U.S. textile industry can continue to produce price-competitive fabrics, the future doesn't look too rosy for manufacturers who are trying to sew garments here. But before you panic and wonder if that means no jobs for you, too, listen to the Secretary of Labor again: "In a wired world, fewer Americans will directly manufacture products. But more of us will devise better methods for making products or will add value through designs, marketing or engineering. In all these endeavors. . . computers are essential partners" [*Rolling Stone*, Oct 20, 1994, "Hire Education"].

Here's a perspective from Fruit of the Loom: "'It's the sewing jobs that are still at issue here in the industry,' he (a spokesman for Fruit of the Loom) said, 'Spinning operations, knitting, and cloth finishing have all remained in the U.S. In many areas, we've been hiring people at an aggressive clip in the U.S., like in management information systems, marketing, manufacturing technology, and production management'" [*Women's Wear Daily*, January 13, 1997, Joanna Ramey].

The U.S. Bureau of Statistics projects employment statistics into the future. The publication is called *Career Guide to Industries.* In their 1994–1995 edition [February 21, 1995], they found that "total employment is projected to increase by 14% or by 17.7 million, from 127.0 million in 1994 to 144.7 million in 2005." But looking at our specific industries, the winners and losers become clear:

Wholesale trade	+19.0% (as fast as average)
Department, clothing, and variety stores	+12.2% (more slowly than average)
Textile mill products manufacturing	-15.0%
Apparel and other textile products manufacturing	-24.4%

That's not a pretty picture! Only wholesale and retail jobs come close to the national growth average. Apparel and textile manufacturing jobs are expected to drop quite dramatically. But again, we say, don't panic! There are companies out there that have been able to buck this trend. Above all, they know what they can make competitively and what they shouldn't even try to do.

Specialized Items Such as Cotton Sweaters

Labor-intensive
Requiring lots of labor.

The United States is a world leader in cotton fiber production and is also very competitive in cotton yarns. Heavy cotton sweaters (using lots of cotton) have tended to be more price-competitive in the United States than overseas. Simple sweaters are usually less **labor-intensive** than cut-sewn woven garments, so more of the cost of a cotton sweater comes from the yarn. With the advantage in yarn cost, U.S. suppliers continue to beat their overseas competition. Domestic market share of cotton sweaters actually grew slightly between 1992 and 1994 [U.S. Imports, Production, Markets Import Production Ratios and Domestic Shares for Textile and Apparel Product Categories. Quarterly Report, May 1995, U.S. Department of Commerce, International Trade Administration Office of Textiles and Apparel].

Low-Labor Items

Some items are so standard that their production can be highly mechanized. T-shirts are a good example of this. In fact, tubular T-shirts (those with no side seams) are almost always cheaper if made in the United States. The production requires costly machinery (different garment sizes, or tubes, require different circular machines), but the labor for assembly is minimal. Then, via either piece dying (the fabric is dyed, then cut) or garment dying (the garment is completed, then dyed), U.S. makers can supply T-shirts very quickly, sometimes within two to five weeks. "Wisconsin children's wear maker, Oshkosh B'Gosh Inc. has decided it can effectively produce knit garments like leggings and tops in the U.S." [*Women's Wear Daily*, January 13, 1997, Joanna Ramey].

Top End of the Market

With production and marketing know-how, there are some companies that continue to thrive in the United States They make the labor costs work for them by producing an especially high-end quality product. On-site control is the key, and having management and the factory in the same building has accomplished that for one of the most famous men's dress shirt makers:

THE INSIDE SCOOP

LAWRENCE AND ALAN BEHAR

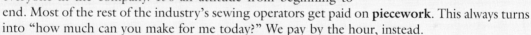

Lawrence, vice president of production, and Alan, vice president of marketing/finance/design, along with their brother Steven, are carrying on the legendary tradition of their famous father, Ike. Sold to Saks, Nieman-Marcus, and specialty stores, Ike Behar shirts are well known as the best of the best. There is also a growing market for his shirts on stage and in films (*Carlito's Way, Cotton Club, Wall Street*). A Japanese study ranked the Ike Behar shirt as the best quality in the world.

On the importance of maintaining quality:

We've always stood for just one thing: quality. It just happens to be made in America. But quality is why we've been able to exist here. We don't have a QC department. Quality is instilled in everyone in the company. It's an attitude from beginning to end. Most of the rest of the industry's sewing operators get paid on **piecework**. This always turns into "how much can you make for me today?" We pay by the hour, instead.

Our father was trained in Cuba as a tailor. He still sits down at the sewing machine and shows the operators how it's done. They know that he can probably do it better than they can! We feel our shirt is an exceptional value, especially next to comparable shirts from Italy which can cost twice as much, or more. And our business grows purely by word of mouth.

Niche Markets

There are some businesses that are so well targeted to their customer, and which dominate their niche of the market, that they can survive using domestic production. A great example, as well as a stirring story, is Malden Mills, in Lawrence, Massachusetts. On December 11, 1995, the mill burned to the ground. Its products, Polarfleece and Polartec, were in tremendous demand (Figure 17-3). Overseas competitors were simply unable to achieve the same silky softness of the fleecy fabric.

> **Piecework**
> Payment is made to workers not by the hours they have worked but by the number of garments they have sewn.

Mr. and Mrs. Feuerstein, the owners, vowed to rebuild in Massachusetts: "Others might have seized the opportunity to move their manufacturing to a developing country, where labor would be cheaper. But the couple were committed to the mill and to Lawrence." Demand for Malden Mills' unique and popular fabrics continued, so by the end of 1996, "the company is again

Figure 17-3

Malden Mills producing its famous Polarfleece. Photo by Ethan Vogt, courtesy of Malden Mills.

turning out its Polartec and Polarfleece fabrics as fast as the machines can run: all but about 400 employees are back on the job, and Mr. Feuerstein hopes to hire them back, too" [*New York Times*, December 26, 1996, "A Mill Community Comes Back to Life," Mitchell Owens] (Figure 17-4).

Figure 17-4

Mr. Feuerstein and Malden Mills employees. Photo by Steve Liss, courtesy of Malden Mills.

UNIT 4

So, After All This, Is the Fashion Business for You?

CHAPTER 18

Aiming for 2000 and Beyond

In Units 1 to 3 we've tried to show you how this business has been done. In this final unit, we're going to ask: Where are you going to take this fashion business in the future?

FIRST PLAN: AIM BIG

Way back in Unit I we told you that the big are getting bigger in this business. We think the biggest will get bigger still, especially among retailers. The giants like Wal-Mart, Sears, Penney's, and Target should continue to fill a large market niche. Their sophisticated computer systems will continue to give them a competitive advantage. "Thank the computer for the increased ability of a Wal-Mart or K-mart to compete with the fashion-oriented Limited. With the faster flow of information from local cash registers to headquarters to manufacturer today, almost any smart merchant can be ready with the trendiest merchandise on short notice" [*Forbes*, December 7, 1992, "Here Come the Cross Shoppers"].

These giants are reaching astounding proportions. "One out of every four American men, women, and children buy their underwear at Wal-Mart. . . Its payroll of 650,000 represents one out of every 200 residents of the U.S., serving the 70 million shoppers who enter Wal-Mart every week" [*Outerwear*, June 1996, "John Lupo of Wal-Mart"]. Sears expects to have 860 stores by the year 2000 [*Daily News Record*, February 14, 1997]. These mega mass merchants and dominant specialty chains such as Gap/Old Navy/Banana Republic and Disney, plus the few remaining but still vital department store chains such as May Co., Dillard's, Federated/Macys, will provide a large proportion of all available fashion jobs in the future. "Since its inception, Gap, Inc., has grown between 15 and 20% a year, doubling its size roughly every four years. If it continues to grow at about 18% a year and doubles every four years, it will do $10 billion in four years and $20 billion four years after that" [*Stores*, January 1997, "Donald G. Fisher," Susan Reda].

As they grow, these chains tend to add private-label product development to their internal operations. Mass merchants such as Wal-Mart are licensing old department store brands such as White Stag, Faded Glory, and Catalina. They've also created brand extensions by licensing McKids and McBaby from McDonald's. As of 1997, Penney's Arizona brand was tracking at about $1 billion in retail sales; Sears' Canyon River Blues, $200 million [*Daily News Record*, February 10, 1997, "A Private Label War Grows More Public," Julie Vargo and Jean Palmieri].

There will be room for fashion forecasters, designers, product managers, sourcers, technical designers, and quality control technicians. This is in addition to the already established jobs of buyer, planner/distributor, and sales. And then the next arena for these giants is the international marketplace. Wal-Mart is perhaps again the leader in this realm. It is planning to buy a controlling stake in its Mexican retail partner, Cifra [*New York Times*, June 4, 1997]. Don't dismiss the mass merchant level of the market as unfashionable. Either directly at these stores, or at wholesalers that produce for them, more jobs will exist here than anywhere else!

Many other retailers are heading overseas as well. "Spain is next on Gap's list. The company plans to open six stores in Japan in November, 10 to 11 stores in the U.K., six in France, and eight in Germany by year's end" [*Women's Wear Daily*, September 11, 1996, "Drexler: Gap Can Grow"]. Eddie Bauer is opening three stores in Britain [*Daily News Record,* April 30, 1997], and Guess is planning 11 more European stores in 1998 [*Daily News Reecord*, April 2, 1997].

International is a new frontier for wholesalers and designers as well. Many American designers have sold in Europe for years. Calvin Klein is a recent addition, with new stores in London and Milan. The explosion is coming with distribution in the Far East. Isaac Mizrahi signed with three partners in Asia in early 1997: "It's a multinational deal expected to generate at least $150 million in retail sales—excluding product extensions or new licenses—over the period from 1997 to 2000. Sources estimated that his Asian business overall will account for a third of Mizrahi's total volume—currently estimated at $60 million to $70 million—over three years" [*Women's Wear Daily*, January 16, 1997, "Mizrahi's Asian Coup," Janet Ozzard].

SECOND PLAN: AIM SMALL

The Alan Stuart folks have found a narrow market niche and have made themselves market leaders for that niche. Michael Stern, vice president of manufacturing for Alan Stuart, explains: "You must identify your market niche. You can't be everything to everybody. Rather than make something that you know nothing about, you should try to enhance the product you know for the customer you know." This philosophy applies to both retail and wholesale. If you're going to start a new store, for example, don't try to take on Penney's or K-mart. Find a little slice of the market that no one else is addressing, and your chances for success will be much greater.

THE INSIDE SCOOP

ALAN GLIST

At age 21, Alan Glist started a business with his father. The line was named Alan Stuart, Inc. Today, Alan is the president and CEO of this Miami-based manufacturer.

On staying competitive by knowing your customer well:

We created a niche for ourselves. We have our own look and target customer. We've never been inundated with a lot of competition in our niche. We sell to better specialty and department stores, where the special look is more important than the price. Of course, every business is price sensitive. But our end is not down and dirty sensitive. With this, we've been able to continue a significant amount of our production in the United States.

The key is getting to know your customer. In our case, it's a mature gentleman—40 to death. I actually walk up to these guys and ask them things like, "Why do you like a banded bottom on your shirt?" (It covers their midsection better.) We also learned that since many of our clothes are actually bought by women (for their husbands) rather than men, we have to appeal to women as well. We've used colors (like mauve) this way—or sometimes we use womenswear fabrics or prints, and recolor them.

Our customer also cares a lot about washing. Ninety-eight percent of them prefer very washable, easy-care garments. We avoid "dry clean only." And our customer must have a pocket! We wouldn't produce a shirt without one!

Photo courtesy of Alan Glist.

Here's how Simon Graj (president of Graj+Gustavson, the marketing company) explains it: "There are always small pockets of opportunity. For example, it's difficult to shop for clothes. . . Therefore, people want clarity and ease when they shop. The number one reason to be a retailer is to be a guide. A small store with a distinct concept, thought through and executed consistently from product to packaging to selling environment, can go up against the big stores and succeed."

Next we discuss two guideposts toward finding such a slice.

Population Shifts

The age breakdown is changing in the United States. Just take a look at the expected growth of people age 65 and older, as a percentage of the total population.

Year	2000	2005	2015	2025
	12.6%	12.3%	14.5%	18.5%

[http://www.census.gov/population/projections/state/stpjage.txt "Projections of the Population, by Age and Sex, of States: 1995 to 2025," accessed February 8, 1997]

It might not look so dramatic as a percentage, but this means that the total number of Americans 65 and over will grow from 34,707,000 in the year 2000 to 61,954,000 in the year 2025. In other words, while you are working in the fashion industry, the number of senior citizens will almost double.

Your baby-boomer mother might still be wearing khaki skirts in 2005 when you start designing or buying, but you'd better plan on adding some elastic to the waist by then. However, she doesn't want to look like her grandmother, either. The boomer "youth culture" is having a very hard time admitting it is growing older. "Today, baby boomers are approaching 50 with less of a sense of settling into a long winter's decline than as a whole new stage in life's adventure" [*New York Times*, November 13, 1996, "Burning at Both Ends, Boomers Turn 50," Karen deWitt].

Also within population shifts, one needs to factor in the (unfortunate) trend that Americans of all ages are getting heavier. This will have a distinct impact on trends; and it should inspire larger-sized clothes that are hip, with-it, but without a large-size stigma attached. "This customer may be bigger, but she wants as many options as her peers. 'Size 14 to 60 is still America's forgotten market, and yet, that's the size of nearly half the women over 30 in this country,' said management consultant R. Fulton MacDonald of International Business Corp" [*Women's Wear Daily,* September 3, 1996, "Fashion Cachet for Large Sizes," Dianne M. Pogoda]. Could you come up with a line like this? The market is worth $20 billion at retail.

A new magazine geared to this customer, *Mode*, was launched in spring 1997. Their research showed that sales of women's large sizes have outpaced sales of regular sizes, and importantly, designers are now getting into plus sizes: Ungaro, Mary McFadden, and Givenchy [*New York Times*, February 23, 1997, "A Magazine Looks at the Plus Side of the Fashion World," Stephen Henderson].

The latest plus-size market to catch the industry's eye is kids! "After years of neglect, the industry is recognizing that overweight children make up an increasing segment of the fashion market, and retail chains from the J.C. Penney Company to Kids "Я" Us are rushing to add larger sizes. . . 10.9% of the total school age population [is overweight], more than double the 5% recorded in 1965" [*New York Times*, May 30, 1997, "Letting Out the Seams for Chubby Children," Dana Canedy]. These kids don't want elastic waists any more! They want to look like everyone else. Could you design this line?

Another opportunity is making clothes for people like you! Clothing for teenagers and young adults changes like lightning—don't expect us old "boomers" to keep up with it! "There are indications that the need for statusy clothes—shirts with polo ponies embroidered on the chest, jeans plastered with designer's initials—diminishes as people grow older. Teenagers, desperate to fit in with the crowd, die if they can't wear what everyone else does" [*Forbes*, December 7, 1992, "Here Come the Cross Shoppers"].

Cultural Shifts

America is changing in other ways as well. Until recently, clothing has been created for the most part with a kind of "northern European" aesthetic and fit. But here's where America is going: "Current trends indicate that by the year 2050, Asians, Hispanics, African-Americans, and other non-Caucasian groups could represent 47% of the total U.S. population" [*Business Week*, July 5, 1993, "Shut Out Immigrants and Trade May Suffer, C. Farrell]. African-American designers such as Patrick Kelly and Byron Lars have already made important contributions to mainstream fashion. There is lots more room!

Our increasingly diverse population will need clothes that, above all, will fit different tastes and body types. Based on the amount of alteration that some customers require, might there not be a market niche for clothes that start out better suited for different physiques? Some retailers are beginning to understand the diversity of their customers: "Last year, Sears appealed to Hispanics with its '*Todo Para Ti*' campaign and is now sponsoring Gloria Estefan's tour. Sears also is believed to be the first major national retailer to test Asian-American marketing efforts and is stepping up its marketing to African-Americans" [*Marketing News*, American Marketing Association, July 15, 1996, Vol. 30. No. 15, "Redux Deluxe"]. In March 1997, Sears introduced a collection aimed at African-American women: Mosaic, designed by Alvin Bell [*New York Times*, February 11, 1997, "Sears Line for Black Women," Constance C. R. White]. Perhaps you could design, or merchandise, or source, or market a specialized wholesale line to Sears or Penney's?

THIRD PLAN: AIM AT SOMEONE ELSE

Marketing is a whole separate study that fills books and courses. But if you're going to join the fashion world, you're going to need a fundamental understanding of marketing. The biggest "name" designers are brilliant marketers. They know how to create an image, an "aura," which in turn creates a demand for their clothing.

Licensing Out Your Name

The other part of marketing which plays a huge role in fashion is licensing. Successful wholesale clothing lines will often employ someone who will go out and find other companies (in cosmetics, sunglasses, sheets, you name it) that will pay a fee to use that name on their products. This is not as easy as it sounds, as it is critical for the designer to make sure that the set level of quality and style be maintained by all licensees. To give you an idea of how big licensing can be, in 1996 the Polo Ralph Lauren Company earned $137.1 million from licensing alone, up 24.5% from the year before [*Daily News Record*, May 23, 1997].

Buying Someone Else's Name

Conversely, a clothing company can buy the license for the name of a sports star, or equipment maker, or even a cartoon character. This becomes the marketing "hook" to sell the clothing. Going one step further, characters are sometimes "invented" to create novelty clothing lines (Big Dog, Fido Dido). You're young—you might know how to create a novelty character that will appeal to the youth of 2005. Or, perhaps you could work for a successful clothing line as the person who selects related products and companies to whom to license the brand.

THE INSIDE SCOOP

Hope Cohen

Hope is the vice president of licensing for Polo Ralph Lauren. Prior to that she was their director of product development for knitwear. Before Polo, Hope worked in product development at Ann Taylor, Anne Klein, AMC, and The Gap.

On setting up a license agreement:

A company to whom you are going to grant a license needs to be a good match-up. They must already have the correct quality, make, and details that will be right for the licensed product. Our company is design-driven, so we provide strong design direction to the licensee. They must be production experts in their field. But it is also critical to know that they will understand our sense of design. We ask that they identify a designer who will be able to work with our team—even before the contract is signed.

After the agreement is set and work starts, our job becomes one of "massaging" the relationship between the two different corporate cultures. We have to establish a good working relationship. We will constantly check up on them, and give them suggestions. In effect, we play their conscience.

The point in all of this is very similar to what we said in Unit I: You need a clear-eyed understanding of who your customer is. In 2005, customers will be different from today. "Futurists" such as author Faith Popcorn can help you visualize some of the changes. You'll need to find a segment of that America, get into their "fashion head," and design, produce, source, market, license, or buy a line that hits their needs exactly. In other words, just as it is today, the triangle of balance (designer–garment–store) will need to be in balance, even if you're aiming at an all new customer.

CHAPTER 19

Garmento Lingo: Talk Like an Insider

WHAT'S A GARMENTO?

One industry veteran defined it this way: "Go into Jimmy's Deli at 1400 Broadway and see who is eating fast. The people gobbling their food and looking at their watches are 'garmentos.'"

One of the pleasant surprises about the garment business is its humor! Things can get pretty tense, so it's a good thing that many people in the industry can stand back and laugh at themselves and at their predicament. "Garmento" for example, has a slightly negative connotation, reflective perhaps of the irony of having to perform miracles just to get a few dozen *"schmattes"* (clothes) shipped!

We thought we should give each of you a head start in the industry. No one taught us the inside terminology that gets used every day. When you're working in fashion, you won't hear people talking about the invention of the bustle in the nineteenth century. But you will hear something like this:

> The color roll style blew out even though that vendor wasn't on the matrix. So my boss made me be a *schnorrer* and get an RTV. Turns out the style was on a rubber band already, so I didn't feel like such a *Chazzer*. The margin came out great. So after all this, my boss let me put it back into four doors!

You're going to need to know what that means! So here's the translation:

> The style that I bought in a wide range of colors sold extremely well. However, the manufacturer who made it was not on the corporate "approved list" of manufacturers. So my boss made me go to the manufacturer and beg to get his authorization to ship back whatever remained of that style. I didn't realize that this style was already prearranged to be returned anyway, so I didn't feel so piggy. As it turns

out, the profit on that item was great. So after all this, my boss let me put the style back into four branches!

INDUSTRY CLASSICS

Big Pencil	Indicates that this buyer can buy very large quantities ("she carries a big pencil").
Going to the Market	When retailers visit the wholesale showrooms or when manufacturers visit their suppliers.
Rag Trade	Sounds negative but it's really affectionate: the garment business.
Paper	When a buyer "leaves paper," she or he is leaving orders with a vendor.
SA	Abbreviation for *Seventh Avenue*.
RTW	Abbreviation for *Ready-to-wear*, apparel for female customers.

RETAIL TRADE TERMINOLOGY

Selling Floor Terms

The Floor	The selling area in a store.
Face Out	A fixture that allows merchandise to be hung so that the entire front of the garment shows.
Four Way	Another selling fixture that holds garments on four arms so that the end garment on each arm is facing out.
Rounder	A large, horizontal ring that holds lots of merchandise but shows only the shoulder of each item.
T Stand	A small fixture with just two arms used to highlight special merchandise.
Jet Rail	Horizontal bar along the wall that holds lots of merchandise but shows only shoulders.
Door	Used to denote a separate store. A department store with one large downtown store plus 15 branches would be said to have 16 doors.

Retail Financial Terms

P.O.	Purchase order; the official paperwork a buyer presents to a wholesaler to order merchandise.
Keystone	Common practice of marking merchandise up 50%. Remember that this refers to 50% of the retail price. So if the cost is $10.00, the retail price would be $20.00 at "keystone" markup.
California Keystone	Historically, retailers on the west coast had to add either an extra 2% markup or an extra $1.00 to cover the additional transportation cost to the west coast.

OTB	Open to buy; an internal accounting dollar figure that represents the amount of open budget a buyer has to buy merchandise in any given month.
Bought Up	A buyer has spent her allocated budget fully.
Out-the-Door Price	The promotional price at which the majority of the inventory of a particular style gets sold.
Sell-Through	Percentage of inventory that has been sold within a specified period of time.
RTV	Return to vendor; merchandise that is faulty or doesn't sell can *sometimes* be returned to the supplier.
MIS	Merchandise information systems; the in-store computer system that keeps track of inventories and sales.

Miscellaneous Retail Terms

Co-op	Advertising moneys contributed by wholesalers.
ROP	Run of paper; advertising that is printed at the same time as the rest of the newspaper.
Wear-Now	Merchandise that can be bought by consumers and worn right away because it matches the season.
Style-Out	An examination of all styles in a department to see if there are duplications or gaps.

FABRICS

Fancy	Any fabric that is not a solid color.
TC	Poly-cotton blend. (Don't ask, it's a long story!)
CVC	Chief value cotton. Still used even though the customs definitions have since changed. It is used for fabrics that are more cotton that any other fiber (for example, cotton/polyester).
Yield	The amount of usable material and/or garments that come out of a set piece or length of fabric.
Head End	The beginning of a new piece or run of fabric in the loom, usually showing identification marks.
Confine a Pattern	If you buy a large enough quantity of a pattern, the mill won't sell it to anyone else (also called an *exclusive*).
Pit Loom	A small swatch, usually woven by hand, to test how the colors selected for the warp and fill (the vertical and horizontal threads) will look when a pattern such as a plaid is woven; also called *trial weave*.

Dye Lot	Large quantities of fabric have to be dyed in separate batches. There is usually a slight shade variation from one batch (lot) to another.
Recovery	The ability (or inability) of a fabric or garment to be stretched out and then to revert naturally to its original shape.
Crocking	When the dye rubs off a dyed fabric.
Self-staining	When one colored panel of a garment "runs" onto another panel of the same garment. Just piece together bright red and white and then wash them!

LINGO

Checked Out	Alternatively, "blew out" or "flew out"; terms used to describe anything that sells fast.
Dog	Alternatively, "had puppies" or "barks"; describes a very bad-selling style.
On a Rubber Band	Alternatively, "on wheels"; merchandise that the wholesaler has agreed (up front) to take back if it doesn't sell.
Flipped	We don't know why, but this is always the description for a positive reaction from a buyer.
Hashed Together	Mixed, as in jumbled sizes or styles on a rounder fixture.
Who Do You Hang With?	No, this does not mean, who are your friends? A buyer would ask this of a wholesaler, meaning "In other stores, which other brands are carried in the department where they also carry your line?"
Garanimals	This is from the famous kidswear brand; used to mean very easy-to-match separates.
Stack 'em High; Watch 'em Fly!	This is what a wholesaler tells a retailer when very sure of success.
Gorilla	An unsophisticated male customer, also known as "Joe Six-Pack."
Granny Bait	Especially cute infantswear.
The Tin Cup	When buyers ask wholesalers for markdown money to help offset deficient retail profits.
Like buttah!	What your leather line feels like.
Like sandpapuh!	What your competitor's leather line feels like.

YIDDISH

There is a wonderfully rich Jewish history and tradition in the garment business. Many Yiddish words are used by everyone. Trust us on this—you will hear these terms and soon you might be using them yourself!

Schmatte	From "rag"; used generically to denote a garment, especially a lower-quality garment.
Mavin	An expert.
Pisher	Someone young and inexperienced.
Gontser Macher or *Big Macher*	A real big shot.
Chutzpa	Nerve, arrogance.
Meshugge	Crazy.
Mishegoss	A situation that is so crazy it defies description.
Schmooz	A friendly chat.
Latke	From "potato pancake"; someone with no energy or spunk.
Mitzvah	A good work, a good deed.
Shmaltzy	Overdone, gaudy, too fancy.
Chazzer	A pig.
Schnorrer	A beggar.
Rachmones	Pity, compassion, as in "He was starting up his own company, so I gave him a *rachmones* order."
Schlep	To drag around, as in "You made me *schlep* these samples all the way from 34th Street?"
Schlepper	Salesperson.
Yenta	A gossip.

(Special acknowledgment to Leo Rosten's book, *The Joys of Yiddish*, Pocket Books, New York, 1968.)

CANTONESE

Don't think there haven't been linguistic influences from around the world! Every new country added to the sourcing list seems to bring in a couple of new words. Everyone in the business has been to Hong Kong at one time or another. So two Cantonese phrases (Cantonese is the version of Chinese that is spoken in Hong Kong) have become universal:

Tai Gui	Too expensive.
Mo Mun Tai	No problem. By the way, we've found that "no problem" in almost any language really means "Start worrying right now!"

TRANSLATIONS

These are a bit of a "stretch," but they might give you just a bit more "local color."

K-mart with a Candelabra	A store that thinks it's better than it really is.

Euro	"Euro" in front of anything means "more stylish than American."
Young Men's Bottoms	A departmental buying responsibility that a young lady on my staff refused to have printed on her business card.
I didn't get your message	This means: "I got your message, I didn't answer it, and now you're going to pester me again, aren't you?"
Understands	"Will put up with," as in "The better customer understands that if her dress is 100% linen, she will be a mass of wrinkles five minutes after putting it on."
Opportunity	The word you use in front of your boss instead of "problem."
Reach	A fashion stretch, as in "These two sweater styles are fine for my customers, but that lycra–chenille–angora crop-top is just too much of a 'reach.'"
How's Business?	Retailers never want to admit that their business might not be terrific. As a result, there has been an "inflation" in the words used to describe retail selling performance:

Description	***Actual Increase***
Tough	-10%
Flat	-3%
Up slightly	0%
Up high single digits	+2%
On fire!	+5%

CHAPTER 20

Words of Wisdom from Industry Pros

After you've been out in the business world for a while, you'll realize (as we all did) that good advice from experienced professionals is the best way to do things right, avoid mistakes, and get ahead. Dina Columbo of DKNY puts it best: "When you graduate, you think you know everything. You want to start at the top. You don't know everything! Be like a sponge. Listen to any idea. It could be a good idea, now or later. Listen to the ideas of successful people. They've gotten where they are by learning themselves!"

Words of Wisdom: Dale Nitschke, Dayton/Hudson/Marshall Field

"To succeed you have to be passionate about the industry, the product, the guest [customer]. It requires lots of time, energy, and focus. You don't appreciate that until you're in it. If you don't have that level of commitment, you won't succeed. Look for a mentor. Someone who is energized by the business. Find out what makes them that way!"

Words of Wisdom: Diann Valentini

Diann (Didi) is chairperson of the Fashion Buying and Merchandising Department at New York's famous Fashion Institute of Technology.

"What separates the students who end up being successful from those who don't?

Drive! Some may not be the best academically, but students with drive, with a real hunger to succeed, do well. They seek out interesting new things, they experiment. Their openminded attitude allows them to be more flexible and see opportunities.

"Of course, there will always be 'stars.' They shine with a special charisma. It's not coincidence that they often end up being in the right place at the right time. But the mainstay of the business will always be the 'troops.' The hard workers. They succeed because of determination and can be very successful. This is a very large business, needing so many different talents and abilities."

Words of Wisdom: Tommy Hilfiger

Photo by Francesco Scavullo, courtesy of Tommy Hilfiger.

"If you know what area you want to focus on—design, marketing, retail, graphics—you should study that in college. However, many young people are unsure of what area they would like to pursue. Therefore, internships are a good way to learn the business—fashion or otherwise. An internship gives you a chance to put what you are learning in school to practical use. It also gives you the flexibility to work within different departments to experience the diversity of the company. This will enable you to more easily decide what you find most interesting. There are many young people at Tommy Hilfiger who started out as interns and were hired in permanent positions after graduation."

Words of Wisdom: Pamela Dennis

"I would tell design students, don't do only fads! They're great for one shot, maybe. But stick with timeless, class, good quality, and good fabrics. Women don't want fine tailoring to be a lost art. This business needs new blood. We want another generation to carry on."

Photo courtesy of Pamela Dennis.

Words of Wisdom: Bob Caplan, Levi Strauss & Co.

"Prospects are more encouraging now. We've gone through a 'flushing out' of a lot of peripheral areas in textiles, manufacturing, and retailing. We're hitting a point where we will see growth and a brighter future in our industry. In the global approach to apparel, there is still a constant mystique for Americana."

Words of Wisdom: Vicky Davis

Photo courtesy of Vicky Davis.

Vicky started her own men's neckwear company in 1969. After the amusing start-up described below, she received the prestigious Coty Award in 1976 and the first Cutty Sark Award in 1979. Two of her largest current accounts are Bloomingdale's and Macy's.

"When I started in this business, I was an insecure little lady from Detroit. My husband Larry had won a cruise, so we went to Hudson's Department Store to find appropriate clothes for the cruise and for New York. All men's ties at the time were very narrow, and they looked funny on heavy-set Larry. I decided to make a few wider ties for him. Through the PTA, I found someone who could sew (I couldn't!), and then located some fabrics at a local fabric store. Well, the 5-inch-wide ties and other novelties that resulted were a big hit on the cruise! People said, 'That tie is great! Where did you get it, Bloomingdale's?' Coming from Detroit, I answered, 'Bloomingdales, is that a nice store?'"

So back home, my PTA partner and I chipped in $23.00 and started our own company! Our first customer was the Claymore Shop, in Birmingham, Michigan. They bought two dozen ties and sold them out. Then four dozen, and on and on! Soon, the entire PTA was sewing in my basement! Still shy and insecure, I suddenly found myself driving to places as far away as Grand Rapids, *alone!*

At first, when a buyer would say 'no' to me, I'd go back out to the car and cry. But in a couple of years, I had built up enough confidence to be able to walk in and sell Bloomingdale's and Sak's *in New York!* Now, if I can do that, *anyone* can!"

Words of Wisdom: S. Miller Harris, Eagle/Nautica Shirtmakers

"In putting together merchandising teams over the years, I've learned early on that the hardest person to find is one with both taste and business skills. You can find creative souls who are flakes—can't read a cost sheet or a line blueprint. Sometimes their talent is such that you hire them anyway. And since you can find good mechanics who don't know green from blue, the solution often is to pair one of each and then make sure they truly do complement one another and are compatible. But the real find—the true five-legged sheep—is someone who can do it all!"

Words of Wisdom: Ed Toro, Product Development Manager, the Harwood Companies, Inc.

"Be accurate and precise in what you do. People are always rushing you, but take the time you need to get it right the first time. Don't rush for half an hour and do it wrong. Take the hour and do it right!"

Words of Wisdom: Lawrence Behar, Ike Behar Inc.

"You can't be afraid to get your hands dirty. You've got to be willing to do anything and everything. Glamor is maybe 5% of your daily routine."

Words of Wisdom: Zach Solomon, AMC

"Never talk down to anyone, no matter what their position. It doesn't matter if it's Louie in receiving. Louie became my bosom buddy. Ingratiate yourself with people, listen to them, ask questions. That's how you'll learn. You've got to be able to work alongside anyone."

Words of Wisdom: Mimi Platcow Lechter

Mimi is yet another of those graduates of Brooklyn's legendary retail training ground: Abraham and Straus. After becoming the buyer of women's sportswear, Mimi transferred to AMC–New York. In her 24 years at AMC, culminating as the vice president, general merchandise manager, Mimi supervised all areas of soft goods. Those of us who worked for her credit Mimi for making us understand what it means "to be a pro."

On being professionally correct. . .
"It's all a matter of P's and C's."

Presentation

You need to present yourself to the world in such a way that people will respect you, listen to you, and want to work with you. Remember that you are representing your company to the public. Even in dress, you should dress in accordance with the practice in your office—if the men are in suits and ties, you have to go with the flow.

Preparation

If you are given an assignment or an activity that you are expected to carry out, you must be prepared to follow through. It's like being in school—you need to come to class prepared for discussions and exams. But in work, don't expect anyone to grant you an extension!

Prepared for the unexpected

Work is fraught with surprises. You will need to deal with the unexpected often!

Positive

You must have a positive attitude in how you deal with the public and with your supervisor. If you are asked to do something that is over your head, approach it with a positive attitude and be open to it as a learning experience.

Pride

You can't be a pro unless you take pride in your job and in doing it well!

Commitment

To do a job well, you have to be committed to do it to the very best of your ability.

Cooperative

It's important not only to come across as cooperative to your boss—you've also got to be cooperative with your co-workers.

There are also some "no-no's" to be avoided if you want to be a pro.

Politics

There are politics in every office. It's OK to be aware of the "intrigue," but it's very bad to get involved. It will almost always come back to haunt you.

Clock-watching

To get the job done, you have to spend as much time as necessary. If you have a 9-to-5 attitude, you won't be successful."

Words of Wisdom: Barbara Dugan

Barbara got her B.S. degree in clothing and textiles from Ohio University. This led to her first job, as assistant fashion director for a large fabric company. From there she went to Bagatelle and then to AMC. After being a merchant for 11 years, Barbara switched over to the personnel department, where she is now vice president of executive recruiting and development.

"If you really want to do your best in an interview:

- Come into the interview already knowing something about the company. Do your homework.
- Bring along any projects, written materials, design portfolios—but less is more!
- Give a nice, firm handshake!

This is the fashion industry, so presentation is key. I like to see someone who is confident, animated, excited about the interview. Someone who makes eye contact. Being a little nervous is perfectly natural. So don't worry about that. But within the first five minutes of the interview, you do need to find a way to establish a rapport with the interviewer. You should steer the interview so that there is an exchange of information. Questions and responses on both sides. I don't want to feel that I'm selling the company to you. You have to think of yourself as one of perhaps 10 candidates. How do you differentiate yourself?"

"And here's a pet peeve: Never, never say you want a job in this industry 'because you love clothes' or 'because you love to shop.' That comes across as terribly superficial. You'll sound much more professional if you say, 'I have always had an interest in the fashion business.' By the way: With the exception of department stores, there are very few 'training programs' left. You're much wiser asking in your cover letter about opening-level positions rather than training programs."

Words of Wisdom: Al Dittrich

Al and Denise Dittrich, and sons Blair, Neal, and Brett. Photo courtesy of Al Dittrich.

Al is the senior vice president and general merchandise manager of the Home Store at Dayton/Hudson/Marshall Field. We consider him one of the most insightful merchants in department stores today.

"Advice for someone starting in retail? I have two answers."

"The short one: Always think like a customer, never compromise your integrity, roll up your sleeves and work hard, find a mentor and be a mentor, and make it fun every day!"

"The long one: I meet with every trainee who joins my team. I try to learn as much as I can about each as a person. I also impart upon them my *six-point expectations speech.* Having worked with trainees in every position I've been in over twenty years, they always ask what my expectations are. Thus, my speech, as if I were giving it to someone new to my team and new to retail."

"First and foremost, I expect you to think! (I usually get a slight rise of the eyebrows as they think to themselves, 'What does that mean? I'm thinking every day in everything I do.') My challenge is that I expect you to think like a customer in everything you do. You're at a point in your career where you can get sucked into the treacherous list of 'To Do's.' You're new, you're inexperienced, and you're at the 'task level' of your job. Your team, and even you yourself, can start to evaluate your self-worth based on how many things you get scratched off your list of 'To Do's.' Let me give you an example. Once, many years ago (so many years, in fact, that cotton was just becoming a fabric for sweaters), I walked into an office, sat on the corner of a trainee's desk, and said, 'What do you think we should do about cotton sweaters?' He looked back at me with a blank stare. I was inquiring because I had just finished reviewing a recap that he had done. In the recap, cotton sweaters had an incredible sell-through and other sweaters had been weak. Our on-order was almost nonexistent in cotton. The person that I'd asked the question of gathered his composure and related that he didn't know anything about cotton sweaters but could do an analysis for me if I wanted. This was a classic case of 'get it off the list of 'To Do's'.' I was disappointed in what we were doing as trainers of new talent. His recap was everything we asked it to be: It was accurate, it was thorough, it was done quickly, etc. This trainee had given us what we asked for. He gave us an effective recap, but we hadn't set the expectation or the environment in which we expected our trainees to think. My expectation of every trainee is that you think. Think about everything you do and how it relates to the customer. If you're doing something that doesn't relate to the customer, challenge us as to why we asked you to do it. Think like a customer. We need your new fresh challenges and ideas."

"My second expectation is that you participate. I've seen many talented people come into the business and hesitate to participate. They seem to be saying, 'There's a lot going on here, some really bright people. I'll listen, absorb, and learn for a while.' Not an option! The beauty of retail is that it is a business everyone knows something about—because everyone shops. This is not nuclear science; this is playing store. I expect everyone to participate, throw out your ideas, throw out your challenges, give your opinion. We need everyone's opinion; we need to know how everyone thinks as a customer. You'll learn easily in this business that a fragile ego will have a tough time succeeding. Retail is part art, part science. We have plenty of computers for the science/analysis part. We need the artists; we need opinions about what's the right color, what's the right button, what's the right price. Like art, the value lies in the eyes of the beholder. The value of the opinion is in the eyes of the customer. Many times you'll feel you are so right, but you're only right if the customer thinks so. Dare to try. If you're not wrong very often, you're not trying enough! The customers can make you very humble; they can also make you feel like a genius, and basically you'll get a little of both each day. Play the game rather than being a 'student' of the game. Participate! It's fun!"

"My third expectation is ownership. Own the store! I remember my second day as a trainee. I went into my buyer's office and relayed a decision that needed to be made. I asked him what criteria one uses to decide something like this. His instant response was, 'What would you do if it was your store?' I gave my answer and he said, 'Then go for it!' He followed with, 'You'll never go wrong in this business if you make decisions as if you owned the store.' Think about your area as if you owned the store. You want it to be the very best, you want customers to think of you first, you want your suppliers to know you're honest and fair, and you want to make money. This store is what provided for your family and you want to run this store as though it were the one thing you'd be able to pass on to your children. If you do that, you'll make the right decisions. If you do that, you'll lead as a steward of the business rather than a manager of someone else's business. I look for people who take ownership, who show accountability, who aren't afraid to say, 'I made that decision.'"

"My fourth expectation deals with training. I've see new trainees enter our teams with seemingly different views on training. One view seems to be 'I wonder how well they'll train me?' The other view is, 'I wonder how fast I can learn?' The latter sounds much better than the former in this business. It works not only when you're a trainee, but every day as well. I look for people who want to learn, people who want to be better today than they were yesterday. I expect everyone on my team to train. I expect everyone on my team to help each other. However, the primary responsibility of training lies with the individual who needs the training. I look for people who dive in and go the extra mile while the learning curve is steep. This is a competitive, fast-paced business. If everyone on the team isn't better today than they were yesterday, the competition will beat us.

"My fifth expectation is to 'have a little fun!' (I usually get a smile, a laugh, and full agreement to live up to that expectation!) My message is one of balance. This is the type of business that can reach out, pull you in, and absorb you. There is always more to do than you can do. There's one more analysis, one more recap, one more market preparation that you can do. Don't get caught up in 'doing' and lose touch with life. In this business, when you lose touch with the customer, you're worthless to us. As I said earlier, we have computers to do the recaps and the analyses. We need merchants to merchandise. Some say retailers and retail hours aren't 'normal.' You need to be out in life, buying groceries when 'normal' people buy groceries, going to movies when 'normal' people go to movies, filling your car with gas when 'normal' people full up with gas. Merchandising is about knowing your customer and you have to experience life to know your customer. Balance and work hard, but take time for family, for friends, for fun. You learn by living. 'Lifestyle' is where all trends start. Have fun."

"My final expectation is that you give your best. I believe that God gave everyone different talents and different levels of talent. All I want is the very best every day of what God gave you. You can't glide in this business. You can't take shortcuts. You have to work hard and give it your best! If you're doing that, there'll be a place in this business where you can contribute, where you can feel good, where you can work with some really great people, and where you can have fun."

"I don't expect anyone coming into this business to have all the answers or to reinvent the wheel of retailing. I expect people to think, participate, take ownership, learn, enjoy, and give it their best. Everyone I know that has followed that formula has done well and enjoyed. I've worked with some wonderful people in this industry and I hope that I have, in some way, helped some of them along. I have been asked many times if I would recommend retailing as a career for any of my three sons. My answer is that I hope I can help them match their talents to whatever is right for them. In whatever they do, however, they'll probably get my six-point expectations speech!"

Words of Wisdom: Evelyn C. Moore

Photo by Zachary T. Moore.

Throughout this book you might have noticed that we have stressed the point that you must really know your customer to be successful in the fashion business. In fact, we took this same point to heart while writing this book: You are our "customer," and we sincerely hope that we have addressed your needs. We wanted to avoid writing a book that just talks "at" you. We hope we have been able to show you "how to" actually begin in the business.

As an instructor, my very best advice is this: The other most important person for you to listen to is yourself! If you start out by knowing yourself, it will be easier to understand that other people will share some of your opinions and not share others. Get to know yourself and discover what is special about you! This will help determine which path is best for you to follow; which "niche" could be especially yours.

Take it slow and easy, and along the way, learn as much as you can from each opportunity and experience—good and bad. Remember the experiences that have given you satisfaction and enjoyment. They will help you identify where you best fit into this business. We hope that as you explore, you will find out (as we did) that the most important measure of success is not necessarily a big commercial breakthrough. It is really a matter of finding day-to-day fulfillment throughout your career, throughout your journey!

Words of Wisdom: Maurice J. Johnson

Photo by Philip Carabetta.

In writing this book, the most fascinating discovery was the consistency between industry members, regardless of location or rank! Either from their own experiences (Ken Master, May Cygan, Tonya Bott) or from their observations (Diann Valentini, Dale Nitschke), they ended up saying essentially the same thing to you: If you want to break into the fashion business and succeed in it, you're going to need push, gumption, and as Didi Valentini put it, drive. No one is going to hand you a career. In fact, it's probably going to be tough.

Some industry veterans, when asked what advice they would give to students just starting out, said, "Tell them to run for their lives!" But then invariably, a softer look would cross their faces and the conversation would turn to the wonderful experiences and rewards that this career had given them. Many talked about a "mentor," someone who had given them extraspecial help along the way. If all the details in this book seem a bit overwhelming, take heart! You don't need to know everything on your first day—and there will no doubt be a "mentor" to help you, too.

The very best advice I would offer is that one secret of success is "caring." If you really, *but really*, care about your career, care about getting ahead, care about your reputation, care about the success of your work, care about seeing your customers and your staff become successful—everything else falls into place. Customers, clients, and even suppliers can always tell when someone sincerely cares. Conversely, they can see through false concern as if it were cellophane. True concern and caring, in my experience, have always made the difference between a job done well enough and a job done with great success."

And now, how will you begin?. . . Chapter 20

Unit 3 was a glimpse at fashion's future. Unit 4 has been a reflection of the experiences, drive, and passion of many industry leaders, plus their guidance for you. In both Units 3 and 4 you were not given exercises on "How to Begin." We wanted you to focus on your course-length notebook during this time. But now it is time to involve you in the "how to begin." Industry leaders worked hand-in-hand with us to bring you to this launching point. Now it is time for you to join in this collaboration and think about where you will fit in this industry.

This last exercise is actually a lot of fun. Make a T-chart for each of the questions below. On the left-hand side, write out the answer, and on the right, discuss why.

First: What Surprised You?

List three things that you learned about the industry that surprised you. Then write out why they were surprising and how this has changed your thinking about the fashion industry.

	Surprises	**Why**
One:	____________	______________________________
	____________	______________________________
	____________	______________________________
	____________	______________________________
	____________	______________________________
Two:	____________	______________________________
	____________	______________________________
	____________	______________________________
	____________	______________________________
	____________	______________________________
Three:	____________	______________________________
	____________	______________________________
	____________	______________________________
	____________	______________________________
	____________	______________________________

Second: What Did You Like Best?

Something has probably grabbed your interest. List three things that you really liked and why you liked them. Are these the areas that fit best with your talents?

	Like Best	Why
One:		
Two:		
Three:		

Third: What Do You Want to Learn More About?

Somewhere in this book we hope that something has sparked a brand-new interest. It could be a job, a company, the background of a leading designer, or even the role of politics in garmentmaking. What would like to learn more about?

	Areas to Explore	Why
One:		

Two:

Three:

Fourth: What's Next?

List the first three steps that YOU will take to "break into" the fashion industry? What, in the book, brought these steps to your attention?

	Plan of Action	Because of. . .
One:		
Two:		
Three:		

So, you want to work in the fashion business? Great! We wish you an enjoyable journey!

INDEX

E

F

G

M

N

O

T

U

V

W

X

Y

Z